THE ROUTLEDGE ATLAS OF AMERICAN HISTORY

This new edition of *The Routledge Atlas of American History* presents a series of clear and detailed maps, accompanied by informative captions, facts, and figures, updated with additional maps and texts. The complete history of America is unrolled through vivid representations of all the significant landmarks, including:

- Politics – from the annexation of Texas to the battle for black voting rights
- Military Events – from the War of Independence and America's standing in two world wars to the conflicts in Korea, Vietnam and the Gulf
- Social History – from the abolition of slavery to the growth of female emancipation
- Transport – from nineteenth century railroads and canals to recent ventures into space
- Economics – from early farming and industry to the state of America today.

Sir **Martin Gilbert** is one of the most prolific historians of his generation. An Honorary Fellow of Merton College, Oxford, he is Churchill's official biographer as well as the author of the three volume *The History of the Twentieth Century* (HarperCollins, 1998–9).

BOOKS BY MARTIN GILBERT

The Routledge Atlas of American History
The Routledge Atlas of the Arab–Israeli Conflict
The Routledge Atlas of British History
The Routledge Atlas of the First World War
The Routledge Atlas of the Holocaust
The Routledge Atlas of Jewish History
The Routledge Atlas of Russian History

Recent History Atlas, 1860–1960
Jerusalem Illustrated History Atlas
Children's Illustrated Bible Atlas
The Appeasers (*with Richard Gott*)
The European Powers, 1900–1945
The Roots of Appeasement
Sir Horace Rumbold, Portrait of a Diplomat
Churchill, A Photographic Portrait
Jerusalem, Rebirth of a City
Exile and Return, The Struggle for Jewish
  Statehood
Auschwitz and the Allies
Shcharansky, Hero of our Time

The Jews of Hope, The Plight of Soviet
  Jewry Today
The Holocaust, The Jewish Tragedy
First World War
Second World War
In Search of Churchill
History of the Twentieth Century (in three
  volumes)
From the Ends of the Earth: The Jews in the
  Twentieth Century
Letters to Auntie Fori: The 5000-Year History of
  the Jewish People and Their Faith
The Righteous: The Unsung Heroes of the
  Holocaust

THE CHURCHILL BIOGRAPHY IS COMPLETE IN EIGHT VOLUMES:

Volume I. Youth, 1874–1900 *by Randolph S. Churchill*
    Volume I. Companion (in two parts)
Volume II. Young Statesman, 1900–1914 *by Randolph S. Churchill*
    Volume II. Companion (in three parts)
Volume III. 1914–1916 *by Martin Gilbert*
    Volume III. Companion (in two parts)
Volume IV. 1917–1922 *by Martin Gilbert*
    Volume IV. Companion (in three parts)
Volume V. 1922–1939 *by Martin Gilbert*
    Volume V. Companion 'The Exchequer Years' 1922–1929
    Volume V. Companion 'The Wilderness Years' 1929–1935
    Volume V. Companion 'The Coming of War' 1936–1939
Volume VI. 1939–1941, 'Finest Hour' *by Martin Gilbert*
    The Churchill War Papers: Volume I 'At the Admiralty'
    The Churchill War Papers: Volume II 'New Surrender', May–December
    The Churchill War Papers: Volume III '1941, The Ever-Widening War'
Volume VII. 1941–1945, 'Road to Victory' *by Martin Gilbert*
Volume VIII. 1945–1965, 'Never Despair' *by Martin Gilbert*

Churchill – A Life *by Martin Gilbert*

Editions of documents
Britain and Germany Between the Wars
Plough My Own Furrow, The Life of Lord Allen of Hurtwood
Servant of India, Diaries of the Viceroy's Private Secretary, 1905–1910

THE ROUTLEDGE ATLAS OF
AMERICAN HISTORY

4th Edition

Martin Gilbert

Routledge
Taylor & Francis Group

LONDON AND NEW YORK

First published 1968 as *The Dent Atlas of American History*
by J. M. Dent Ltd
Revised edition published 1985
Third edition published 1993

Reprinted 1995
by Routledge
11 New Fetter Lane, London EC4P 4EE

Simultaneously published in the USA and Canada
by Routledge
29 West 35th Street, New York, NY 10001

Fourth edition first published 2003

Routledge is an imprint of the Taylor & Francis Group

Printed and bound in Great Britain by
Bell & Bain Ltd, Glasgow

British Library Cataloguing in Publication Data
A catalogue record for this book is available from the British Library

Library of Congress Cataloging in Publication Data
A catalog record for this book has been requested

ISBN 0–415–28151–2 (Hbk)
ISBN 0–415–28152–0 (Pbk)

Preface

The idea for this atlas came to me while I was teaching at the University of South Carolina. Its aim is to provide a short but informative visual guide to American history. I have tried to make use of maps in the widest possible way, designing each one individually, and seeking to transform statistics and facts into something easily seen and grasped. My material has been obtained from a wide range of historical works, encyclopaedias, and newspaper and Government reports.

More than twenty-five years have passed since the first publication of this atlas. It was a period marked first by the intensification and then by the ending of the Vietnam war, with more than 55,000 American dead. It was also a period marked by a substantial increase in the population of the United States, and continued immigration. This same period has seen the development of outer space as a region of defence policy. New maps cover these recent developments.

Since the revised edition was published in 1985, the pattern of events has led me to draw twenty-six new maps, to cover, among recent developments, the continuing growth of immigration, new ethnic and population changes, and the military and humanitarian actions of the United States overseas, culminating in the Gulf War (1991), aid to Somalia (1992), and air drops to Bosnia (1993). New domestic maps show the natural and accidental disasters of the past two decades, the continuing high death rate from motor accidents (more than a million dead in twenty years), murder (a quarter of a million dead in a single decade), and the new scourge of Aids (170,000 deaths in a decade).

The United States has also been the pioneer in exploring the solar system and in defence preparedness in space, for both of which I have drawn a special map. United States' arms sales, and economic help to poorer countries, as well as the ending of the Cold War confrontation, also required new maps, as did pollution. The continuing United States' presence in the Pacific, and her defence preparedness at home and abroad, are also mapped.

I have been helped considerably in the task of updating this atlas by Abe Eisenstat and Kay Thomson. Many individuals and institutions have provided extra material for the maps. I am particularly grateful to:

Martin Adams, Bureau of Political-Military Affairs, State Department, Washington DC
James T. Hackett, Member of the President's General Advisory Committee on Arms Control
Louan Hall, National Highway Traffic Safety Administration
Michael Hoeffer, Statistics Division, Immigration and Naturalisation Services
John Richter, Agency for International Development, State Department
Joshua Gilbert (for help on the space map)

For the first and second edition of this atlas, my draft maps were turned into clear and striking artwork by Arthur Banks and Terry Bicknell. For this new edition, I am grateful to the cartographic skills of Tim Aspden. At my publishers, JM Dent, David Swarbrick has made it possible to realise my ambition to re-issue all of my historical atlases updated. It is my hope that they will be of interest and service to teachers, students, and the general reader for whom the past is not a forbidden planet, but an integral part of today's world.

MARTIN GILBERT
Merton College, Oxford

14 June 1993

Note to the Fourth Edition

For this fourth edition, I have prepared eleven new maps, which bring the story of the United States into the twenty-first century. As with the previous edition, this could not have been done without the cartographic expertise of Tim Aspden. I am also grateful to the Librarian at the United States Embassy, London, for access to reference material.

12 July 2002

MARTIN GILBERT
Merton College, Oxford

Maps

1 The Origin of Settlement in America 50,000–1,000 BC
2 The Indian Tribes of North America Before 1492
3 The Vikings and America 800–1015
4 European Exploration 1492–1534
5 Spanish Exploration 1513–1543
6 De Soto's March 1539–1543
7 Spanish America 1609
8 Puritan Emigration from England 1612–1646
9 The English Origins of the Puritans 1620–1675
10 European Settlements 1526–1642
11 English Land Grants 1606–1620
12 English Land Grants 1621–1682
13 The Pequot War 1636–1637
14 King Philip's War 1675–1676
15 The Thirteen Colonies 1624–1774
16 California Missions 1769–1848
17 Trade and Transport 1696–1774
18 Queen Anne's War 1702–1713
19 European Settlements by 1742
20 The British Conquest of Canada 1758–1763
21 North America 1758
22 North America 1763–1774
23 The North Atlantic 1770
24 The Triangular Trade 1752
25 The War of Independence 1775–1783
26 Proposed Boundaries 1779–1782
27 The Ratification of the Federal Constitution 1787–1790
28 North America 1783
29 Medicine and Public Health 1738–1886
30 National Origins and Religious Groups 1790
31 Social Problems 1792–1860
32 The Barbary Wars 1801–1815
33 Colonial South America 1495–1810

34 Independent South America 1810–1938
35 The Declaration of War Against Britain 1812
36 The War Against Britain 1812–1815
37 Indian Battles and Cessions 1784–1820
38 The Expulsion of the Indians from the South 1820–1840
39 The Expanding Frontier 1783–1840
40 The Opening of the West 1803–1864
41 Texan Independence 1836–1845
42 The Annexation of Texas 1845
43 The War Against Mexico 1846–1848
44 The Mormons 1830–1851
45 Education 1784–1888
46 The Missouri Compromise 1820
47 Canals and the Cumberland Road 1785–1850
48 Railroads by 1860
49 The Growth of the United States by 1860
50 King Cotton 1801–1860
51 The Abolition of Slavery 1777–1858
52 The Spread of Slavery 1808–1860
53 The Underground Railroad 1786–1860
54 The Coming of Civil War 1858–1861
55 The Union Advance 1861–1865
56 The Battles of the Civil War 1861–1865
57 The South 1865–1915
58 Indian Reservations 1788–1894
59 Alaska 1728–1958
60 Social Discontent 1876–1932
61 Public Lands and Railway Grants 1796–1890
62 Indian Lands Lost 1850–1890
63 The Americas 1823–1916
64 The United States in the Pacific 1857–1911
65 European Emigration 1820–1920

66 Immigration 1820–1920
67 The Caribbean 1625–1939
68 The Panama Canal Zone Protectorate 1903
69 The Opening of the West 1864–1912
70 The Federal Reserve Bank 1914
71 Votes for Women 1890–1919
72 War in Europe 1914–1918
73 The American Expeditionary Force 1918
74 Intervention in Russia 1918–1919
75 The Proposed United States' Mandates 1919
76 Senate Voting on the Versailles Treaty 1919
77 European War Debts to the United States 1920
78 The Spread of Prohibition 1845–1933
79 Farming in 1920
80 Civil Aviation 1918–1940
81 Industry by 1920
82 The Tennessee Valley Authority 1933
83 The United States 1914–1945
84 The United States and the War in Europe 1939–1941
85 Lend-Lease 1941–1945
86 The North Atlantic 1939–1943
87 Big Week 19–25 February 1944
88 The Oil Campaign June–September 1944
89 The Allied Advance 1942–1945
90 Wartime Conferences 1941–1945
91 The War in Asia 1941–1942
92 The Defeat of Japan 1942–1945
93 The United States and the Pacific 1945–1965
94 The Korean War June–November 1950
95 The Korean War November 1950–November 1951
96 United States Aid 1948–1965
97 The United States 1945–1965
98 From Lake Superior to the Atlantic 1959
99 Berlin Airlift 1948–1949
100 The Search for Open Skies 1957–1958
101 The Bay of Pigs 1961
102 The Cuban Missile Crisis 1962
103 Indo-China 1945–1954
104 Vietnam 1955–1968
105 School Segregation 1954–1965

106 Negro Voting Rights 1964–1965
107 The American Negro 1965
108 The Negro Revolt 1965–1967
109 The Death of Martin Luther King April 1968
110 United States Alliances 1948–1965
111 Polaris Power 1960
112 American Preparedness 1960
113 American Land Based Surveillance Systems 1982
114 The United States and the Soviet Union in Outer Space
115 Immigrants to the United States 1963–1983
116 The United States in the Pacific, 1823–1993
117 Great Power Confrontation and Conciliation, 1972–1986
118 The Cold War and Arms Suplies, 1984–1988
119 The End of the Cold War, 1987–1993
120 Military, Economic and Humanitarian Missions, 1975–1993
121 Major Natural and Accidental Disasters, 1972–1993
122 Pollution: Hazardous Waste Sites, 1990
123 Murder in the United States, 1991
124 Death from AIDS, 1982–1992
125 Immigration to the United States, 1991
126 Leading States Taking Immigrants, 1989
127 National Ancestry of United States Citizens
128 Cities with Large Ethnic Groups
129 United States Citizens Resident Abroad, 1989
130 The Visa Lottery Program, 1990–1993
131 The Gulf War, 1991
132 "No-Fly Zones" Iraq, 1991–1993
133 United States Arms Sales, 1992
134 Main Recipients of United States Economic Aid, 1992
135 Defence Preparedness on Land, 1991
136 United States Forces in Somalia, 1992–1993
137 Exploring the Solar System, 1962–1992
138 Defence Preparedness in Space, 1992–1993

THE TWENTY-FIRST CENTURY

139 Foreign Born Population of the United States, 2000
140 Immigration to the United States, 1998 (Census of 2000)
141 United States Military Personnel Overseas, 2000: Europe
142 United States Military Personnel Overseas, 2000: Global
143 Oil Imports to the United States, 2000
144 Principal United States Military Sales, 1990–1998
145 The Urbanization of the United States by 2000
146 Pollution: Hazardous Waste Sites, 2000
147 United States Caribbean and Pacific Territories: 2000
148 Domestic Airport Passengers, 2000
149 September 11

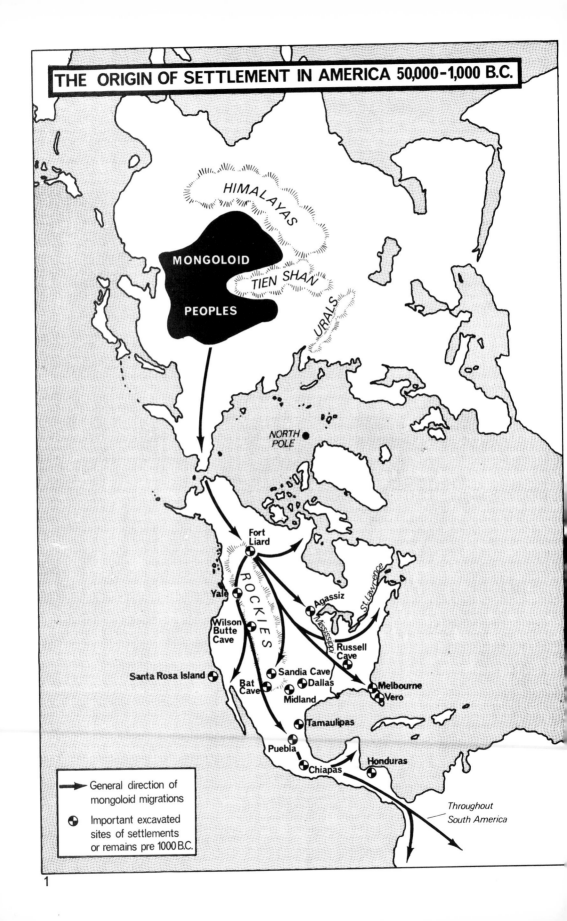

THE ORIGIN OF SETTLEMENT IN AMERICA 50,000–1,000 B.C.

HIMALAYAS

MONGOLOID

TIEN SHAN

PEOPLES

URALS

NORTH POLE

Fort Liard

ROCKIES

Yale

Wilson Butte Cave

Agassiz

St. Lawrence

Mississippi

Russell Cave

Santa Rosa Island

Bat Cave

Sandia Cave

Dallas

Midland

Melbourne

Vero

Tamaulipas

Puebla

Chiapas

Honduras

Throughout South America

→ General direction of mongoloid migrations

✦ Important excavated sites of settlements or remains pre 1000 B.C.

THE INDIAN TRIBES OF NORTH AMERICA BEFORE 1492

Eskimo
Koyukon
Ingalik
Tanaina
Aleut
Kutchin
Han
Tanana
Nabesna
Tuchone
Ahtena
Kaska
Tahltan
Tlingit

Tsimshian
Bella Coola
Haida
Bella Bella
Kwakiutl
Nootka
Salish
Makah Puyallup
Nisqually
Chehalis
Chinook
Cowlitz
Tillamook
Yakima
Klikitat
Molala
Kalapuya
Coos
Umpqua
Takelma
Karok
Yurok
Wiyot
Shasta
Hupa
Yana
Mattole
Maidu
Yuki
Pomo
Wintun
Miwok
Costanoan
Yokuts
Salinan
Chumash

Hare
Bear Lake
Dogrib
Yellowknife
Slave
Sekani
Beaver

Carrier
Chilcotin
Shuswap
Lillooet
Thompson
Okanagan
Sanpoil
Colville
Spokane
Palouse
Walla Walla

Klamath
Modoc
Chomawi
Tsugewi
Kawaiisu
Mono
Panamint

Cayuse

Mohave
Serrano
Yavapai
Cahuilla
Yuma
Pima
Maricopa
Papago

Chipewyan

Sarsi
Siksika (Blackfoot)
Cree

Kaigani
Piegan
Kutenai
Kalispel
Atsina
Coeur D'Alene
Flathead
Crow
Nez Perce
Bannock
Shoshoni
Paviotso
Washo
Ute
Gosiute
N. Paiute
S. Paiute

Navaho
Kavasupai
Chemehuevi
Walapai

Cochimi
Seri

Hidatsa
Arikara
Teton
Yankton
Dakota
Ponca
Pawnee
N. Cheyenne
Oto
Arapaho
S. Cheyenne
Jicarilla Apache
Pueblo
Mescalero Apache
Hopi
Zuni
W. Apache
Lipan Apache
Opata
Concho
Tarahumara
Cahita
Acaxee

Mandan
Menomini
Dakota
Sauk
Fox
Iowa
Omaha
Kansa
Osage
Missouri
Kiowa
Kiowa Apache
Comanche
Waco
Kichai
Tonkawa
Karankawa

Walcuri
Pericu
Yaqui
Huichol

Ojibwa (Chippewa)
Ottawa
Plains Cree
Assiniboin
Winnebago

Kickapoo
Wea
Peoria
Quapaw

Tuskegee
Choctaw
Tawakoni Wichita
Caddo Natchez
Tunica
Atakapa
Chitimacha
Coahuiltec
Tamaulipec

Huastec
Totonac
Tlaxcalan
Aztec
Mixtec
Zapotec
Chontal

Tobacco
Neutral

Naskapi Montagnais
Micmac
Malecite
Passamaquoddy
Penobscot
Abnaki
Huron

Beothuk

Pennacook

Mahican
Mohawk
Nipmuc Oneida
Massachuset
Wampanoag
Narraganset
Pequot
Mohegan
Wappinger
Onondaga
Cayuga
Seneca
Delaware
Nanticoke
Powhatan
Chickahominy
Mattapony
Tutelo
Pamlico
Nottoway
Tuscarora
Catawba

Erie

Potawatomie
Miami
Susquehanna
Pamunkey
Piankashaw
Illinois
Shawnee
Cherokee
Yuchi
Creek
Alabama
Chickasaw

Mobile
Apalachee
Yucatan Maya

Lacandon
Maya
Quiche
Maya

Mosquito

Yamasee
Guale
Timucua
Hichiti

Calusa

Seminole

Taino

Ciboney

Toltec
Tarascan
Otomi

0   600
Miles

There were approximately one million Indians
north of Mexico in 1492

2

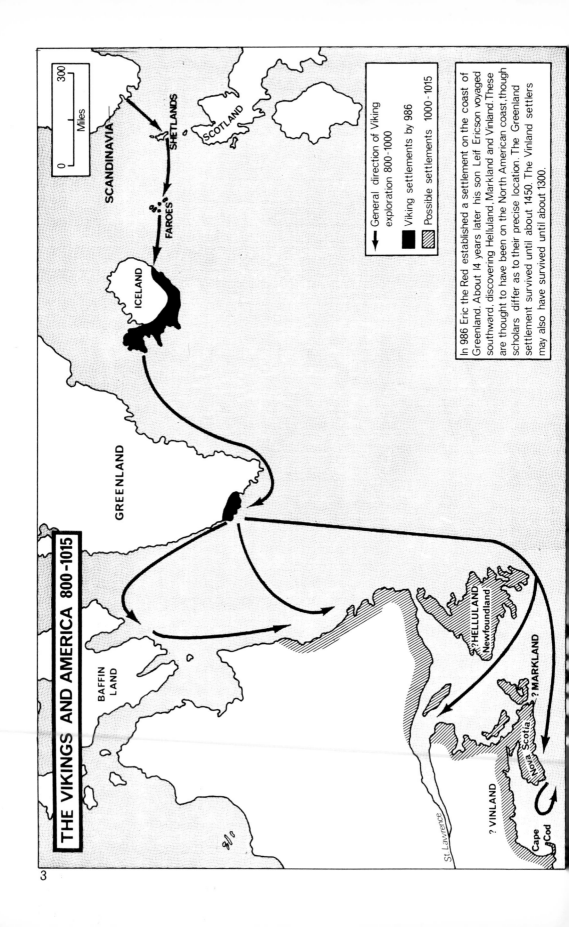

THE VIKINGS AND AMERICA 800-1015

SCANDINAVIA

SHETLANDS

SCOTLAND

FAROES

ICELAND

GREENLAND

BAFFIN
LAND

St. Lawrence

? HELLULAND

Newfoundland

? MARKLAND

? VINLAND

Nova Scotia

Cape
Cod

0   300

Miles

General direction of Viking
exploration 800-1000

Viking settlements by 986

Possible settlements 1000-1015

In 986 Eric the Red established a settlement on the coast of
Greenland. About 14 years later his son Leif Ericson voyaged
southward, discovering Helluland, Markland and Vinland. These
are thought to have been on the North American coast, though
scholars differ as to their precise location. The Greenland
settlement survived until about 1450. The Vinland settlers
may also have survived until about 1300.

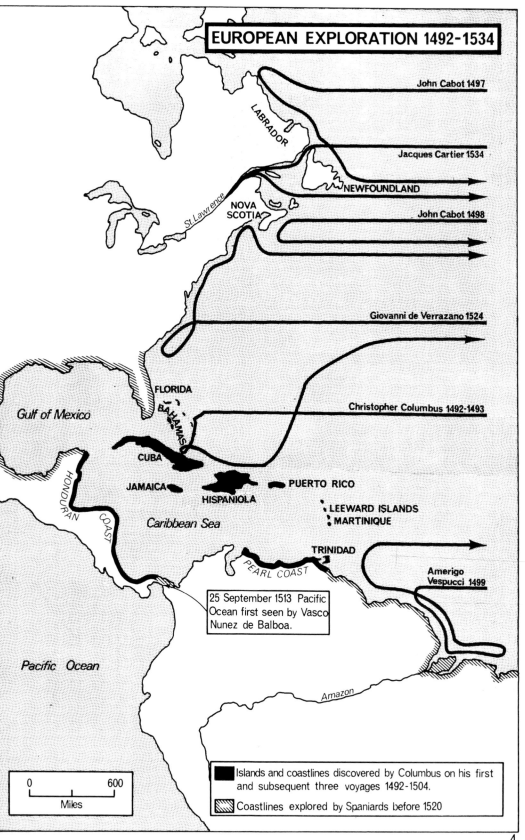

EUROPEAN EXPLORATION 1492-1534

John Cabot 1497

LABRADOR

Jacques Cartier 1534

NEWFOUNDLAND

St. Lawrence

NOVA SCOTIA

John Cabot 1498

Giovanni de Verrazano 1524

FLORIDA

BAHAMAS

Gulf of Mexico

Christopher Columbus 1492-1493

CUBA

JAMAICA

HISPANIOLA

PUERTO RICO

HONDURAN COAST

LEEWARD ISLANDS

MARTINIQUE

Caribbean Sea

TRINIDAD

PEARL COAST

Amerigo Vespucci 1499

25 September 1513 Pacific Ocean first seen by Vasco Nunez de Balboa.

Pacific Ocean

Amazon

0   600

Miles

■ Islands and coastlines discovered by Columbus on his first and subsequent three voyages 1492-1504.

▨ Coastlines explored by Spaniards before 1520

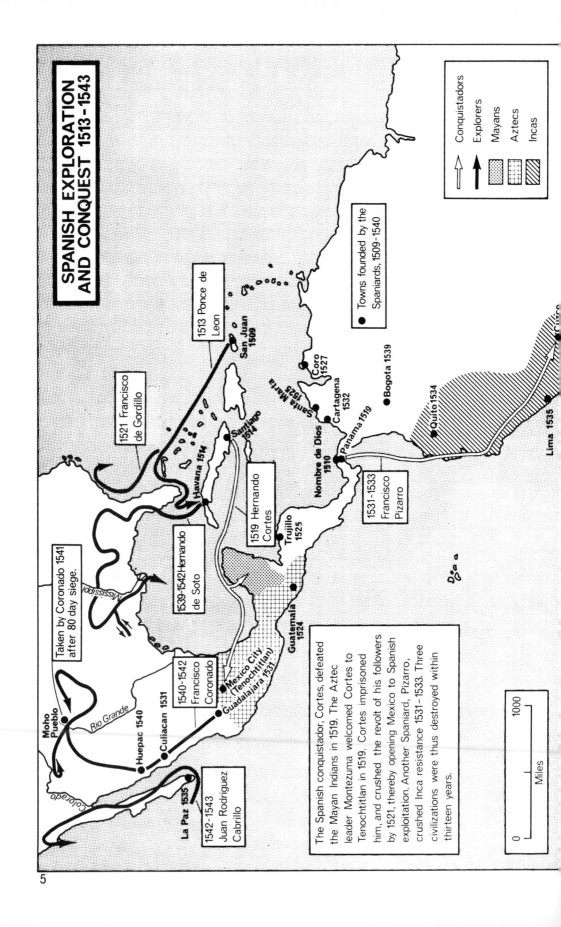

SPANISH EXPLORATION AND CONQUEST 1513-1543

Legend:
- ⬆ Conquistadors (outline arrow)
- ⬆ Explorers (solid arrow)
- Mayans (dotted pattern)
- Aztecs (grid pattern)
- Incas (diagonal lines pattern)

● Towns founded by the Spaniards, 1509-1540

1513 Ponce de Leon

1521 Francisco de Gordillo

1539-1542 Hernando de Soto

1519 Hernando Cortes

Taken by Coronado 1541 after 80 day siege.

1540-1542 Francisco Coronado

1542-1543 Juan Rodriguez Cabrillo

1531-1533 Francisco Pizarro

San Juan 1509

Coro 1527

Santa Maria 1525

Cartagena 1532

Bogota 1539

Panama 1519

Nombre de Dios 1510

Quito 1534

Lima 1535

Cuzco

Havana 1514

Santiago 1514

Trujillo 1525

Guatemala 1524

Mexico City (Tenochtitlan)

Guadalajara 1531

Culiacan 1531

Huepac 1540

Moho Pueblo

Rio Grande

Colorado

Mississippi

La Paz 1535

The Spanish conquistador, Cortes, defeated the Mayan Indians in 1519. The Aztec leader Montezuma welcomed Cortes to Tenochtitlan in 1519. Cortes imprisoned him, and crushed the revolt of his followers by 1521, thereby opening Mexico to Spanish exploitation. Another Spaniard, Pizarro, crushed Inca resistance 1531-1533. Three civilizations were thus destroyed within thirteen years.

0   Miles   1000

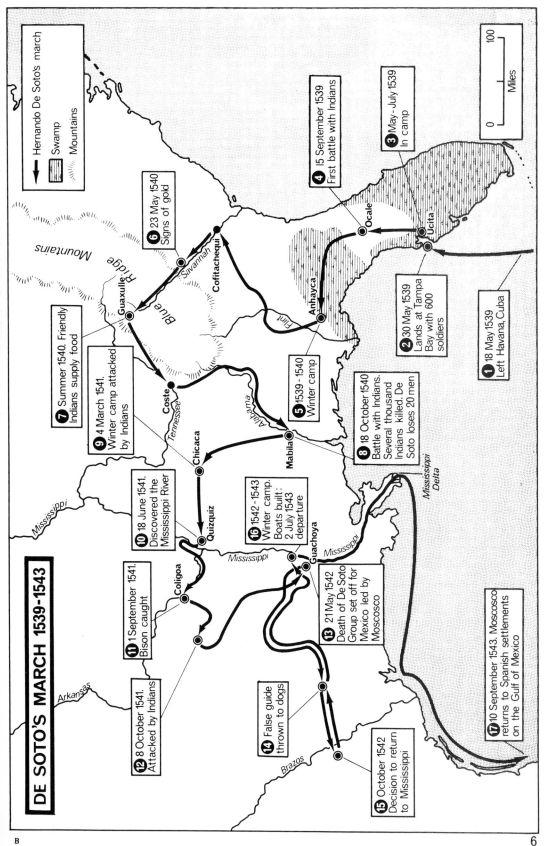

DE SOTO'S MARCH 1539-1543

Hernando De Soto's march
Swamp
Mountains

Miles
0 100

1 18 May 1539 Left Havana, Cuba

2 30 May 1539 Lands at Tampa Bay with 600 soldiers

3 May–July 1539 In camp

4 15 September 1539 First battle with Indians

5 1539–1540 Winter camp

6 23 May 1540 Signs of gold

7 Summer 1540. Friendly Indians supply food

8 18 October 1540 Battle with Indians. Several thousand Indians killed. De Soto loses 20 men

9 4 March 1541. Winter camp attacked by Indians

10 18 June 1541. Discovered the Mississippi River

11 1 September 1541. Bison caught

12 8 October 1541. Attacked by Indians

13 21 May 1542 Death of De Soto Group set off for Mexico led by Moscosco

14 False guide thrown to dogs

15 October 1542 Decision to return to Mississippi

16 1542–1543 Winter camp. Boats built: 2 July 1543 departure

17 10 September 1543. Moscosco returns to Spanish settlements on the Gulf of Mexico

Ucita
Ocale
Anhayca
Cofitachequi
Savannah
Guaxulle
Blue Ridge
Mountains
Coste
Tennessee
Chicaca
Mabila
Quizquiz
Coligoa
Guachoya
Mississippi
Mississippi Delta
Flint
Alabama
Arkansas
Brazos

B

6

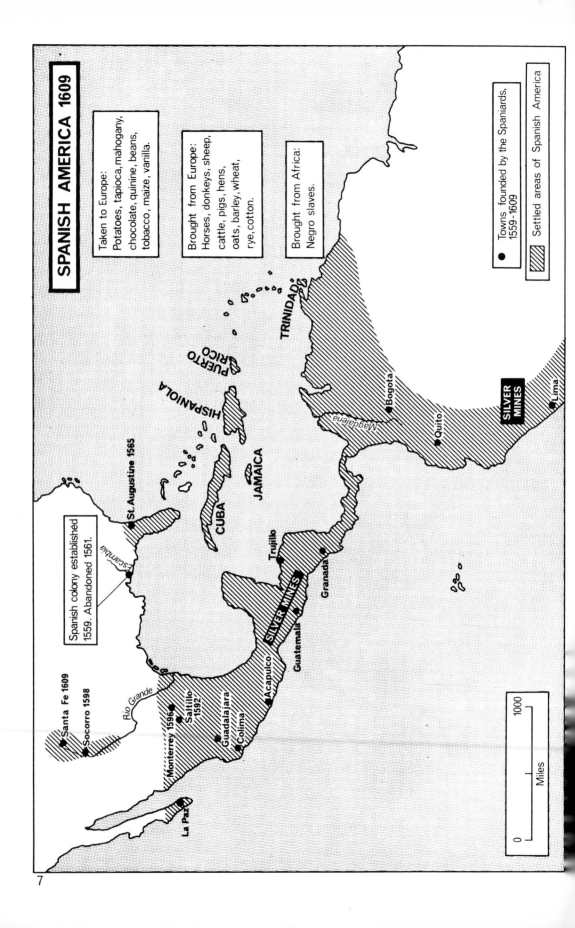

SPANISH AMERICA 1609

Taken to Europe:
Potatoes, tapioca, mahogany, chocolate, quinine, beans, tobacco, maize, vanilla.

Brought from Europe:
Horses, donkeys, sheep, cattle, pigs, hens, oats, barley, wheat, rye, cotton.

Brought from Africa:
Negro slaves.

● Towns founded by the Spaniards, 1559-1609

▨ Settled areas of Spanish America

TRINIDAD

PUERTO RICO

HISPANIOLA

St. Augustine 1565

Spanish colony established 1559. Abandoned 1561.

Escambia

CUBA

JAMAICA

Magdalena

Bogota

Quito

SILVER MINES

Lima

Trujillo

Granada

SILVER MINES

Guatemala

Acapulco

Colima

Guadalajara

Monterrey 1596

Saltillo 1592

Rio Grande

Santa Fe 1609

Socorro 1598

La Paz

0   1000

Miles

7

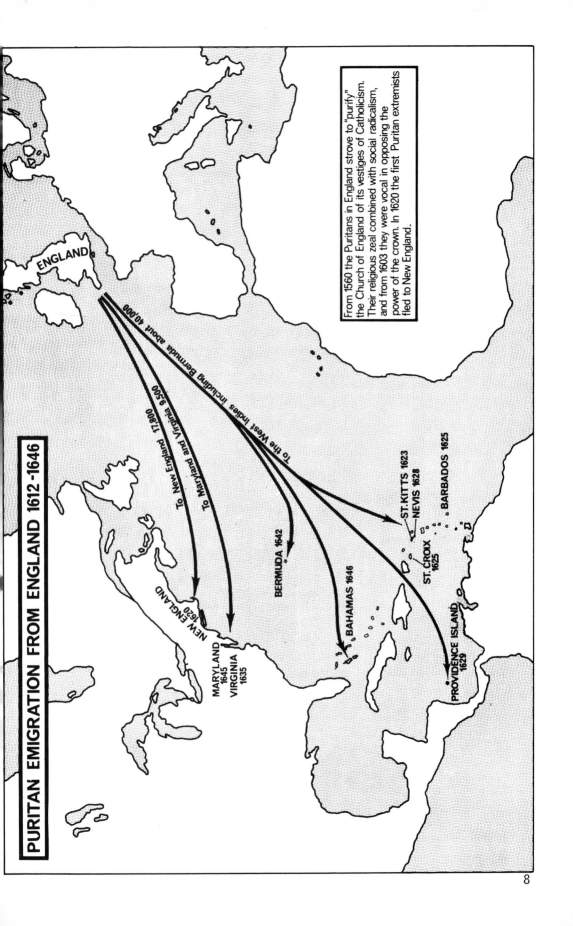

PURITAN EMIGRATION FROM ENGLAND 1612-1646

ENGLAND

From 1560 the Puritans in England strove to "purify" the Church of England of its vestiges of Catholicism. Their religious zeal combined with social radicalism, and from 1603 they were vocal in opposing the power of the crown. In 1620 the first Puritan extremists fled to New England.

To New England 17,800

To Maryland and Virginia 9,500

To the West Indies including Bermuda about 40,000

NEW ENGLAND
1620

MARYLAND
1645

VIRGINIA
1635

BERMUDA 1642

BAHAMAS 1646

ST. KITTS 1623

NEVIS 1628

BARBADOS 1625

ST. CROIX
1625

PROVIDENCE ISLAND
1629

8

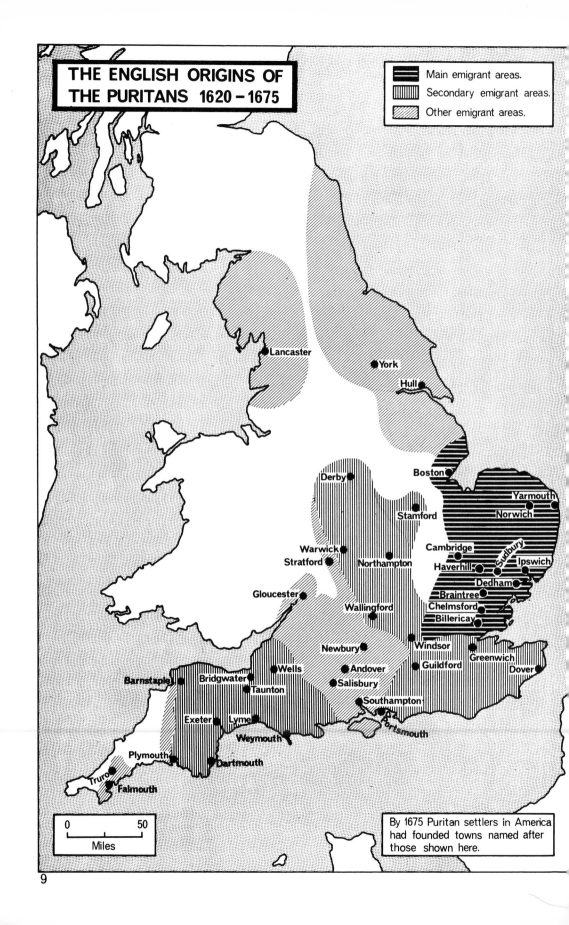

THE ENGLISH ORIGINS OF THE PURITANS 1620–1675

Main emigrant areas.
Secondary emigrant areas.
Other emigrant areas.

Lancaster
York
Hull
Derby
Boston
Yarmouth
Norwich
Stamford
Warwick
Cambridge
Stratford
Northampton
Sudbury
Ipswich
Haverhill
Dedham
Gloucester
Braintree
Wallingford
Chelmsford
Billericay
Newbury
Windsor
Greenwich
Wells
Andover
Guildford
Dover
Barnstaples
Bridgwater
Salisbury
Taunton
Southampton
Exeter
Lyme
Portsmouth
Weymouth
Plymouth
Dartmouth
Truro
Falmouth

0   50
Miles

By 1675 Puritan settlers in America had founded towns named after those shown here.

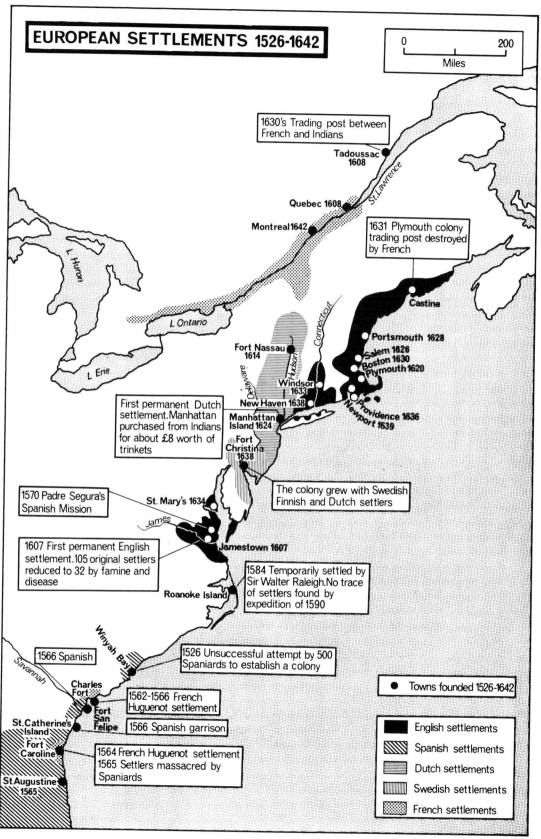

EUROPEAN SETTLEMENTS 1526-1642

0   200
Miles

1630's Trading post between French and Indians

Tadoussac 1608

Quebec 1608

St.Lawrence

Montreal 1642

1631 Plymouth colony trading post destroyed by French

Castine

L Huron

L Ontario

L Erie

Portsmouth 1628
Salem 1626
Boston 1630
Plymouth 1620

Fort Nassau 1614

Connecticut

Hudson

Delaware

Windsor 1633

New Haven 1638

Providence 1636
Newport 1639

First permanent Dutch settlement. Manhattan purchased from Indians for about £8 worth of trinkets

Manhattan Island 1624

Fort Christina 1638

The colony grew with Swedish Finnish and Dutch settlers

1570 Padre Segura's Spanish Mission

St. Mary's 1634

James

1607 First permanent English settlement. 105 original settlers reduced to 32 by famine and disease

Jamestown 1607

1584 Temporarily settled by Sir Walter Raleigh. No trace of settlers found by expedition of 1590

Roanoke Island

Winyah Bay

Savannah

1566 Spanish

1526 Unsuccessful attempt by 500 Spaniards to establish a colony

Charles Fort

1562-1566 French Huguenot settlement

Fort San Felipe

1566 Spanish garrison

St.Catherine's Island

Fort Caroline

1564 French Huguenot settlement
1565 Settlers massacred by Spaniards

St.Augustine 1565

● Towns founded 1526-1642

■ English settlements
▨ Spanish settlements
▤ Dutch settlements
▥ Swedish settlements
▦ French settlements

10

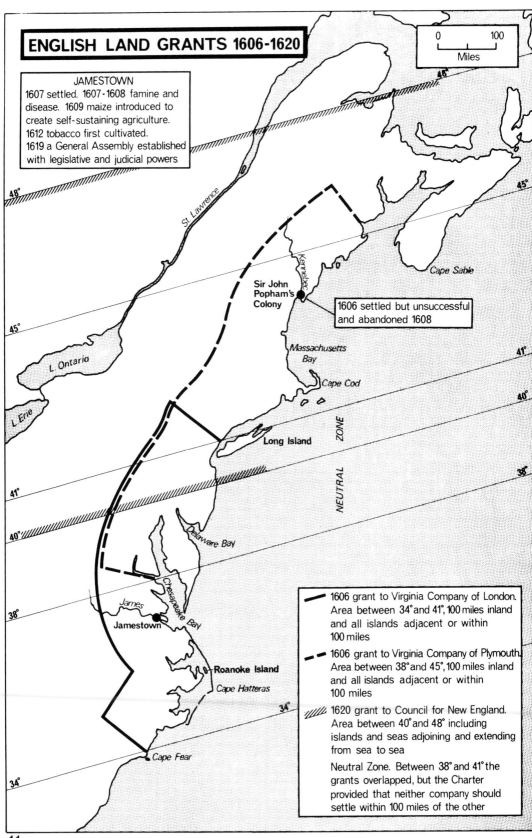

ENGLISH LAND GRANTS 1606-1620

0   100
Miles

JAMESTOWN
1607 settled. 1607-1608 famine and
disease. 1609 maize introduced to
create self-sustaining agriculture.
1612 tobacco first cultivated.
1619 a General Assembly established
with legislative and judicial powers

St. Lawrence

48°

45°

45°

41°

L. Ontario

L. Erie

41°

40°

38°

34°

Kennebec

Sir John
Popham's
Colony

1606 settled but unsuccessful
and abandoned 1608

Cape Sable

Massachusetts
Bay

Cape Cod

Long Island

Delaware Bay

NEUTRAL ZONE

James

Jamestown

Chesapeake Bay

Roanoke Island

Cape Hatteras

Cape Fear

46°

45°

41°

40°

38°

34°

—— 1606 grant to Virginia Company of London.
Area between 34° and 41°, 100 miles inland
and all islands adjacent or within
100 miles

– – – 1606 grant to Virginia Company of Plymouth.
Area between 38° and 45°, 100 miles inland
and all islands adjacent or within
100 miles

///// 1620 grant to Council for New England.
Area between 40° and 48° including
islands and seas adjoining and extending
from sea to sea

Neutral Zone. Between 38° and 41° the
grants overlapped, but the Charter
provided that neither company should
settle within 100 miles of the other

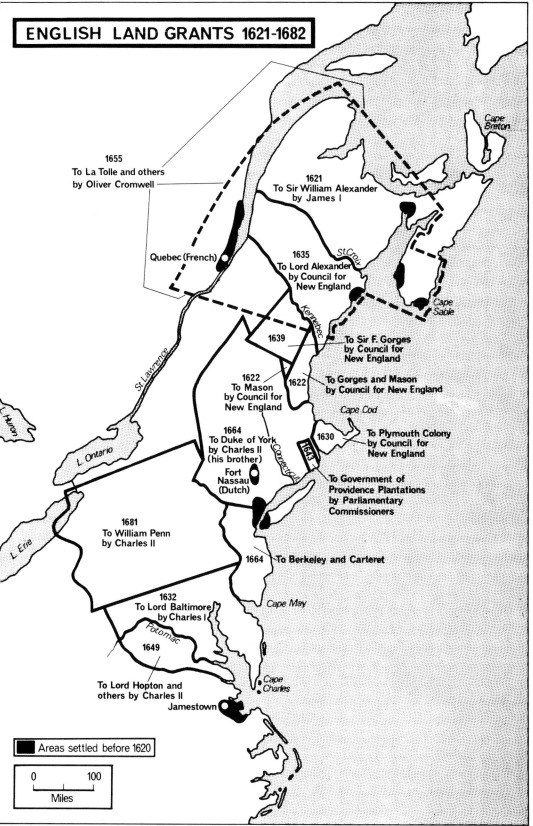

ENGLISH LAND GRANTS 1621-1682

Cape Breton

1655
To La Tolle and others
by Oliver Cromwell

1621
To Sir William Alexander
by James I

Quebec (French)

St Croix

1635
To Lord Alexander
by Council for
New England

Cape Sable

Kennebec

1639

To Sir F. Gorges
by Council for
New England

1622
To Mason
by Council for
New England

1622

To Gorges and Mason
by Council for New England

Cape Cod

St. Lawrence

1664
To Duke of York
by Charles II
(his brother)

Fort
Nassau
(Dutch)

Connecticut

1630

To Plymouth Colony
by Council for
New England

1643

To Government of
Providence Plantations
by Parliamentary
Commissioners

L. Huron

L. Ontario

1681
To William Penn
by Charles II

L. Erie

1664 To Berkeley and Carteret

Cape May

1632
To Lord Baltimore
by Charles I

Potomac

1649

Cape
Charles

To Lord Hopton and
others by Charles II
Jamestown

■ Areas settled before 1620

0   100
Miles

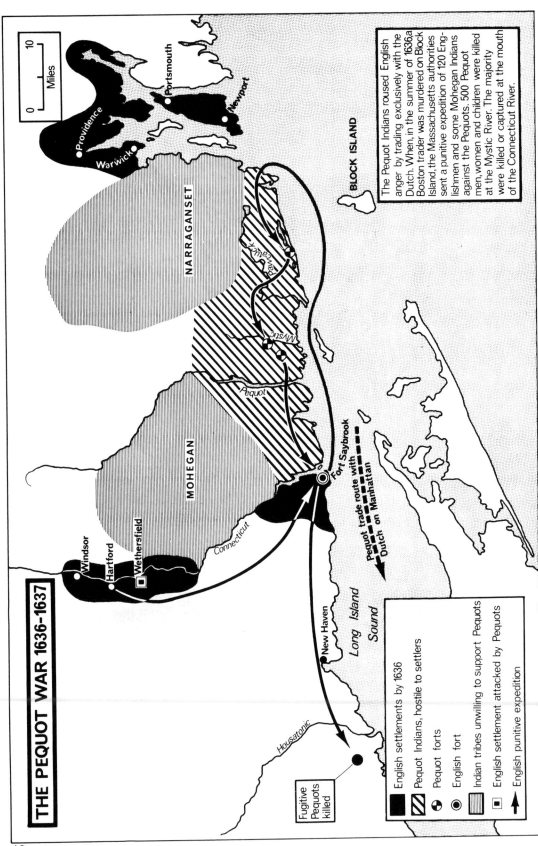

THE PEQUOT WAR 1636-1637

The Pequot Indians roused English anger by trading exclusively with the Dutch. When, in the summer of 1636 a Boston trader was murdered on Block Island, the Massachusetts authorities sent a punitive expedition of 120 Englishmen and some Mohegan Indians against the Pequots. 500 Pequot men, women and children were killed at the Mystic River. The majority were killed or captured at the mouth of the Connecticut River.

Miles
0   10

Providence
Warwick
Portsmouth
Newport

NARRAGANSET

BLOCK ISLAND

MOHEGAN

Mystic

Pequot

Pawcatuck

Fort Saybrook

Pequot trade route with
Dutch on Manhattan

Windsor
Hartford
Wethersfield

Connecticut

New Haven

Long Island Sound

Housatonic

Fugitive
Pequots
killed

■ English settlements by 1636

▨ Pequot Indians, hostile to settlers

◑ Pequot forts

◉ English fort

▥ Indian tribes unwilling to support Pequots

▣ English settlement attacked by Pequots

↑ English punitive expedition

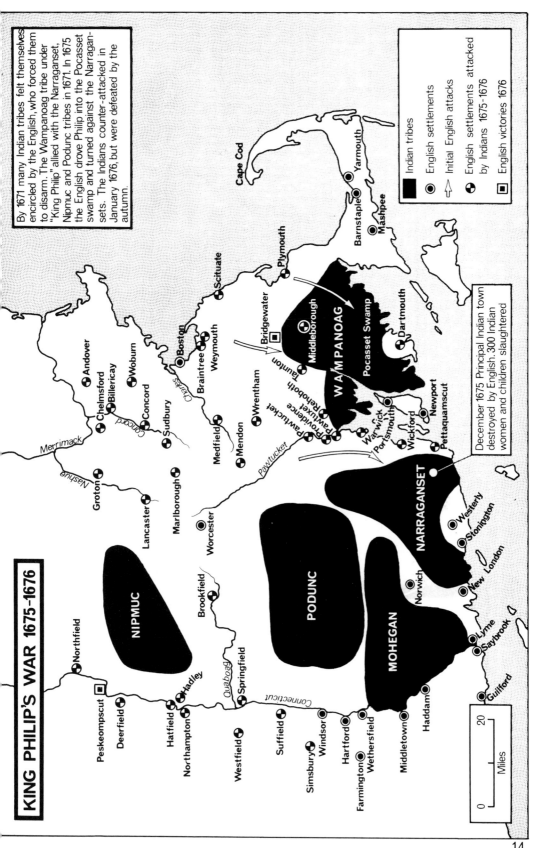

KING PHILIP'S WAR 1675-1676

By 1671 many Indian tribes felt themselves encircled by the English, who forced them to disarm. The Wampanoag tribe under "King Philip" allied with the Narraganset, Nipmuc and Podunc tribes in 1671. In 1675 the English drove Philip into the Pocasset swamp and turned against the Narragansets. The Indians counter-attacked in January 1676, but were defeated by the autumn.

Legend:
- Indian tribes
- ◉ English settlements
- ⇨ Initial English attacks
- ◒ English settlements attacked by Indians 1675-1676
- ▣ English victories 1676

December 1675 Principal Indian town destroyed by English. 300 Indian women and children slaughtered

Tribes: NIPMUC, PODUNC, MOHEGAN, NARRAGANSET, WAMPANOAG

Places: Northfield, Peskeompscut, Deerfield, Hatfield, Northampton, Hadley, Westfield, Suffield, Simsbury, Windsor, Farmington, Hartford, Wethersfield, Middletown, Haddam, Guilford, Saybrook, Lyme, New London, Norwich, Stonington, Westerly, Pettaquamscut, Newport, Wickford, Portsmouth, Warwick, Providence, Pawtuxet, Pawtucket, Rehoboth, Taunton, Dartmouth, Pocasset Swamp, Middleborough, Bridgewater, Plymouth, Barnstaple, Mashpee, Yarmouth, Scituate, Weymouth, Braintree, Boston, Woburn, Andover, Billericay, Chelmsford, Concord, Sudbury, Groton, Lancaster, Marlborough, Worcester, Brookfield, Springfield, Mendon, Medfield, Wrentham

Rivers: Merrimack, Nashua, Concord, Charles, Pawtucket, Quaboag, Connecticut

Cape Cod

Miles 0 — 20

14

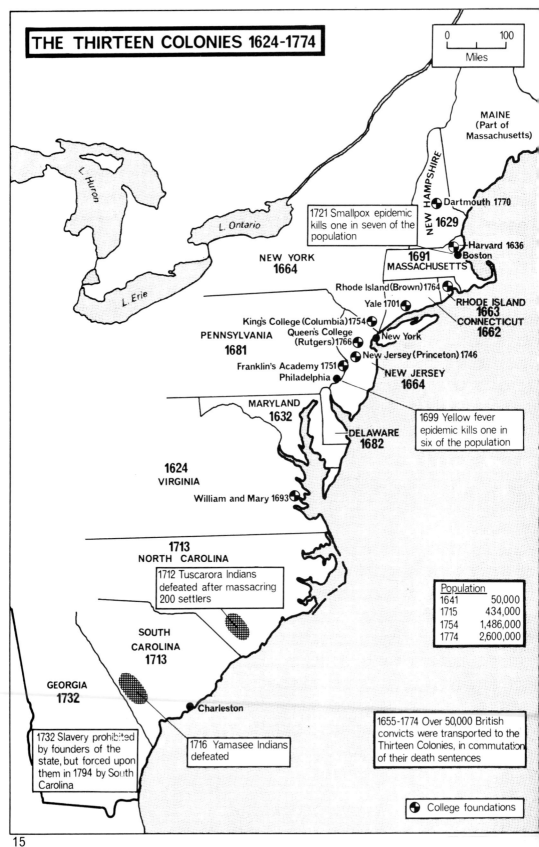

THE THIRTEEN COLONIES 1624-1774

0   100
Miles

MAINE
(Part of
Massachusetts)

NEW HAMPSHIRE

Dartmouth 1770

1629

1721 Smallpox epidemic
kills one in seven of the
population

NEW YORK
1664

Harvard 1636
Boston
1691
MASSACHUSETTS

Rhode Island (Brown) 1764

Yale 1701

King's College (Columbia) 1754

RHODE ISLAND
1663
CONNECTICUT
1662

PENNSYLVANIA
1681

Queen's College
(Rutgers) 1766

New York

Franklin's Academy 1751

New Jersey (Princeton) 1746

Philadelphia

NEW JERSEY
1664

MARYLAND
1632

DELAWARE
1682

1699 Yellow fever
epidemic kills one in
six of the population

1624
VIRGINIA

William and Mary 1693

1713
NORTH CAROLINA

1712 Tuscarora Indians
defeated after massacring
200 settlers

Population	
1641	50,000
1715	434,000
1754	1,486,000
1774	2,600,000

SOUTH
CAROLINA
1713

GEORGIA
1732

Charleston

1732 Slavery prohibited
by founders of the
state, but forced upon
them in 1794 by South
Carolina

1716 Yamasee Indians
defeated

1655-1774 Over 50,000 British
convicts were transported to the
Thirteen Colonies, in commutation
of their death sentences

College foundations

L. Huron

L. Ontario

L. Erie

15

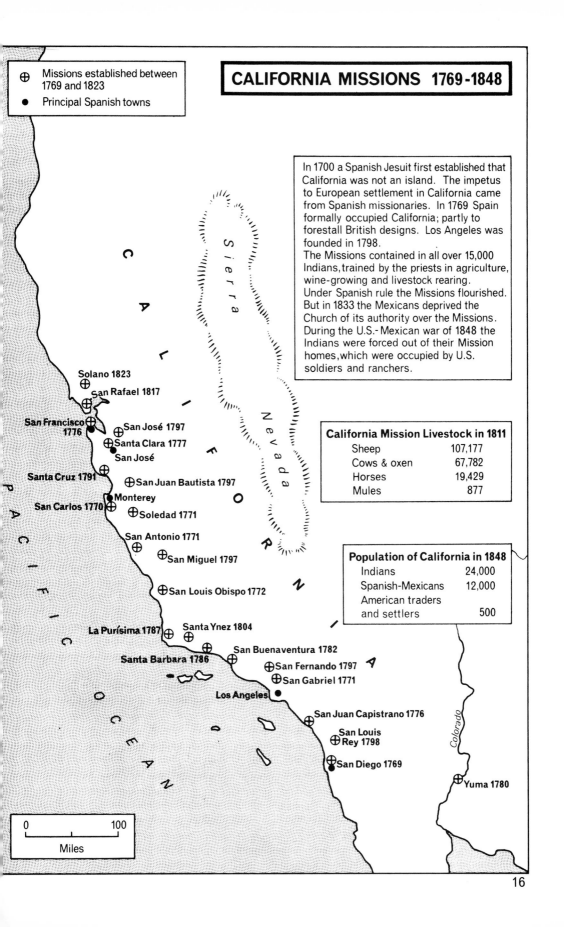

CALIFORNIA MISSIONS 1769-1848

⊕ Missions established between 1769 and 1823

● Principal Spanish towns

In 1700 a Spanish Jesuit first established that California was not an island. The impetus to European settlement in California came from Spanish missionaries. In 1769 Spain formally occupied California; partly to forestall British designs. Los Angeles was founded in 1798.

The Missions contained in all over 15,000 Indians, trained by the priests in agriculture, wine-growing and livestock rearing.

Under Spanish rule the Missions flourished. But in 1833 the Mexicans deprived the Church of its authority over the Missions. During the U.S.-Mexican war of 1848 the Indians were forced out of their Mission homes, which were occupied by U.S. soldiers and ranchers.

California Mission Livestock in 1811

Sheep	107,177
Cows & oxen	67,782
Horses	19,429
Mules	877

Population of California in 1848

Indians	24,000
Spanish-Mexicans	12,000
American traders and settlers	500

C A L I F O R N I A

Sierra Nevada

Solano 1823
San Rafael 1817
San Francisco 1776
San José 1797
Santa Clara 1777
San José
Santa Cruz 1791
San Juan Bautista 1797
Monterey
San Carlos 1770
Soledad 1771
San Antonio 1771
San Miguel 1797
San Louis Obispo 1772
La Purísima 1787
Santa Ynez 1804
Santa Barbara 1786
San Buenaventura 1782
San Fernando 1797
San Gabriel 1771
Los Angeles
San Juan Capistrano 1776
San Louis Rey 1798
San Diego 1769
Yuma 1780

Colorado

PACIFIC OCEAN

0 ___ 100
Miles

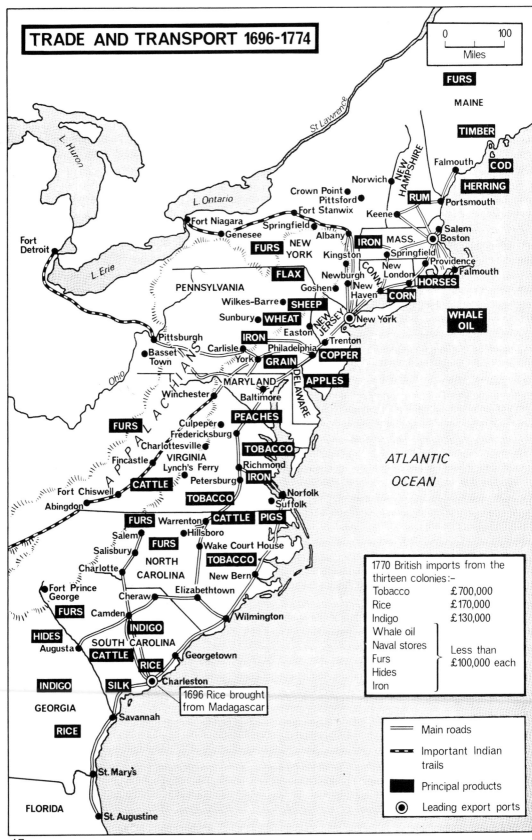

TRADE AND TRANSPORT 1696-1774

0 — 100
Miles

FURS
MAINE

TIMBER

St.Lawrence

COD

HERRING

L. Huron

Fort Detroit

L. Ontario

Crown Point
Pittsford
Fort Stanwix
Fort Niagara
Springfield
Genesee
Albany
Norwich
Keene
RUM
Portsmouth
Salem
Boston
IRON MASS.
Springfield
Providence
Falmouth

FURS NEW YORK
Kingston
New London
HORSES

FLAX
Newburgh
Goshen
New Haven
CORN

PENNSYLVANIA
Wilkes-Barre
SHEEP
Sunbury
WHEAT
Easton
NEW JERSEY
New York

WHALE OIL

Pittsburgh
Carlisle
IRON
Trenton
Basset Town
York
Philadelphia
COPPER

Ohio

GRAIN

MARYLAND
APPLES
Winchester
Baltimore
DELAWARE

FURS
Culpeper
Fredericksburg
Charlottesville
Fincastle
VIRGINIA
Lynch's Ferry
Petersburg
Richmond
IRON
PEACHES

TOBACCO

ATLANTIC OCEAN

Fort Chiswell
Abingdon
CATTLE
TOBACCO
Norfolk
Suffolk

FURS Warrenton
CATTLE **PIGS**
Salem
Hillsboro
Salisbury
FURS
Wake Court House
Charlotte
NORTH CAROLINA
TOBACCO
New Bern
Elizabethtown

Fort Prince George
Cheraw
Wilmington

FURS Camden

HIDES
Augusta
INDIGO
SOUTH CAROLINA
CATTLE
RICE
Georgetown

INDIGO
SILK
Charleston

1696 Rice brought from Madagascar

GEORGIA
Savannah

RICE

St. Mary's

FLORIDA
St. Augustine

1770 British imports from the thirteen colonies:-
Tobacco   £700,000
Rice   £170,000
Indigo   £130,000
Whale oil
Naval stores
Furs   Less than
Hides   £100,000 each
Iron

——— Main roads

▄▄▄▄ Important Indian trails

█ Principal products

◉ Leading export ports

17

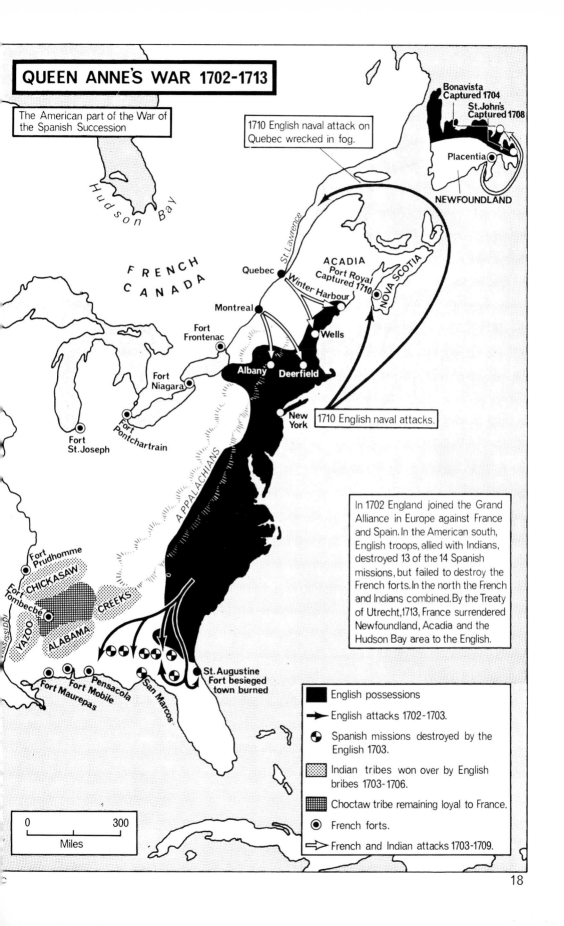

QUEEN ANNE'S WAR 1702-1713

The American part of the War of the Spanish Succession

1710 English naval attack on Quebec wrecked in fog.

Bonavista
Captured 1704
St.John's
Captured 1708

Placentia

NEWFOUNDLAND

Hudson Bay

FRENCH CANADA

St. Lawrence

Quebec

ACADIA
Port Royal
Captured 1710

NOVA SCOTIA

Winter Harbour

Montreal

Fort Frontenac

Wells

Fort Niagara

Albany   Deerfield

Fort Pontchartrain

New York

1710 English naval attacks.

Fort St.Joseph

APPALACHIANS

In 1702 England joined the Grand Alliance in Europe against France and Spain. In the American south, English troops, allied with Indians, destroyed 13 of the 14 Spanish missions, but failed to destroy the French forts. In the north the French and Indians combined. By the Treaty of Utrecht, 1713, France surrendered Newfoundland, Acadia and the Hudson Bay area to the English.

Fort Prudhomme

CHICKASAW

Fort Tombecbe

CREEKS

Mississippi

YAZOO

ALABAMA

Fort Maurepas   Fort Mobile   Pensacola   San Marcos

St. Augustine
Fort besieged
town burned

	English possessions
→	English attacks 1702-1703.
◑	Spanish missions destroyed by the English 1703.
	Indian tribes won over by English bribes 1703-1706.
	Choctaw tribe remaining loyal to France.
◉	French forts.
⇨	French and Indian attacks 1703-1709.

0   300
Miles

18

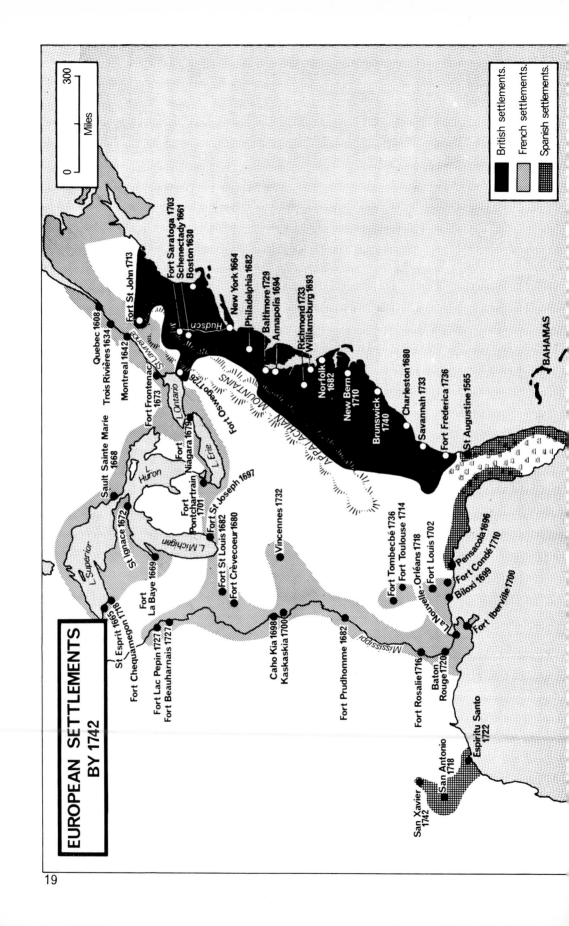

EUROPEAN SETTLEMENTS BY 1742

Scale: 300 Miles (0 – 300)

Legend:
- British settlements.
- French settlements.
- Spanish settlements.

BAHAMAS

Fort Saratoga 1703
Schenectady 1661
Boston 1630
Fort St John 1713
Quebec 1608
Trois Rivières 1634
Montreal 1642
New York 1664
Philadelphia 1682
Baltimore 1729
Annapolis 1694
Richmond 1733
Williamsburg 1693
Hudson
St Lawrence
Fort Frontenac 1673
L. Ontario
Fort Oswego 1726
Fort Niagara 1679
L. Erie
APPALACHIAN MOUNTAINS
Norfolk 1682
New Bern 1710
Brunswick 1740
Charleston 1680
Savannah 1733
Fort Frederica 1736
St Augustine 1565

Sault Sainte Marie 1668
St Ignace 1672
Huron
L. Superior
L. Michigan
Fort Pontchartrain 1701
Fort St Joseph 1697
Fort St Louis 1682
Fort Crèvecoeur 1680
Vincennes 1732
Fort Tombecbé 1736
Fort Toulouse 1714
Fort Louis 1702
Pensacola 1696
Fort Condé 1710
Biloxi 1699

St Esprit 1665
Fort Chequamegon 1718
Fort La Baye 1669
Fort Lac Pepin 1727
Fort Beauharnais 1727
Caho Kia 1698
Kaskaskia 1700
Fort Prudhomme 1682
Mississippi
Fort Rosalie 1716
Baton Rouge 1720
La Nouvelle Orléans 1718
Fort Iberville 1700

San Xavier 1742
San Antonio 1718
Espiritu Santo 1722

19

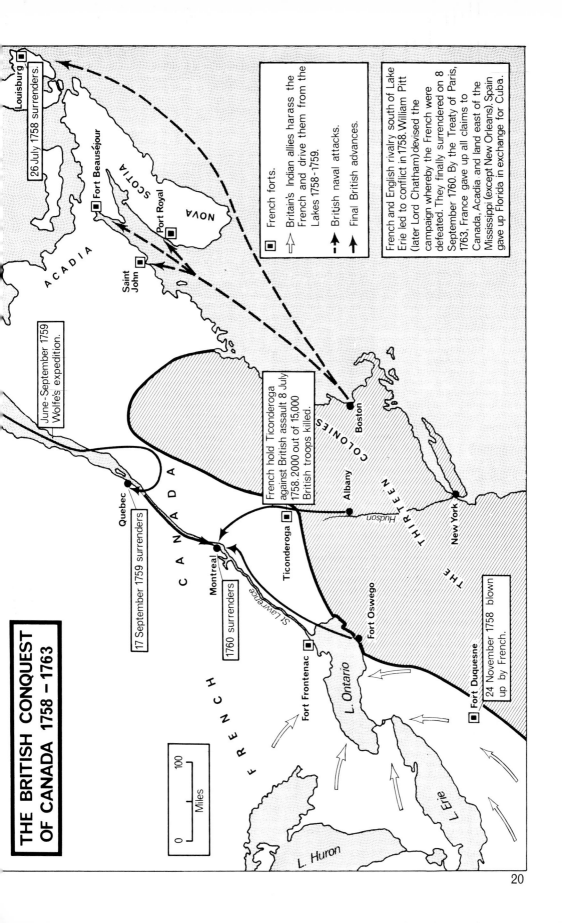

THE BRITISH CONQUEST OF CANADA 1758 – 1763

Louisburg. 26 July 1758 surrenders.

Fort Beauséjour

Port Royal

NOVA SCOTIA

Saint John

ACADIA

French forts.

Britain's Indian allies harass the French and drive them from the Lakes 1758-1759.

British naval attacks.

Final British advances.

French and English rivalry south of Lake Erie led to conflict in 1758. William Pitt (later Lord Chatham) devised the campaign whereby the French were defeated. They finally surrendered on 8 September 1760. By the Treaty of Paris, 1763, France gave up all claims to Canada, Acadia and land east of the Mississippi (except New Orleans). Spain gave up Florida in exchange for Cuba.

June-September 1759 Wolfe's expedition.

French hold Ticonderoga against British assault 8 July 1758. 2000 out of 15,000 British troops killed.

Boston

THE THIRTEEN COLONIES

Albany

Hudson

New York

Quebec

17 September 1759 surrenders

CANADA

Montreal

1760 surrenders

Ticonderoga

St Lawrence

Fort Oswego

FRENCH

Fort Frontenac

Fort Duquesne

24 November 1758 blown up by French.

L. Ontario

L. Erie

L. Huron

0   100
Miles

20

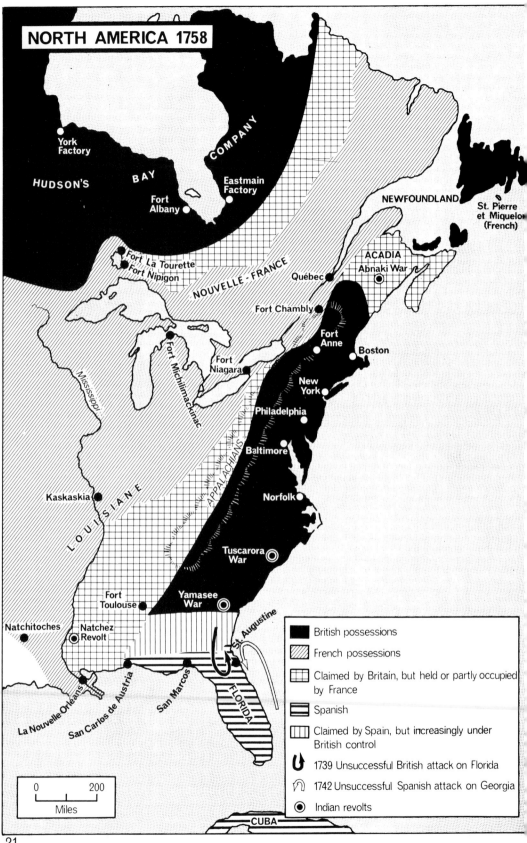

NORTH AMERICA 1758

York Factory

HUDSON'S BAY COMPANY

Eastmain Factory

Fort Albany

NEWFOUNDLAND

St. Pierre et Miquelon (French)

Fort La Tourette
Fort Nipigon

NOUVELLE - FRANCE

ACADIA
Abnaki War

Québec

Fort Chambly

Fort Anne

Fort Michilimackinac

Fort Niagara

Boston

Fort Niagara

New York

Mississippi

Philadelphia

Baltimore

Kaskaskia

LOUISIANE

APPALACHIANS

Norfolk

Tuscarora War

Yamasee War

Fort Toulouse

Natchitoches

Natchez Revolt

St. Augustine

La Nouvelle-Orléans

San Carlos de Austria

San Marcos

FLORIDA

CUBA

■	British possessions
▨	French possessions
▦	Claimed by Britain, but held or partly occupied by France
▤	Spanish
▥	Claimed by Spain, but increasingly under British control
↻	1739 Unsuccessful British attack on Florida
↱	1742 Unsuccessful Spanish attack on Georgia
◉	Indian revolts

0   200
Miles

21

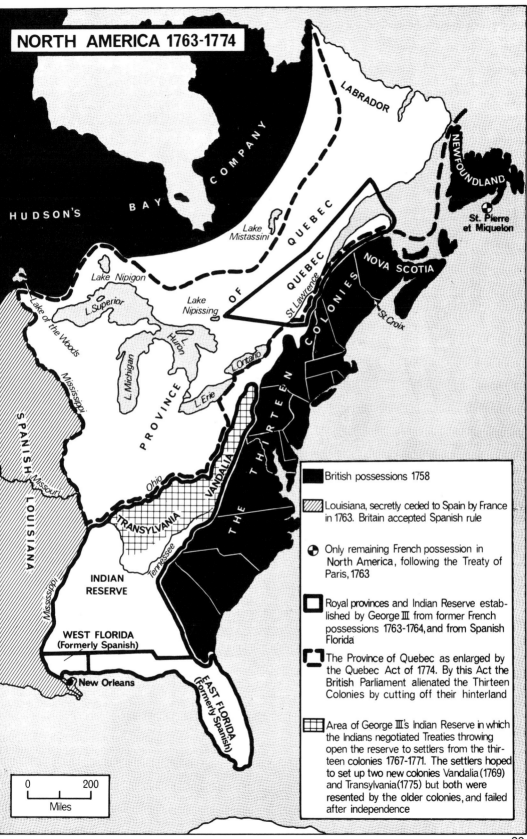

NORTH AMERICA 1763-1774

LABRADOR

NEWFOUNDLAND

HUDSON'S BAY COMPANY

Lake Mistassini

QUEBEC

St. Pierre et Miquelon

Lake Nipigon

L. Superior

Lake of the Woods

Lake Nipissing

QUEBEC

St Lawrence

NOVA SCOTIA

St Croix

L. Michigan

Huron

PROVINCE

L. Ontario

L. Erie

THE THIRTEEN COLONIES

Mississippi

SPANISH LOUISIANA

Missouri

Ohio

VANDALIA

TRANSYLVANIA

Tennessee

INDIAN RESERVE

WEST FLORIDA
(Formerly Spanish)

Mississippi

New Orleans

EAST FLORIDA
(Formerly Spanish)

■	British possessions 1758
▨	Louisiana, secretly ceded to Spain by France in 1763. Britain accepted Spanish rule
◕	Only remaining French possession in North America, following the Treaty of Paris, 1763
□	Royal provinces and Indian Reserve established by George III from former French possessions 1763-1764, and from Spanish Florida
⌐¬	The Province of Quebec as enlarged by the Quebec Act of 1774. By this Act the British Parliament alienated the Thirteen Colonies by cutting off their hinterland
▦	Area of George III's Indian Reserve in which the Indians negotiated Treaties throwing open the reserve to settlers from the thirteen colonies 1767-1771. The settlers hoped to set up two new colonies Vandalia (1769) and Transylvania (1775) but both were resented by the older colonies, and failed after independence

0   200
Miles

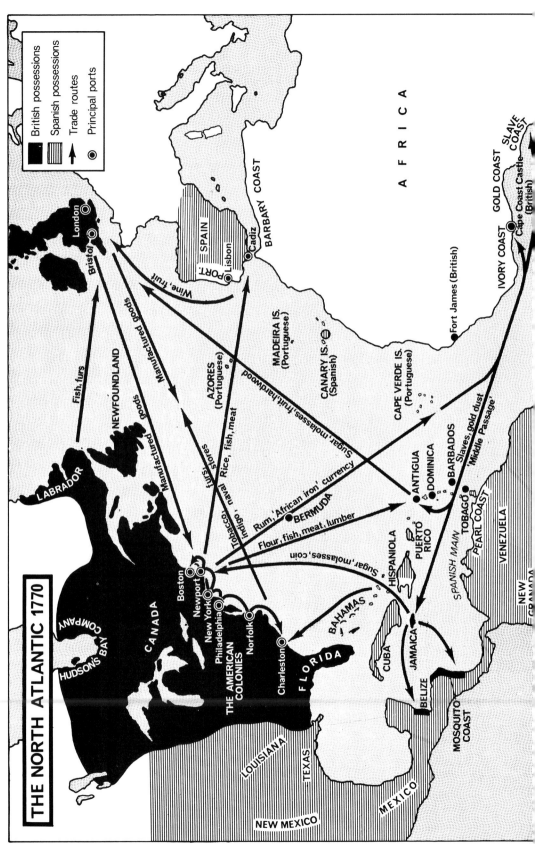

THE NORTH ATLANTIC 1770

Legend:
- British possessions
- Spanish possessions
- Trade routes
- Principal ports

Labels on map:

LABRADOR

NEWFOUNDLAND

HUDSON'S BAY COMPANY

CANADA

THE AMERICAN COLONIES

Boston
Newport
New York
Philadelphia
Norfolk
Charleston

FLORIDA

LOUISIANA

TEXAS

NEW MEXICO

MEXICO

BAHAMAS

CUBA

JAMAICA

BELIZE

MOSQUITO COAST

NEW GRANADA

VENEZUELA

SPANISH MAIN

PEARL COAST

TOBAGO

BARBADOS

DOMINICA

ANTIGUA

PUERTO RICO

HISPANIOLA

BERMUDA

AZORES (Portuguese)

MADEIRA IS. (Portuguese)

CANARY IS. (Spanish)

CAPE VERDE IS. (Portuguese)

AFRICA

SLAVE COAST

GOLD COAST

IVORY COAST

Cape Coast Castle (British)

Fort James (British)

SPAIN

PORT. (Portugal)

Lisbon
Cadiz

BARBARY COAST

London
Bristol

Trade route annotations:

Fish, furs

Manufactured goods

Manufactured goods

furs, stores

naval stores

Tobacco, naval stores, Rice, fish, meat

indigo, Rice, fish, meat

Rum, 'African iron' currency

Wine, fruit

Sugar, molasses, fruit, hardwood

Flour, fish, meat, lumber

Sugar, molasses, coin

Slaves, gold dust 'Middle Passage'

23

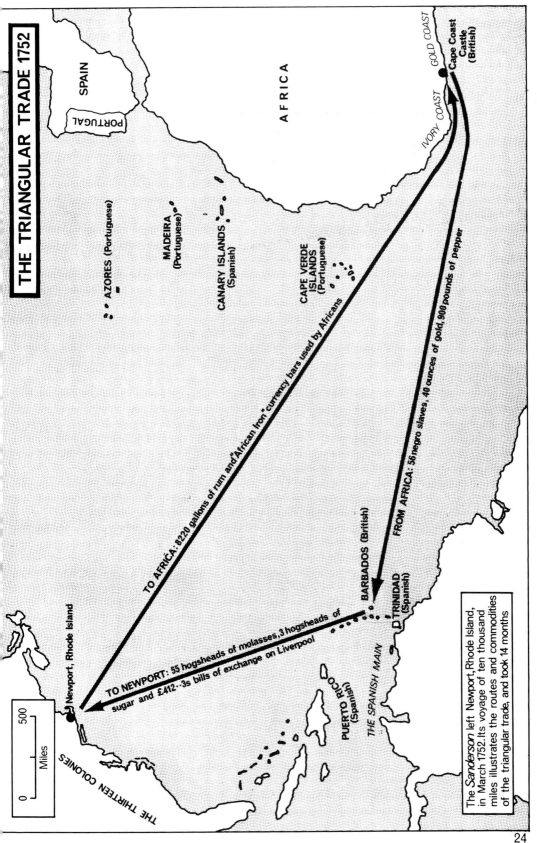

THE TRIANGULAR TRADE 1752

SPAIN

PORTUGAL

AZORES (Portuguese)

MADEIRA (Portuguese)

CANARY ISLANDS (Spanish)

CAPE VERDE ISLANDS (Portuguese)

AFRICA

GOLD COAST

IVORY COAST

Cape Coast Castle (British)

TO AFRICA: 8220 gallons of rum and "African Iron" currency bars used by Africans

FROM AFRICA: 56 negro slaves, 40 ounces of gold, 900 pounds of pepper

Newport, Rhode Island

THE THIRTEEN COLONIES

TO NEWPORT: 55 hogsheads of molasses, 3 hogsheads of sugar and £412··3s bills of exchange on Liverpool

BARBADOS (British)

TRINIDAD (Spanish)

PUERTO RICO (Spanish)

THE SPANISH MAIN

0   500

Miles

The *Sanderson* left Newport, Rhode Island, in March 1752. Its voyage of ten thousand miles illustrates the routes and commodities of the triangular trade, and took 14 months

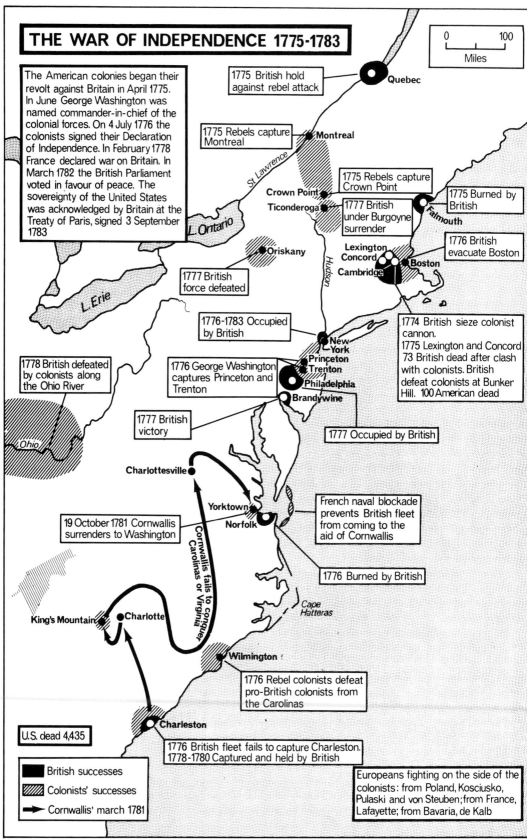

THE WAR OF INDEPENDENCE 1775-1783

0   100

Miles

The American colonies began their revolt against Britain in April 1775. In June George Washington was named commander-in-chief of the colonial forces. On 4 July 1776 the colonists signed their Declaration of Independence. In February 1778 France declared war on Britain. In March 1782 the British Parliament voted in favour of peace. The sovereignty of the United States was acknowledged by Britain at the Treaty of Paris, signed 3 September 1783

1775 British hold against rebel attack

Quebec

1775 Rebels capture Montreal

Montreal

St Lawrence

1775 Rebels capture Crown Point

Crown Point

Ticonderoga

1777 British under Burgoyne surrender

1775 Burned by British

Falmouth

L. Ontario

1776 British evacuate Boston

Oriskany

Lexington Concord

Cambridge

Boston

1777 British force defeated

Hudson

L. Erie

1776-1783 Occupied by British

1774 British sieze colonist cannon.
1775 Lexington and Concord 73 British dead after clash with colonists. British defeat colonists at Bunker Hill. 100 American dead

New York

Princeton

1776 George Washington captures Princeton and Trenton

Trenton

Philadelphia

Brandywine

1778 British defeated by colonists along the Ohio River

Ohio

1777 British victory

1777 Occupied by British

Charlottesville

Yorktown

Norfolk

French naval blockade prevents British fleet from coming to the aid of Cornwallis

19 October 1781 Cornwallis surrenders to Washington

Cornwallis fails to conquer Carolinas or Virginia

1776 Burned by British

Cape Hatteras

King's Mountain

Charlotte

Wilmington

1776 Rebel colonists defeat pro-British colonists from the Carolinas

U.S. dead 4,435

Charleston

1776 British fleet fails to capture Charleston. 1778-1780 Captured and held by British

■ British successes

▨ Colonists' successes

➤ Cornwallis' march 1781

Europeans fighting on the side of the colonists: from Poland, Kosciusko, Pulaski and von Steuben; from France, Lafayette; from Bavaria, de Kalb

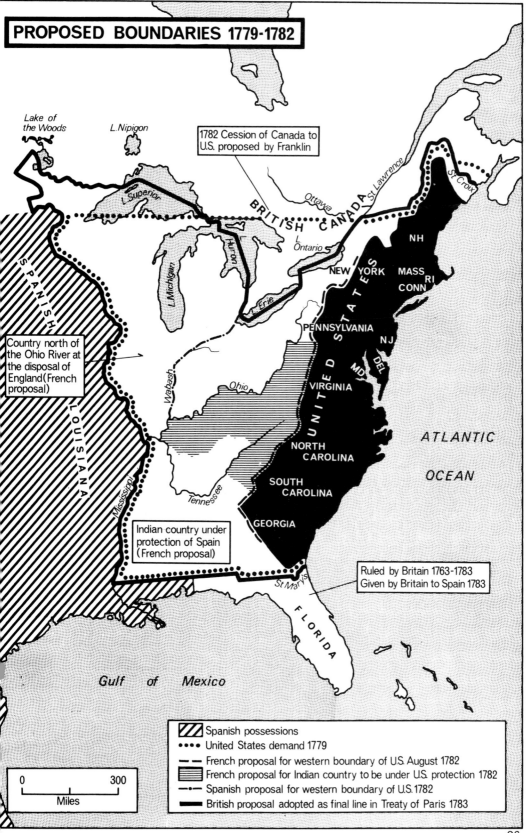

PROPOSED BOUNDARIES 1779-1782

Lake of the Woods

L. Nipigon

1782 Cession of Canada to U.S. proposed by Franklin

BRITISH CANADA

Ottawa

St. Lawrence

St. Croix

L. Superior

L. Huron

L. Michigan

L. Ontario

Erie

SPANISH

LOUISIANA

Country north of the Ohio River at the disposal of England (French proposal)

UNITED STATES

NH

NEW YORK

MASS

RI

CONN

PENNSYLVANIA

NJ

DEL

MD

VIRGINIA

Wabash

Ohio

NORTH CAROLINA

SOUTH CAROLINA

Tennessee

Mississippi

Indian country under protection of Spain (French proposal)

GEORGIA

St Mary's

FLORIDA

ATLANTIC

OCEAN

Ruled by Britain 1763-1783 Given by Britain to Spain 1783

Gulf of Mexico

Spanish possessions
•••• United States demand 1779
– – – French proposal for western boundary of U.S. August 1782
≡≡≡ French proposal for Indian country to be under U.S. protection 1782
–•–• Spanish proposal for western boundary of U.S. 1782
▬▬▬ British proposal adopted as final line in Treaty of Paris 1783

0   300
Miles

26

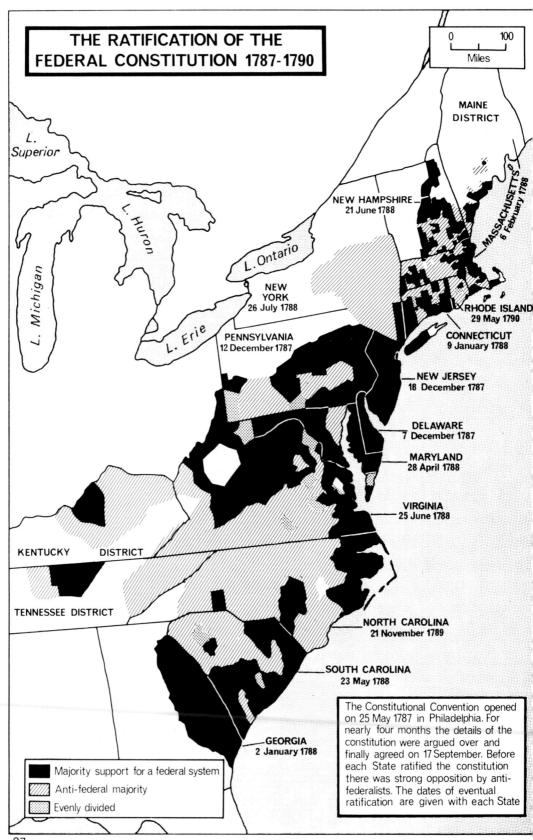

THE RATIFICATION OF THE FEDERAL CONSTITUTION 1787-1790

0   100

Miles

L. Superior

L. Huron

L. Michigan

L. Ontario

L. Erie

MAINE DISTRICT

NEW HAMPSHIRE
21 June 1788

MASSACHUSETTS
6 February 1788

NEW YORK
26 July 1788

RHODE ISLAND
29 May 1790

CONNECTICUT
9 January 1788

PENNSYLVANIA
12 December 1787

NEW JERSEY
18 December 1787

DELAWARE
7 December 1787

MARYLAND
28 April 1788

VIRGINIA
25 June 1788

KENTUCKY   DISTRICT

TENNESSEE DISTRICT

NORTH CAROLINA
21 November 1789

SOUTH CAROLINA
23 May 1788

GEORGIA
2 January 1788

The Constitutional Convention opened
on 25 May 1787 in Philadelphia. For
nearly four months the details of the
constitution were argued over and
finally agreed on 17 September. Before
each State ratified the constitution
there was strong opposition by anti-
federalists. The dates of eventual
ratification are given with each State

■   Majority support for a federal system

▨   Anti-federal majority

▦   Evenly divided

NORTH AMERICA 1783

Legend:
- ■ The United States of America.
- ▦ British claims not finally ceded to U.S. until the Jay Treaty of 1795.
- ▤ British possessions.
- ▨ Spanish possessions.
- ▥ Disputed and unsettled frontiers

ALASKA

Kodiak

1784 Russian settlement founded

UNEXPLORED TERRITORY

BAFFIN LAND

NEWFOUNDLAND

HUDSON BAY

NEW SOUTH WALES

NEW BRITAIN

LABRADOR

ACADIA

NOVA SCOTIA

CANADA

Northern limit of Spanish claims

Columbia

Snake

CALIFORNIA

Mississippi

THE UNITED STATES

TEXAS

Rio Grande

FLORIDA

BAHAMAS

MEXICO

CUBA

JAMAICA

BELIZE

MOSQUITO COAST

PANAMA

By the Treaty of Paris, 3 September 1783, Britain recognised the independence of the United States, withdrew all military and naval forces, agreed to fix the boundary of Canada by negotiation, and returned Florida to Spain.

0   1000

Miles

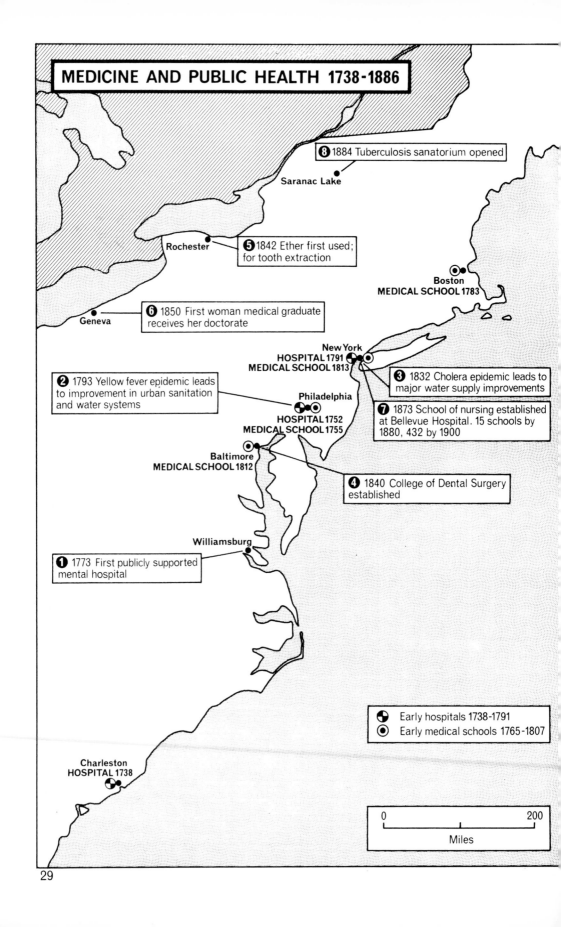

MEDICINE AND PUBLIC HEALTH 1738-1886

8 1884 Tuberculosis sanatorium opened

Saranac Lake

Rochester

5 1842 Ether first used; for tooth extraction

Boston
MEDICAL SCHOOL 1783

6 1850 First woman medical graduate receives her doctorate

Geneva

New York
HOSPITAL 1791
MEDICAL SCHOOL 1813

2 1793 Yellow fever epidemic leads to improvement in urban sanitation and water systems

Philadelphia
HOSPITAL 1752
MEDICAL SCHOOL 1755

3 1832 Cholera epidemic leads to major water supply improvements

7 1873 School of nursing established at Bellevue Hospital. 15 schools by 1880, 432 by 1900

Baltimore
MEDICAL SCHOOL 1812

4 1840 College of Dental Surgery established

Williamsburg

1 1773 First publicly supported mental hospital

⊕ Early hospitals 1738-1791
◉ Early medical schools 1765-1807

Charleston
HOSPITAL 1738

0   200
Miles

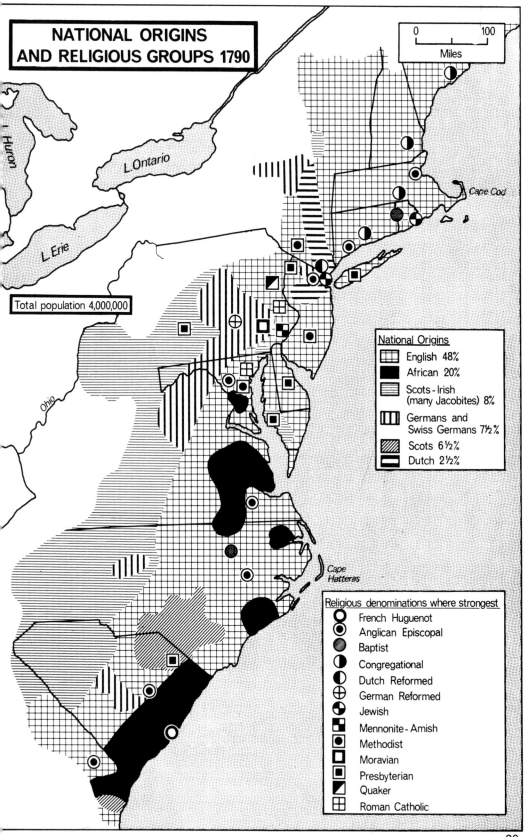

NATIONAL ORIGINS AND RELIGIOUS GROUPS 1790

0 — 100
Miles

L. Huron

L. Ontario

L. Erie

Cape Cod

Total population 4,000,000

Ohio

Cape Hatteras

National Origins

⊞	English 48%
■	African 20%
≡	Scots - Irish (many Jacobites) 8%
⦀	Germans and Swiss Germans 7½%
▨	Scots 6½%
▭	Dutch 2½%

Religious denominations where strongest

◐	French Huguenot
◉	Anglican Episcopal
◓	Baptist
◑	Congregational
◖	Dutch Reformed
⊕	German Reformed
◒	Jewish
▣	Mennonite - Amish
▣	Methodist
▢	Moravian
▪	Presbyterian
◣	Quaker
⊞	Roman Catholic

D

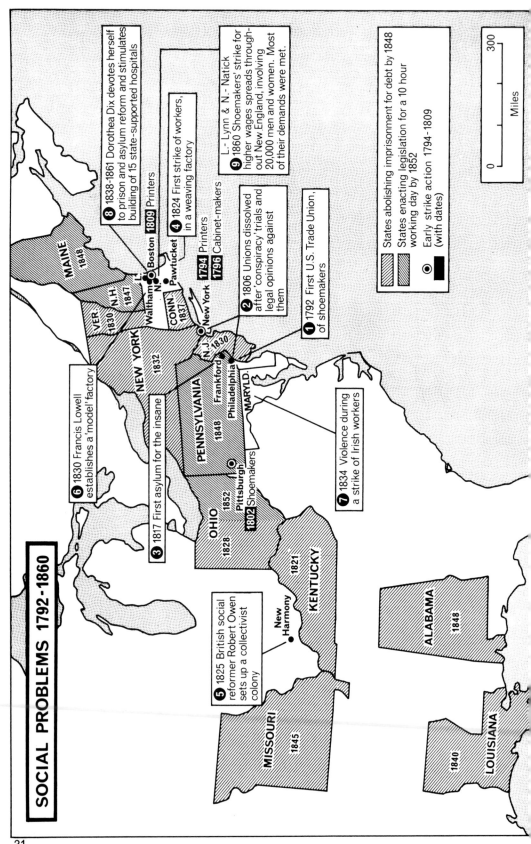

SOCIAL PROBLEMS 1792-1860

8 1838-1861 Dorothea Dix devotes herself to prison and asylum reform and stimulates building of 15 state-supported hospitals

1809 Printers

4 1824 First strike of workers, in a weaving factory

L - Lynn & N - Natick
9 1860 Shoemakers' strike for higher wages spreads throughout New England, involving 20,000 men and women. Most of their demands were met.

1794 Printers
1796 Cabinet-makers

2 1806 Unions dissolved after 'conspiracy' trials and legal opinions against them

1 1792 First U.S. Trade Union, of shoemakers

6 1830 Francis Lowell establishes a 'model' factory

3 1817 First asylum for the insane

7 1834 Violence during a strike of Irish workers

5 1825 British social reformer Robert Owen sets up a collectivist colony

MAINE
1848

VER
1830

N.H.
1847

CONN
1837

NEW YORK
1832

N.J.
1830

PENNSYLVANIA
1848

Frankford

Philadelphia

MARYLD.

OHIO
1828   1852

1802 Shoemakers

Pittsburgh

Boston

Waltham

N.

Pawtucket

New York

KENTUCKY
1821

New Harmony

MISSOURI
1845

ALABAMA
1848

LOUISIANA
1840

States abolishing imprisonment for debt by 1848

States enacting legislation for a 10 hour working day by 1852

⊙ Early strike action 1794-1809 (with dates)

0   300

Miles

31

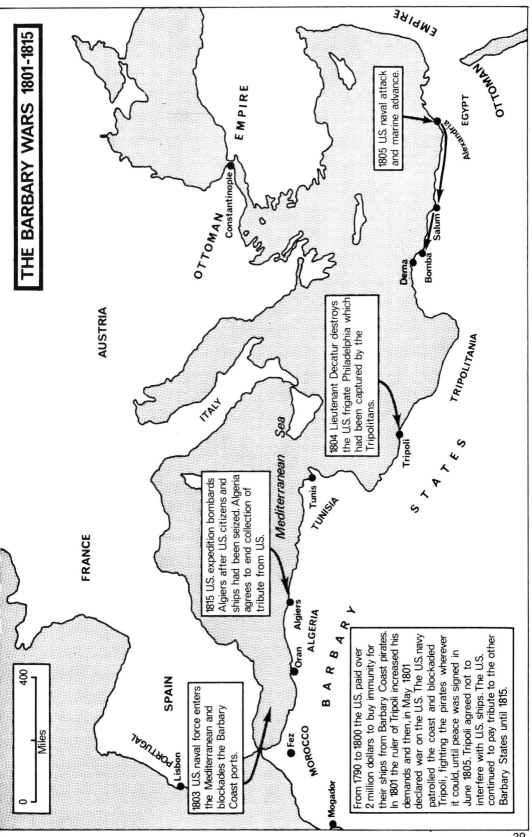

THE BARBARY WARS 1801-1815

1805 U.S. naval attack and marine advance.

1804 Lieutenant Decatur destroys the U.S. frigate Philadelphia which had been captured by the Tripolitans.

1815 U.S. expedition bombards Algiers after U.S. citizens and ships had been seized. Algeria agrees to end collection of tribute from U.S.

1803 U.S. naval force enters the Mediterranean and blockades the Barbary Coast ports.

From 1790 to 1800 the U.S. paid over 2 million dollars to buy immunity for their ships from Barbary Coast pirates. In 1801 the ruler of Tripoli increased his demands and then, in May 1801 declared war on the U.S. The U.S. navy patrolled the coast and blockaded Tripoli, fighting the pirates wherever it could, until peace was signed in June 1805. Tripoli agreed not to interfere with U.S. ships. The U.S. continued to pay tribute to the other Barbary States until 1815.

OTTOMAN EMPIRE

OTTOMAN EMPIRE

AUSTRIA

FRANCE

SPAIN

PORTUGAL

Lisbon

ITALY

Mediterranean Sea

Constantinople

EGYPT

Alexandria

Salum

Bomba

Derna

TRIPOLITANIA

Tripoli

S T A T E S

B A R B A R Y

Tunis

TUNISIA

Algiers

Oran

ALGERIA

Fez

MOROCCO

Mogador

0 — 400
Miles

32

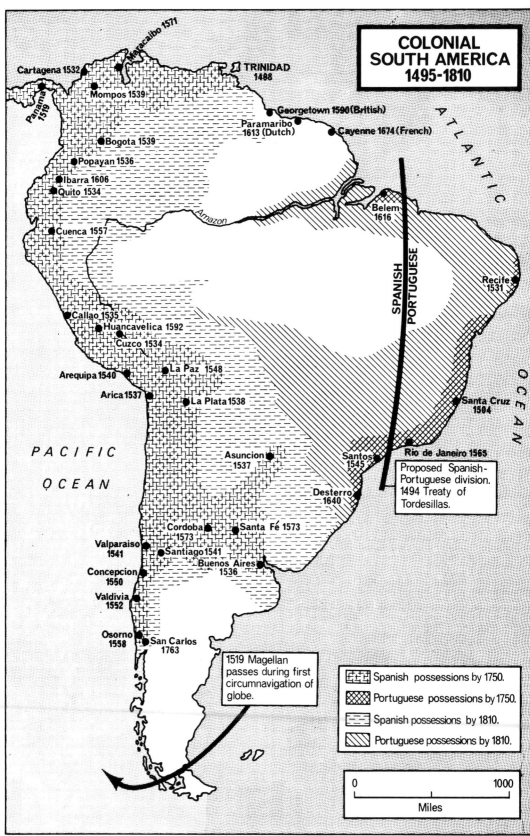

COLONIAL SOUTH AMERICA 1495-1810

Maracaibo 1571

Cartagena 1532

TRINIDAD 1488

Mompos 1539

Georgetown 1590 (British)

Paramaribo 1613 (Dutch)

Cayenne 1674 (French)

Panama 1519

Bogota 1539

Popayan 1536

Ibarra 1606

Quito 1534

Amazon

Belem 1616

Cuenca 1557

SPANISH

PORTUGUESE

Recife 1531

Callao 1535

Huancavelica 1592

Cuzco 1534

Arequipa 1540

La Paz 1548

Arica 1537

La Plata 1538

Santa Cruz 1504

PACIFIC

OCEAN

Asuncion 1537

Santos 1545

Rio de Janeiro 1565

Proposed Spanish-Portuguese division. 1494 Treaty of Tordesillas.

Desterro 1640

Cordoba 1573

Santa Fé 1573

Valparaiso 1541

Santiago 1541

Concepcion 1550

Buenos Aires 1536

Valdivia 1552

Osorno 1558

San Carlos 1763

1519 Magellan passes during first circumnavigation of globe.

ATLANTIC

OCEAN

Spanish possessions by 1750.

Portuguese possessions by 1750.

Spanish possessions by 1810.

Portuguese possessions by 1810.

0   1000

Miles

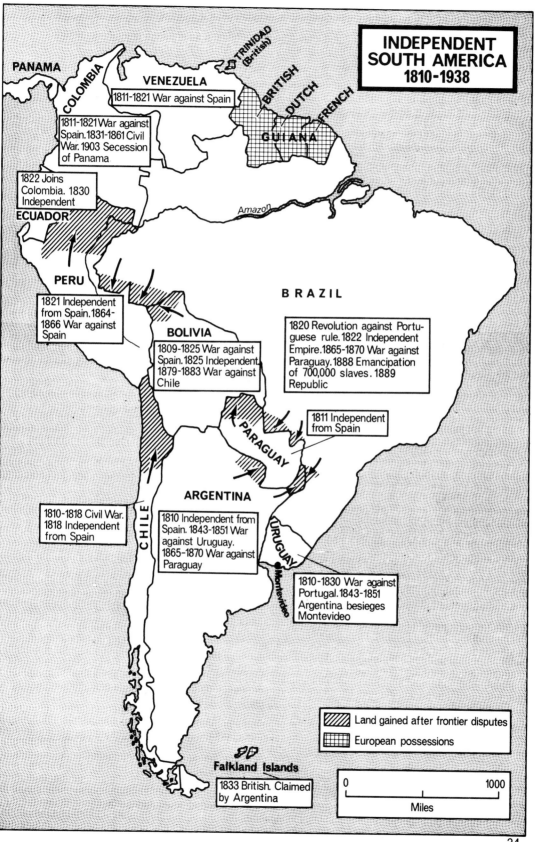

INDEPENDENT SOUTH AMERICA 1810-1938

PANAMA

COLOMBIA

VENEZUELA

1811-1821 War against Spain

1811-1821 War against Spain. 1831-1861 Civil War. 1903 Secession of Panama

TRINIDAD (British)

BRITISH DUTCH FRENCH

GUIANA

1822 Joins Colombia. 1830 Independent

ECUADOR

Amazon

PERU

1821 Independent from Spain. 1864-1866 War against Spain

BOLIVIA

1809-1825 War against Spain. 1825 Independent. 1879-1883 War against Chile

BRAZIL

1820 Revolution against Portuguese rule. 1822 Independent Empire. 1865-1870 War against Paraguay. 1888 Emancipation of 700,000 slaves. 1889 Republic

PARAGUAY

1811 Independent from Spain

1810-1818 Civil War. 1818 Independent from Spain

CHILE

ARGENTINA

1810 Independent from Spain. 1843-1851 War against Uruguay. 1865-1870 War against Paraguay

URUGUAY

Montevideo

1810-1830 War against Portugal. 1843-1851 Argentina besieges Montevideo

⬜ Land gained after frontier disputes

⬜ European possessions

Falkland Islands

1833 British. Claimed by Argentina

0 ————————— 1000

Miles

34

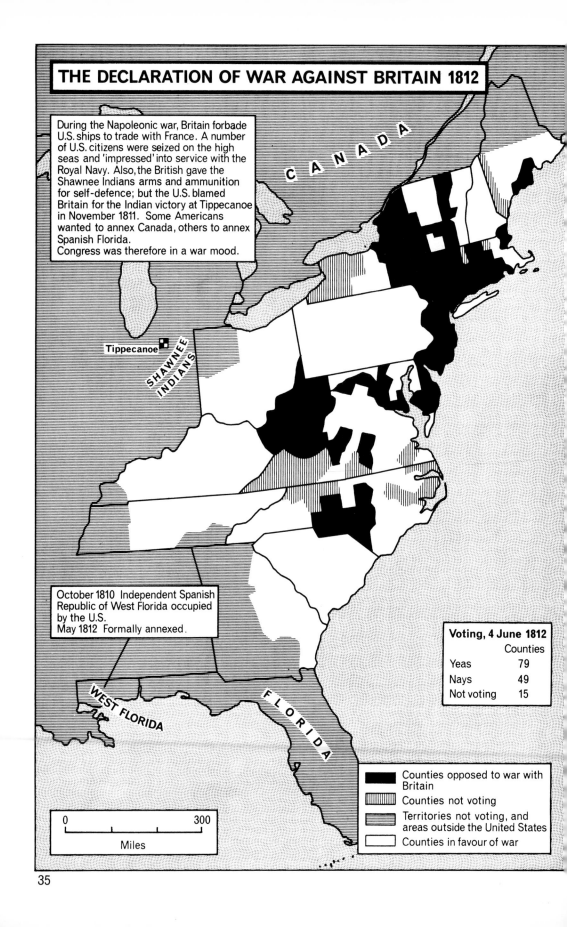

THE DECLARATION OF WAR AGAINST BRITAIN 1812

During the Napoleonic war, Britain forbade U.S. ships to trade with France. A number of U.S. citizens were seized on the high seas and 'impressed' into service with the Royal Navy. Also, the British gave the Shawnee Indians arms and ammunition for self-defence; but the U.S. blamed Britain for the Indian victory at Tippecanoe in November 1811. Some Americans wanted to annex Canada, others to annex Spanish Florida.
Congress was therefore in a war mood.

CANADA

Tippecanoe

SHAWNEE INDIANS

October 1810 Independent Spanish Republic of West Florida occupied by the U.S.
May 1812 Formally annexed.

WEST FLORIDA

FLORIDA

Voting, 4 June 1812

	Counties
Yeas	79
Nays	49
Not voting	15

Counties opposed to war with Britain

Counties not voting

Territories not voting, and areas outside the United States

Counties in favour of war

0 — 300
Miles

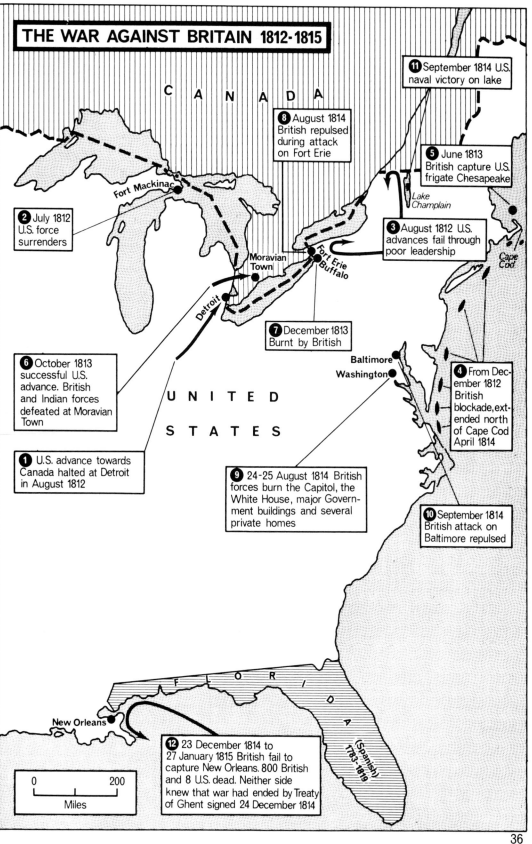

THE WAR AGAINST BRITAIN 1812-1815

C A N A D A

11 September 1814 U.S. naval victory on lake

8 August 1814 British repulsed during attack on Fort Erie

5 June 1813 British capture U.S. frigate Chesapeake

Fort Mackinac

Lake Champlain

2 July 1812 U.S. force surrenders

3 August 1812 U.S. advances fail through poor leadership

Cape Cod

Moravian Town

Fort Erie
Buffalo

Detroit

7 December 1813 Burnt by British

Baltimore

Washington

6 October 1813 successful U.S. advance. British and Indian forces defeated at Moravian Town

4 From December 1812 British blockade, extended north of Cape Cod April 1814

U N I T E D

S T A T E S

1 U.S. advance towards Canada halted at Detroit in August 1812

9 24-25 August 1814 British forces burn the Capitol, the White House, major Government buildings and several private homes

10 September 1814 British attack on Baltimore repulsed

F L O R I D A

New Orleans

(Spanish) 1783-1819

12 23 December 1814 to 27 January 1815 British fail to capture New Orleans. 800 British and 8 U.S. dead. Neither side knew that war had ended by Treaty of Ghent signed 24 December 1814

0   200
Miles

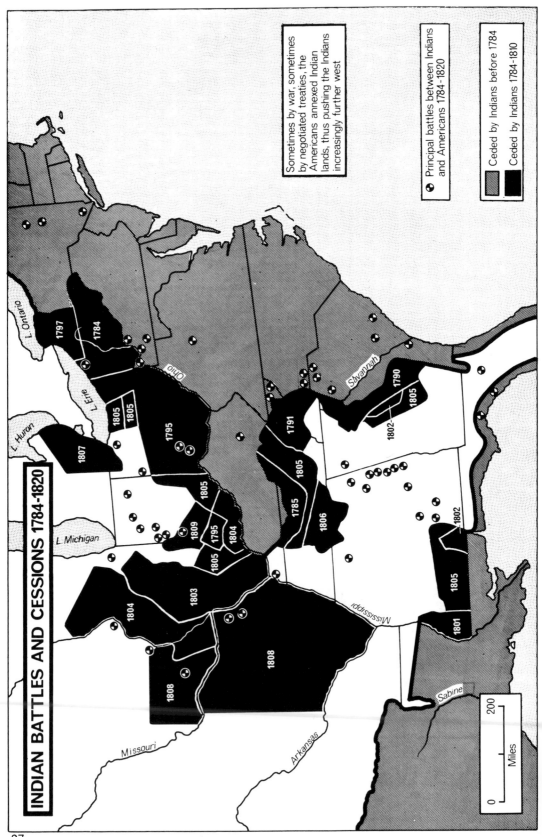

INDIAN BATTLES AND CESSIONS 1784-1820

Sometimes by war, sometimes by negotiated treaties, the Americans annexed Indian lands, thus pushing the Indians increasingly further west

⊕ Principal battles between Indians and Americans 1784-1820

Ceded by Indians before 1784

Ceded by Indians 1784-1810

L. Ontario

L. Erie

L. Huron

L. Michigan

Ohio

Savannah

Mississippi

Missouri

Arkansas

Sabine

1797
1784
1805
1805
1807
1795
1805
1809
1795
1804
1805
1803
1804
1808
1808
1791
1805
1785
1806
1790
1805
1802
1802
1805
1801

0 — 200
Miles

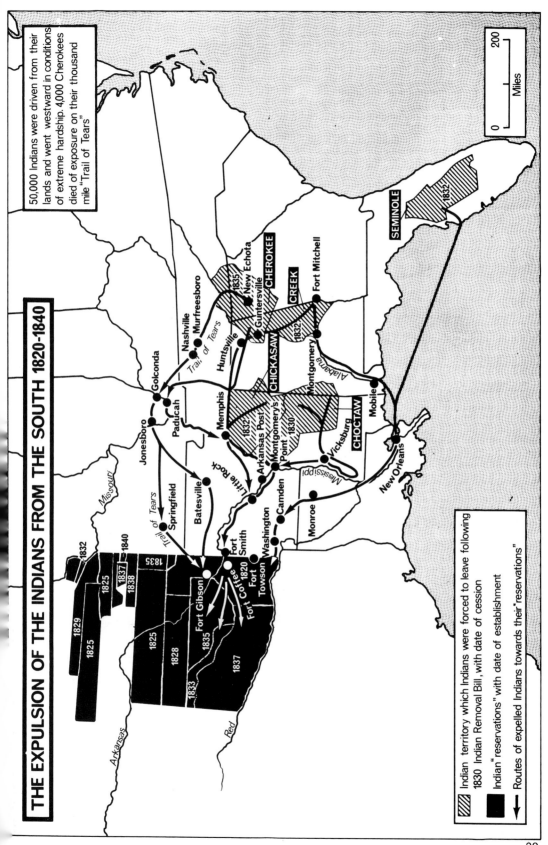

THE EXPULSION OF THE INDIANS FROM THE SOUTH 1820-1840

50,000 Indians were driven from their lands and went westward in conditions of extreme hardship. 4,000 Cherokees died of exposure on their thousand mile "Trail of Tears"

Miles
0   200

SEMINOLE
1835

CHEROKEE
New Echota
1835
Guntersville

CREEK
Fort Mitchell
1832

Nashville
Murfreesboro
Trail of Tears
Huntsville

CHICKASAW
Montgomery
Alabama

Golconda

Paducah
Memphis
1832
Arkansas Post
Montgomery's
Point 1830

CHOCTAW
Mobile

Jonesboro
Little Rock
Vicksburg
Mississippi

Trail of Tears
Springfield
Batesville
Camden
New Orleans

Missouri

Fort
Smith
Washington
Monroe

1832
1825
1840
1838
1837
1835

Fort Gibson
1835
Fort
Coffee 1820
Fort
Towson

1825
1828
1833
1837

Arkansas
Red

Indian territory which Indians were forced to leave following 1830 Indian Removal Bill, with date of cession

Indian "reservations" with date of establishment

Routes of expelled Indians towards their "reservations"

38

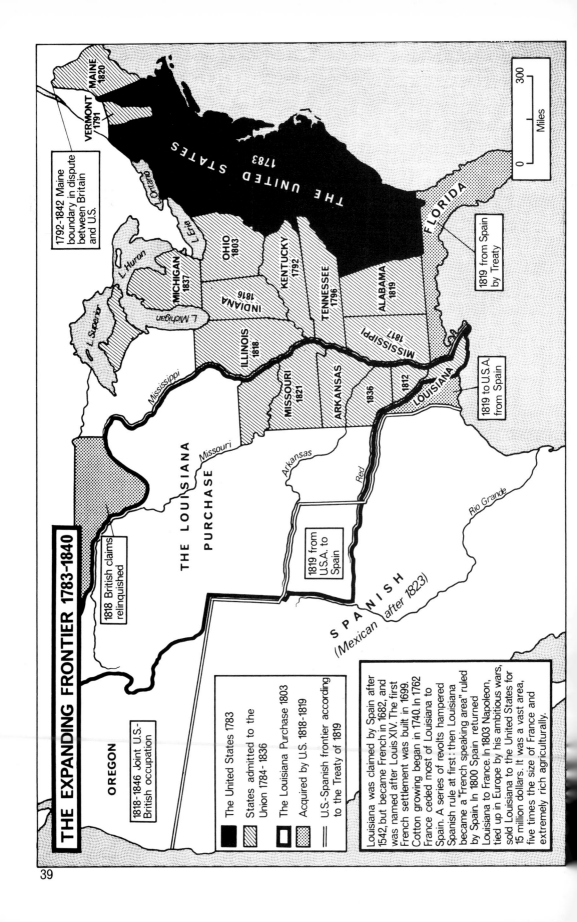

THE EXPANDING FRONTIER 1783-1840

OREGON

1818-1846 Joint U.S.-British occupation

■ The United States 1783

▨ States admitted to the Union 1784-1836

☐ The Louisiana Purchase 1803

▦ Acquired by U.S. 1818-1819

‖ U.S.-Spanish frontier according to the Treaty of 1819

Louisiana was claimed by Spain after 1542, but became French in 1682, and was named after Louis XIV. The first French settlement was built in 1699. Cotton growing began in 1740. In 1762 France ceded most of Louisiana to Spain. A series of revolts hampered Spanish rule at first: then Louisiana became a "French speaking area" ruled by Spain. In 1800 Spain returned Louisiana to France. In 1803 Napoleon, tied up in Europe by his ambitious wars, sold Louisiana to the United States for 15 million dollars. It was a vast area, five times the size of France and extremely rich agriculturally.

THE LOUISIANA PURCHASE

SPANISH
(Mexican after 1823)

1819 from U.S.A. to Spain

1818 British claims relinquished

1819 from U.S.A. to Spain

1819 to U.S.A. from Spain

1819 from Spain by Treaty

1792-1842 Maine boundary in dispute between Britain and U.S.

THE UNITED STATES 1783

VERMONT 1791

MAINE 1820

MICHIGAN 1837

OHIO 1803

INDIANA 1816

KENTUCKY 1792

TENNESSEE 1796

ILLINOIS 1818

MISSOURI 1821

ARKANSAS 1836

MISSISSIPPI 1817

ALABAMA 1819

LOUISIANA 1812

FLORIDA

L. Superior

L. Huron

L. Michigan

L. Erie

L. Ontario

Mississippi

Missouri

Arkansas

Red

Rio Grande

0   300
Miles

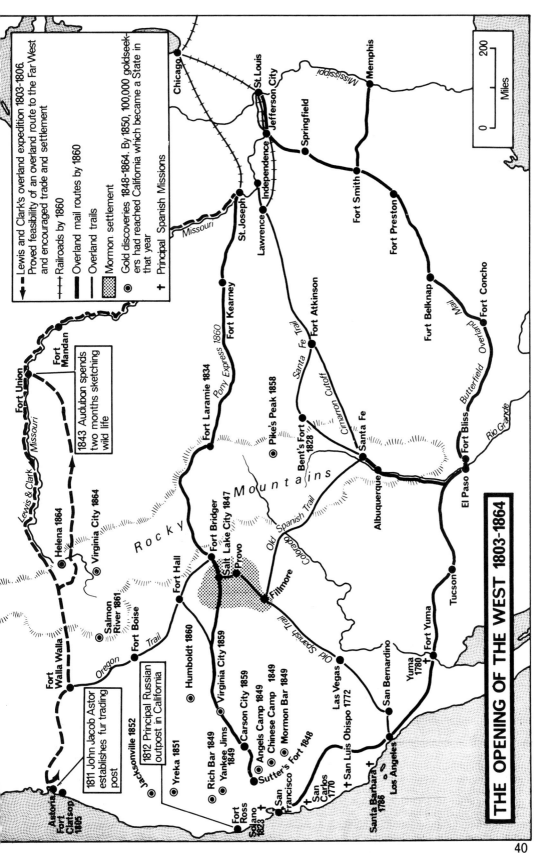

THE OPENING OF THE WEST 1803-1864

Lewis and Clark's overland expedition 1803-1806 Proved feasibility of an overland route to the Far West and encouraged trade and settlement

Railroads by 1860

Overland mail routes by 1860

Overland trails

Mormon settlement

Gold discoveries 1848-1864. By 1850, 100,000 goldseekers had reached California which became a State in that year

Principal Spanish Missions

1811 John Jacob Astor establishes fur trading post

1812 Principal Russian outpost in California

1843 Audubon spends two months sketching wild life

200 Miles

Chicago
St.Louis
Jefferson City
Springfield
Independence
Lawrence
St.Joseph
Fort Smith
Fort Preston
Fort Belknap
Fort Concho
Fort Bliss
El Paso
Rio Grande
Albuquerque
Santa Fe
Tucson
Fort Yuma
Yuma 1780
San Bernardino
Las Vegas
Los Angeles
Santa Barbara 1786
San Luis Obispo 1772
San Carlos 1770
San Francisco
Sutter's Fort 1848
Mormon Bar 1849
Chinese Camp 1849
Angels Camp 1849
Carson City 1859
Yankee Jims 1849
Rich Bar 1849
Yreka 1851
Fort Ross
Solano 1823
Jacksonville 1852
Virginia City 1859
Humboldt 1860
Fort Boise
Salmon River 1861
Fort Walla Walla
Astoria Fort Clatsop 1805
Fort Union
Fort Mandan
Helena 1864
Virginia City 1864
Fort Hall
Fort Bridger
Salt Lake City 1847
Provo
Fillmore
Rocky Mountains
Old Spanish Trail
Colorado
Oregon Trail
Pony Express 1860
Fort Laramie 1834
Fort Kearney
Pike's Peak 1858
Bent's Fort 1828
Fort Atkinson
Santa Fe Trail
Cimarron Cutoff
Butterfield Overland Mail
Missouri
Mississippi
Memphis
Lewis & Clark
Missouri

40

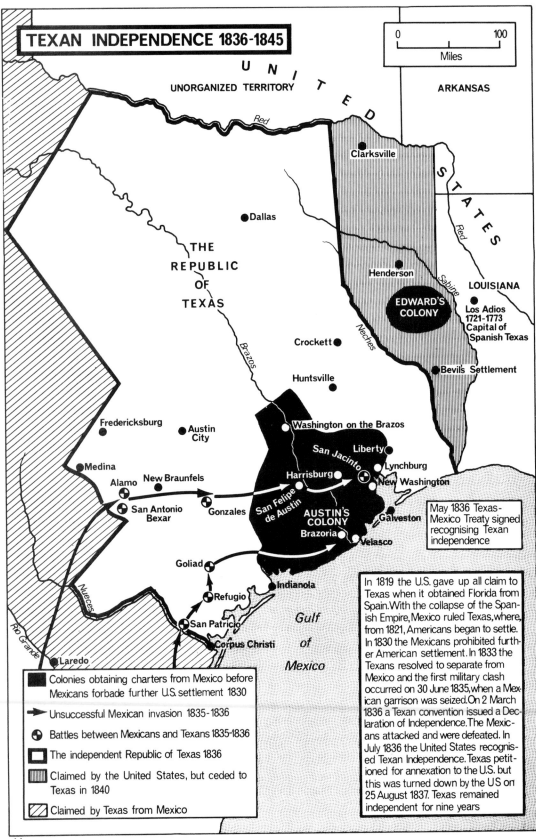

TEXAN INDEPENDENCE 1836-1845

0   100
Miles

U N I T E D
UNORGANIZED TERRITORY   ARKANSAS
S T A T E S

Red

●Clarksville

●Dallas

THE
REPUBLIC
OF
TEXAS

Henderson●

EDWARD'S
COLONY

LOUISIANA

●Los Adios
1721-1773
Capital of
Spanish Texas

Crockett●

●Bevils Settlement

Huntsville
●

Brazos

Neches

Sabine

Red

●Fredericksburg   ●Austin
City

Washington on the Brazos ○

San Jacinto   Liberty○

●Medina

Alamo ✚   ●New Braunfels

✚ San Antonio
Bexar

Harrisburg ●   ⊕   Lynchburg○
✚   ●New Washington

San Felipe
de Austin

AUSTIN'S
COLONY

Gonzales

●Galveston

Brazoria ●

●Velasco

May 1836 Texas-
Mexico Treaty signed
recognising Texan
independence

Goliad ✚

●Indianola

✚ Refugio

Gulf

✚ San Patricio

of

●Corpus Christi

Mexico

Rio Grande

Nueces

●Laredo

In 1819 the U.S. gave up all claim to
Texas when it obtained Florida from
Spain.With the collapse of the Spanish Empire, Mexico ruled Texas, where,
from 1821, Americans began to settle.
In 1830 the Mexicans prohibited further American settlement. In 1833 the
Texans resolved to separate from
Mexico and the first military clash
occurred on 30 June 1835, when a Mexican garrison was seized.On 2 March
1836 a Texan convention issued a Declaration of Independence.The Mexicans attacked and were defeated. In
July 1836 the United States recognised Texan Independence.Texas petit-
ioned for annexation to the U.S. but
this was turned down by the US on
25 August 1837. Texas remained
independent for nine years

■ Colonies obtaining charters from Mexico before
Mexicans forbade further U.S. settlement 1830

➤ Unsuccessful Mexican invasion 1835-1836

⊕ Battles between Mexicans and Texans 1835-1836

□ The independent Republic of Texas 1836

▦ Claimed by the United States, but ceded to
Texas in 1840

▨ Claimed by Texas from Mexico

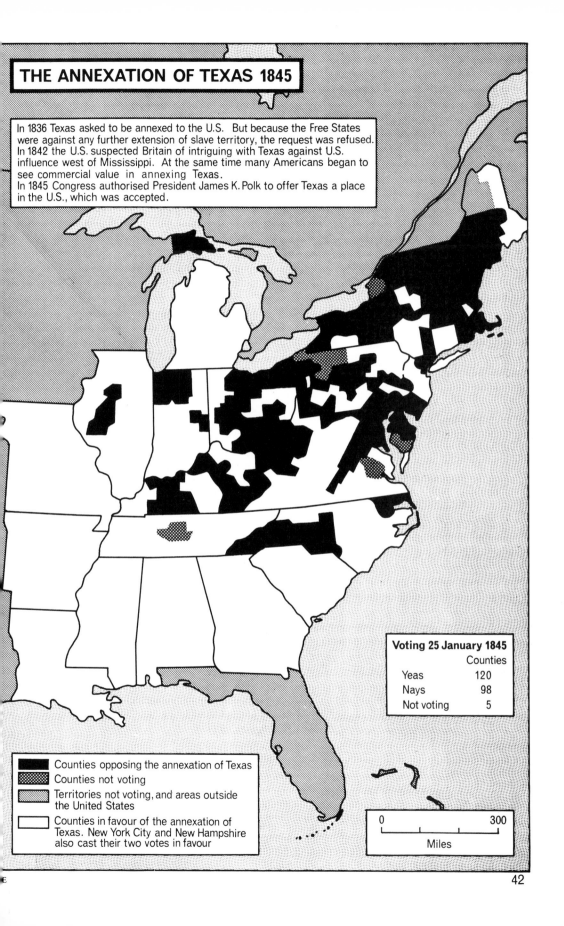

THE ANNEXATION OF TEXAS 1845

In 1836 Texas asked to be annexed to the U.S. But because the Free States were against any further extension of slave territory, the request was refused. In 1842 the U.S. suspected Britain of intriguing with Texas against U.S. influence west of Mississippi. At the same time many Americans began to see commercial value in annexing Texas.
In 1845 Congress authorised President James K. Polk to offer Texas a place in the U.S., which was accepted.

Voting 25 January 1845

	Counties
Yeas	120
Nays	98
Not voting	5

- ■ Counties opposing the annexation of Texas
- ▨ Counties not voting
- ▨ Territories not voting, and areas outside the United States
- □ Counties in favour of the annexation of Texas. New York City and New Hampshire also cast their two votes in favour

0 ⊢——⊣ 300
Miles

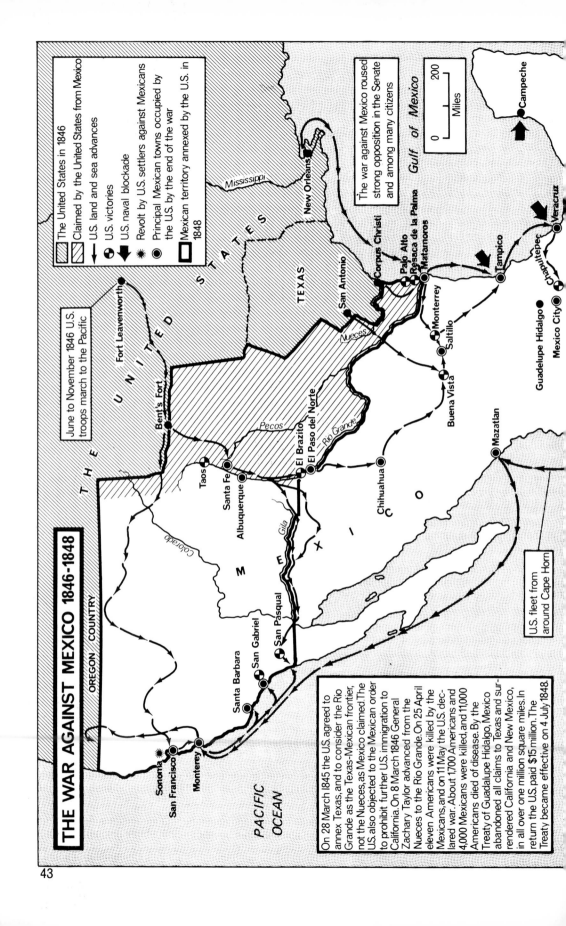

THE WAR AGAINST MEXICO 1846-1848

The United States in 1846

Claimed by the United States from Mexico

U.S. land and sea advances

U.S. victories

U.S. naval blockade

Revolt by U.S. settlers against Mexicans

Principal Mexican towns occupied by the U.S. by the end of the war

Mexican territory annexed by the U.S. in 1848

June to November 1846 U.S. troops march to the Pacific

The war against Mexico roused strong opposition in the Senate and among many citizens

U.S. fleet from around Cape Horn

0   200
Miles

OREGON COUNTRY

THE UNITED STATES

TEXAS

Gulf of Mexico

PACIFIC OCEAN

M E X I C O

Mississippi
New Orleans
Corpus Christi
Palo Alto
Resaca de la Palma
Matamoros
Campeche
Veracruz
Chapultepec
Tampico
Guadalupe Hidalgo
Mexico City
Mazatlan
Saltillo
Monterrey
Buena Vista
San Antonio
Nueces
Fort Leavenworth
Bent's Fort
Pecos
Rio Grande
El Brazito
El Paso del Norte
Chihuahua
Santa Fe
Taos
Albuquerque
Gila
Colorado
Santa Barbara
San Gabriel
San Pasqual
Monterey
San Francisco
Sonoma

On 28 March 1845 the U.S. agreed to annex Texas, and to consider the Rio Grande as the Texas-Mexican frontier, not the Nueces, as Mexico claimed. The U.S. also objected to the Mexican order to prohibit further U.S. immigration to California. On 8 March 1846 General Zachary Taylor advanced from the Nueces to the Rio Grande. On 25 April eleven Americans were killed by the Mexicans, and on 11 May the U.S. declared war. About 1,700 Americans and 4,000 Mexicans were killed, and 11,000 Americans died of disease. By the Treaty of Guadalupe Hidalgo, Mexico abandoned all claims to Texas and surrendered California and New Mexico, in all over one million square miles. In return the U.S. paid $15 million. The Treaty became effective on 4 July 1848.

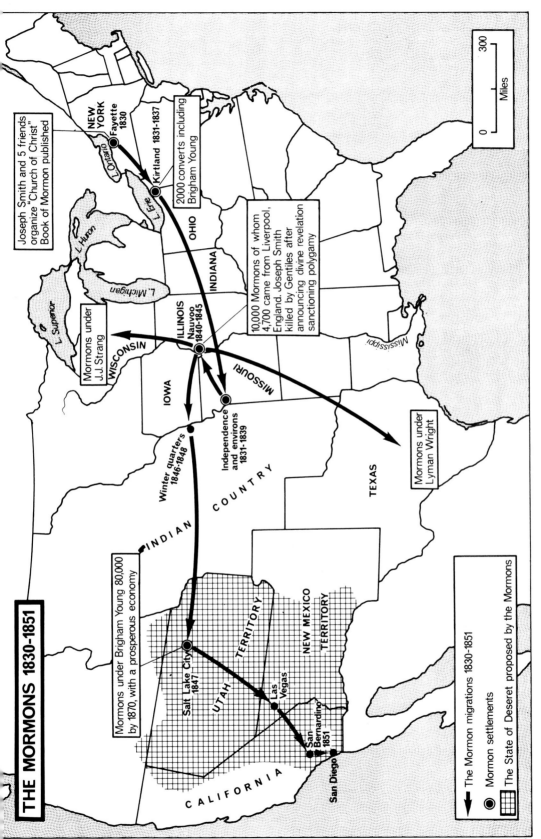

THE MORMONS 1830-1851

Joseph Smith and 5 friends organize "Church of Christ" Book of Mormon published

NEW YORK
Fayette 1830

Kirtland 1831-1837

2000 converts including Brigham Young

OHIO

INDIANA

10,000 Mormons of whom 4,700 came from Liverpool, England. Joseph Smith killed by Gentiles after announcing divine revelation sanctioning polygamy

L. Superior

L. Michigan

L. Huron

L. Erie

L. Ontario

Mormons under J.J. Strang

WISCONSIN

ILLINOIS
Nauvoo 1840-1845

IOWA

Winter quarters 1846-1848

MISSOURI

Independence and environs 1831-1839

INDIAN COUNTRY

Mississippi

Mormons under Lyman Wright

TEXAS

Mormons under Brigham Young 80,000 by 1870, with a prosperous economy

Salt Lake City 1847

UTAH TERRITORY

Las Vegas

NEW MEXICO TERRITORY

San Bernardino 1851

San Diego

CALIFORNIA

0   300
Miles

The Mormon migrations 1830-1851

● Mormon settlements

The State of Deseret proposed by the Mormons

44

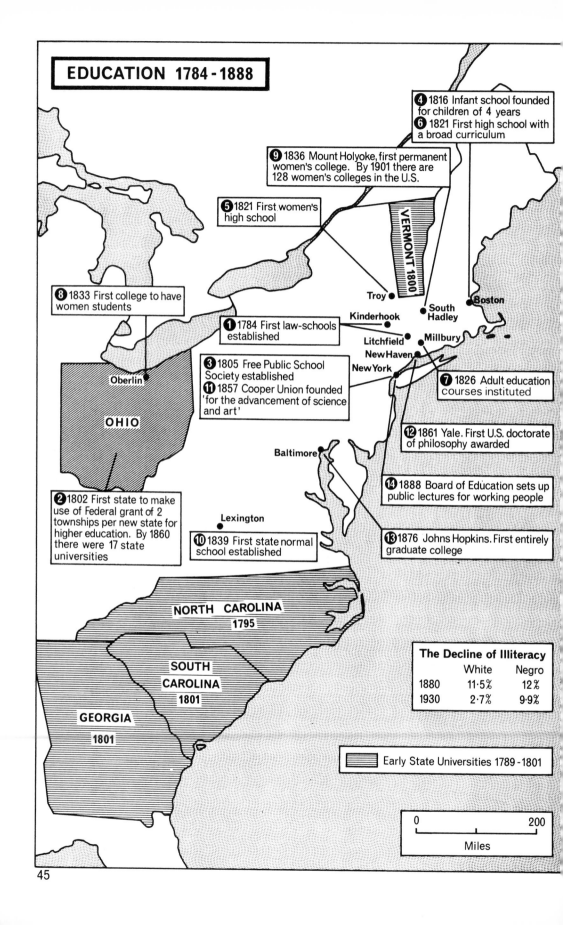

EDUCATION 1784-1888

4 1816 Infant school founded for children of 4 years
6 1821 First high school with a broad curriculum

9 1836 Mount Holyoke, first permanent women's college. By 1901 there are 128 women's colleges in the U.S.

5 1821 First women's high school

VERMONT 1800

8 1833 First college to have women students

1 1784 First law-schools established

Troy
South Hadley
Boston
Kinderhook
Litchfield Millbury
New Haven
New York

3 1805 Free Public School Society established
11 1857 Cooper Union founded 'for the advancement of science and art'

Oberlin

OHIO

7 1826 Adult education courses instituted

12 1861 Yale. First U.S. doctorate of philosophy awarded

Baltimore

14 1888 Board of Education sets up public lectures for working people

2 1802 First state to make use of Federal grant of 2 townships per new state for higher education. By 1860 there were 17 state universities

Lexington

10 1839 First state normal school established

13 1876 Johns Hopkins. First entirely graduate college

NORTH CAROLINA
1795

The Decline of Illiteracy		
	White	Negro
1880	11·5%	12%
1930	2·7%	9·9%

SOUTH CAROLINA
1801

GEORGIA
1801

Early State Universities 1789-1801

0 ————————— 200
Miles

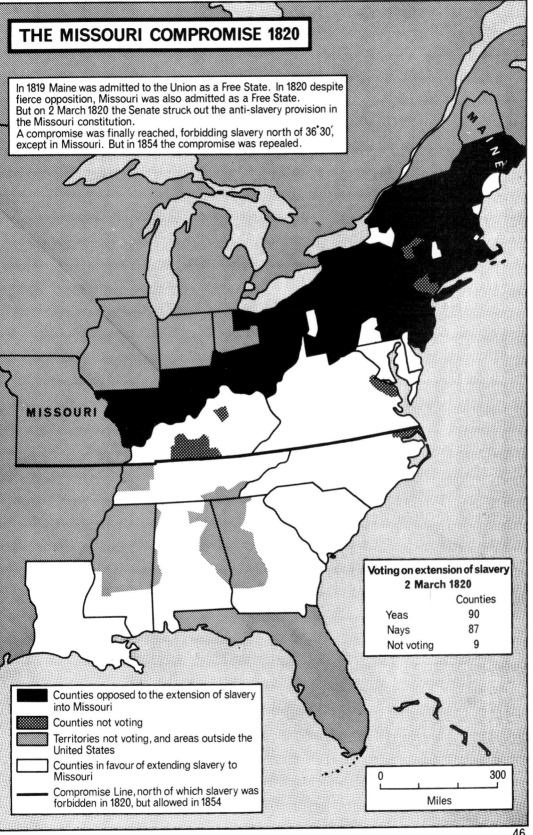

THE MISSOURI COMPROMISE 1820

In 1819 Maine was admitted to the Union as a Free State. In 1820 despite fierce opposition, Missouri was also admitted as a Free State.
But on 2 March 1820 the Senate struck out the anti-slavery provision in the Missouri constitution.
A compromise was finally reached, forbidding slavery north of 36°30', except in Missouri. But in 1854 the compromise was repealed.

MAINE

MISSOURI

Voting on extension of slavery
2 March 1820

	Counties
Yeas	90
Nays	87
Not voting	9

■ Counties opposed to the extension of slavery into Missouri

▨ Counties not voting

▨ Territories not voting, and areas outside the United States

☐ Counties in favour of extending slavery to Missouri

— Compromise Line, north of which slavery was forbidden in 1820, but allowed in 1854

0   300
Miles

46

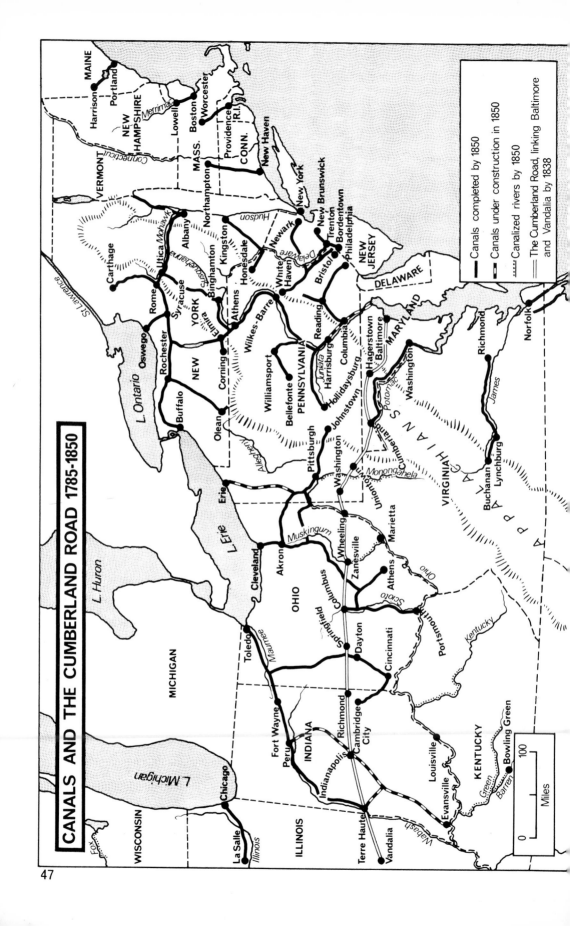

CANALS AND THE CUMBERLAND ROAD 1785-1850

Legend:
- Canals completed by 1850
- Canals under construction in 1850
- Canalized rivers by 1850
- The Cumberland Road, linking Baltimore and Vandalia by 1838

47

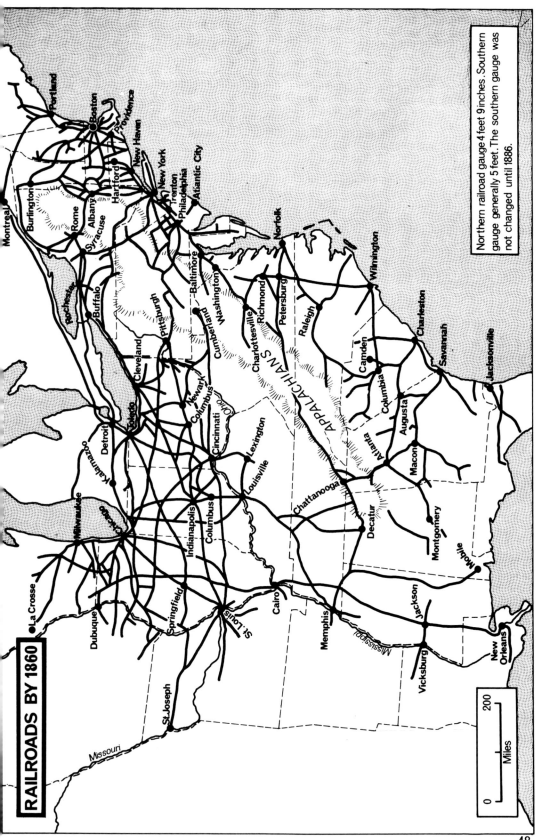

RAILROADS BY 1860

Northern railroad gauge 4 feet 9 inches. Southern gauge generally 5 feet. The southern gauge was not changed until 1886.

La Crosse

Montreal

Portland

Burlington

Boston

Providence

Rome

Albany

Syracuse

Hartford

New Haven

New York

Trenton

Philadelphia

Atlantic City

Rochester

Buffalo

Pittsburgh

Baltimore

Cumberland

Washington

Norfolk

Cleveland

Charlottesville

Richmond

Petersburg

Raleigh

Wilmington

Detroit

Kalamazoo

Toledo

Newark

Columbus

Cincinnati

Lexington

Louisville

APPALACHIANS

Ohio

Camden

Columbia

Augusta

Charleston

Savannah

Jacksonville

Milwaukee

Chicago

Indianapolis

Columbus

Chattanooga

Atlanta

Macon

Decatur

Montgomery

Mobile

Dubuque

Springfield

St. Louis

Cairo

Memphis

Jackson

New Orleans

Vicksburg

Mississippi

St. Joseph

Missouri

0   200

Miles

48

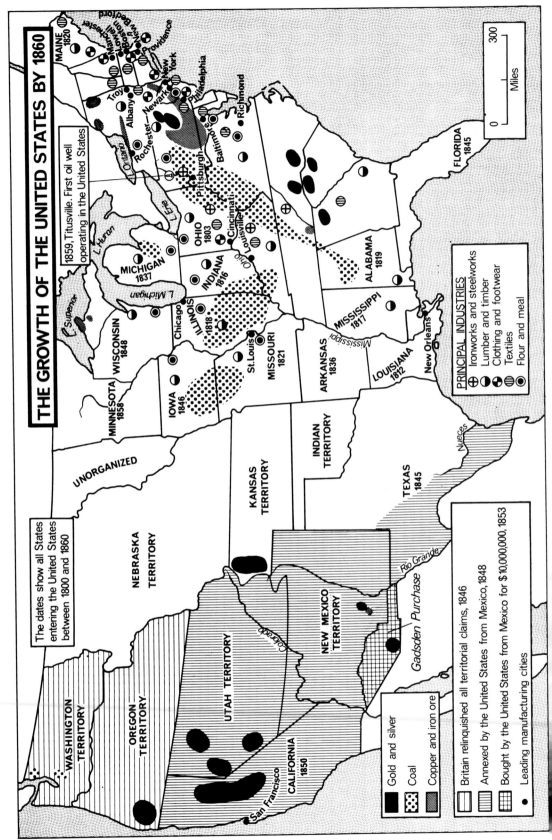

THE GROWTH OF THE UNITED STATES BY 1860

1859. Titusville. First oil well operating in the United States

The dates show all States entering the United States between 1800 and 1860

MAINE 1820

New Bedford

Providence

New York

Troy

Albany

Newark

Philadelphia

Rochester

Baltimore

Richmond

Pittsburgh

L. Ontario

L. Erie

OHIO 1803

Cincinnati

Louisville

MICHIGAN 1837

L. Huron

L. Michigan

INDIANA 1816

ILLINOIS 1818

Chicago

L. Superior

WISCONSIN 1848

MINNESOTA 1858

IOWA 1846

St.Louis

MISSOURI 1821

Ohio

ALABAMA 1819

MISSISSIPPI 1817

ARKANSAS 1836

Mississippi

LOUISIANA 1812

New Orleans

FLORIDA 1845

UNORGANIZED

NEBRASKA TERRITORY

KANSAS TERRITORY

INDIAN TERRITORY

TEXAS 1845

Nueces

Rio Grande

Gadsden Purchase

NEW MEXICO TERRITORY

Colorado

UTAH TERRITORY

CALIFORNIA 1850

San Francisco

WASHINGTON TERRITORY

OREGON TERRITORY

PRINCIPAL INDUSTRIES

- Ironworks and steelworks
- Lumber and timber
- Clothing and footwear
- Textiles
- Flour and meal

Gold and silver

Coal

Copper and iron ore

Britain relinquished all territorial claims, 1846

Annexed by the United States from Mexico, 1848

Bought by the United States from Mexico for $10,000,000, 1853

· Leading manufacturing cities

0 — 300 Miles

49

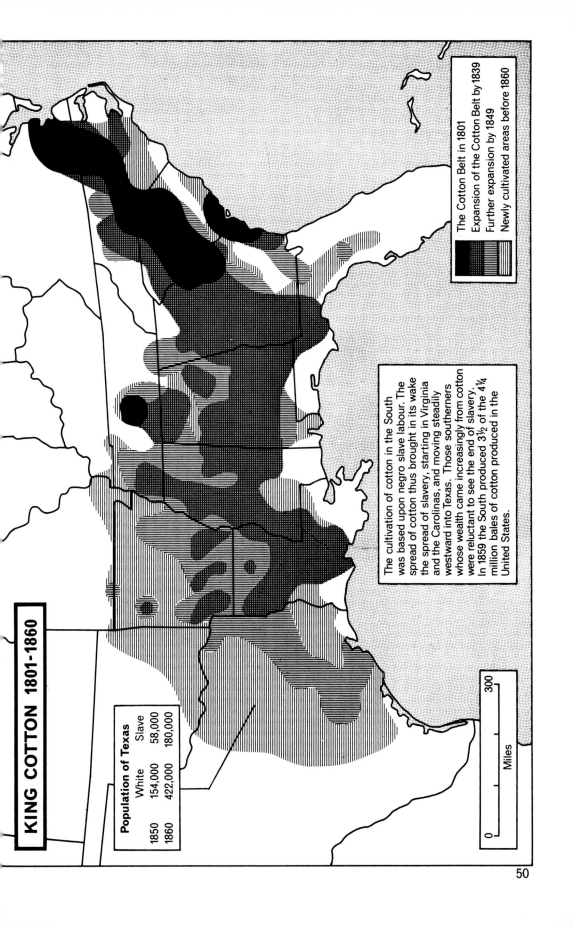

KING COTTON 1801-1860

Population of Texas

	White	Slave
1850	154,000	58,000
1860	422,000	180,000

The cultivation of cotton in the South was based upon negro slave labour. The spread of cotton thus brought in its wake the spread of slavery, starting in Virginia and the Carolinas, and moving steadily westward into Texas. Those southerners whose wealth came increasingly from cotton were reluctant to see the end of slavery. In 1859 the South produced 3½ of the 4¼ million bales of cotton produced in the United States.

The Cotton Belt in 1801
Expansion of the Cotton Belt by 1839
Further expansion by 1849
Newly cultivated areas before 1860

0   Miles   300

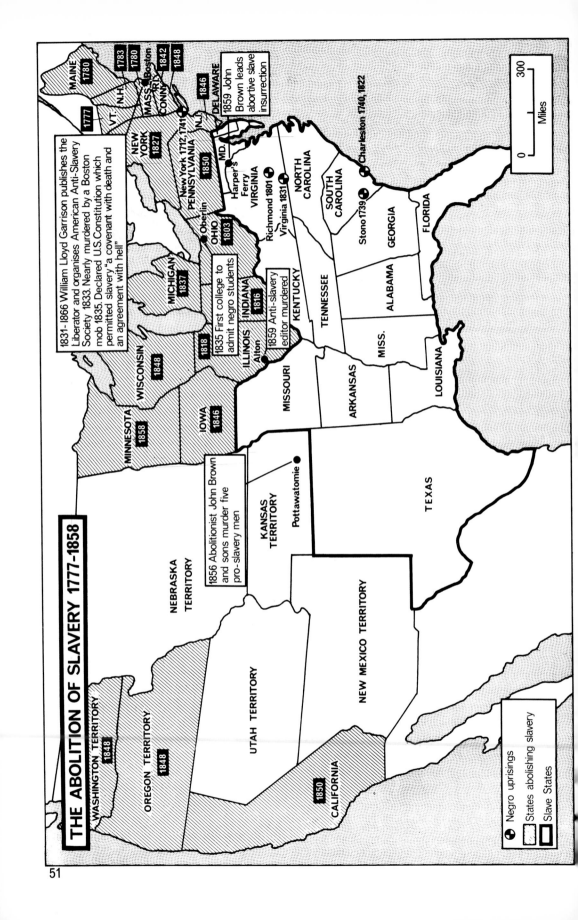

THE ABOLITION OF SLAVERY 1777-1858

1831- 1866 William Lloyd Garrison publishes the Liberator and organises American Anti-Slavery Society 1833. Nearly murdered by a Boston mob 1835. Declared U.S.Constitution which permitted slavery "a covenant with death and an agreement with hell"

1835 First college to admit negro students

1859 Anti-Slavery editor murdered

1856 Abolitionist John Brown and sons murder five pro-slavery men

1859 John Brown leads abortive slave insurrection

MAINE **1833**
1780
N.H. **1783** **1780**
MASS. Boston **1842** **1848**
VT. **1777**
CONN.
NEW YORK **1827**
New York 1712, 1741
PENNSYLVANIA
N.J. **1846**
DELAWARE
MD. **1850**
Oberlin ● OHIO **1803**
Harper's Ferry ⊕ VIRGINIA
Richmond 1801 ⊕ Virginia 1831 ⊕
NORTH CAROLINA
SOUTH CAROLINA
Charleston 1740, 1822 ⊕
Stono 1739 ⊕ GEORGIA
FLORIDA
ALABAMA
MISS.
TENNESSEE
KENTUCKY
INDIANA **1816**
ILLINOIS Alton ● **1818**
MICHIGAN **1837**
WISCONSIN **1848**
MINNESOTA **1858**
IOWA **1846**
MISSOURI
ARKANSAS
LOUISIANA
KANSAS TERRITORY
Pottawatomie ●
TEXAS
NEBRASKA TERRITORY
WASHINGTON TERRITORY **1848**
OREGON TERRITORY **1848**
UTAH TERRITORY
NEW MEXICO TERRITORY
CALIFORNIA **1850**

0 ——— 300
Miles

⊕ Negro uprisings
☐ States abolishing slavery
■ Slave States

51

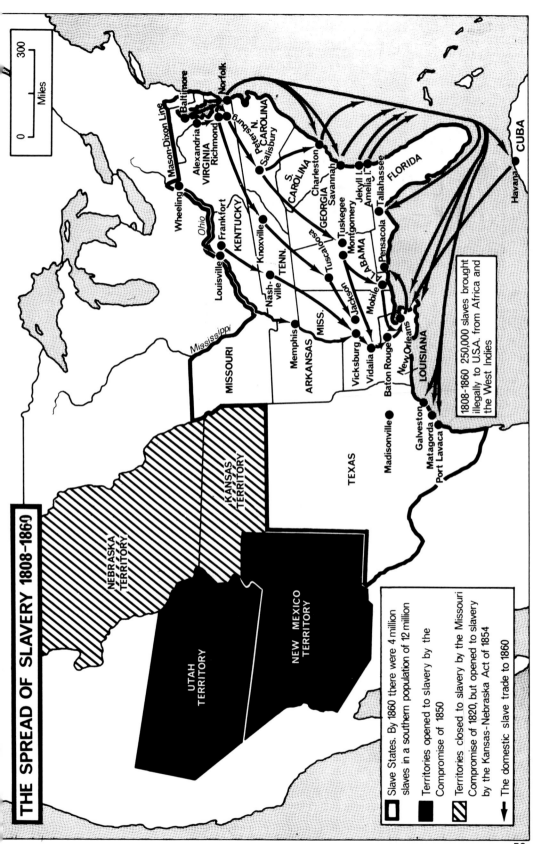

THE SPREAD OF SLAVERY 1808-1860

Miles
0 — 300

CUBA
Havana

FLORIDA
Tallahassee
Amelia I.
Jekyll I.
Pensacola
Mobile
Montgomery
Tuskegee
ALABAMA
Savannah
Charleston
GEORGIA
S. CAROLINA
Salisbury
Peters N. CAROLINA
Norfolk
Baltimore
Mason-Dixon Line
Alexandria
VIRGINIA
Richmond
Burks?
Wheeling
Ohio
Frankfort
KENTUCKY
Louisville
Knoxville
TENN.
Nashville
Tuscaloosa
Jackson
MISS.
Memphis
ARKANSAS
Vicksburg
Vidalia
Baton Rouge
New Orleans
LOUISIANA
Galveston
Matagorda
Port Lavaca
Madisonville
TEXAS
Mississippi
MISSOURI

KANSAS TERRITORY
NEBRASKA TERRITORY
UTAH TERRITORY
NEW MEXICO TERRITORY

1808-1860 250,000 slaves brought illegally to U.S.A. from Africa and the West Indies

☐ Slave States. By 1860 there were 4 million slaves in a southern population of 12 million

■ Territories opened to slavery by the Compromise of 1850

▨ Territories closed to slavery by the Missouri Compromise of 1820, but opened to slavery by the Kansas-Nebraska Act of 1854

→ The domestic slave trade to 1860

52

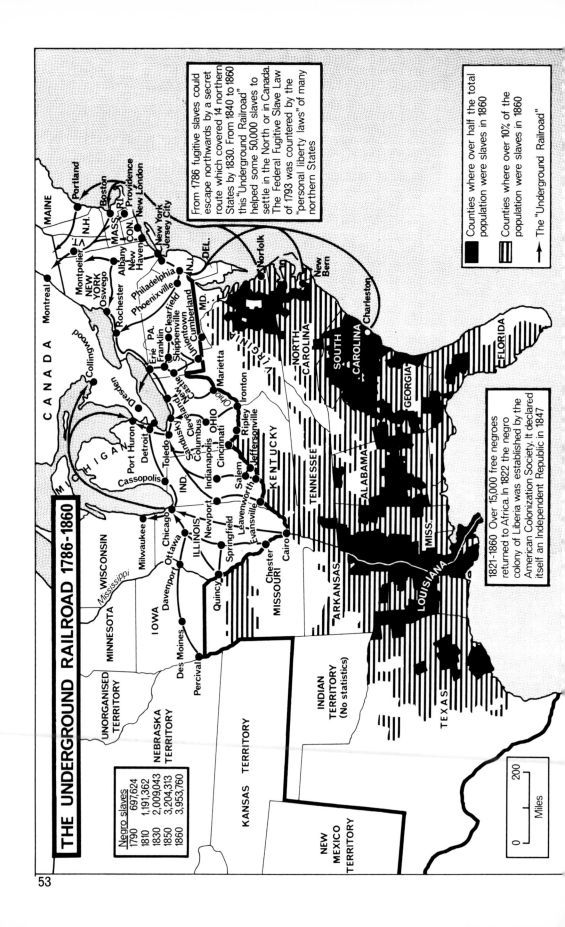

THE UNDERGROUND RAILROAD 1786-1860

Negro slaves
1790	697,624
1810	1,191,362
1830	2,009,043
1850	3,204,313
1860	3,953,760

From 1786 fugitive slaves could escape northwards by a secret route which covered 14 northern States by 1830. From 1840 to 1860 this "Underground Railroad" helped some 50,000 slaves to settle in the North or in Canada. The Federal Fugitive Slave Law of 1793 was countered by the "personal liberty laws" of many northern States

1821-1860 Over 15,000 free negroes returned to Africa. In 1822 the negro colony of Liberia was established by the American Colonization Society. It declared itself an Independent Republic in 1847

■ Counties where over half the total population were slaves in 1860

▥ Counties where over 10% of the population were slaves in 1860

→ The "Underground Railroad"

0   200
Miles

THE COMING OF CIVIL WAR 1858-1861

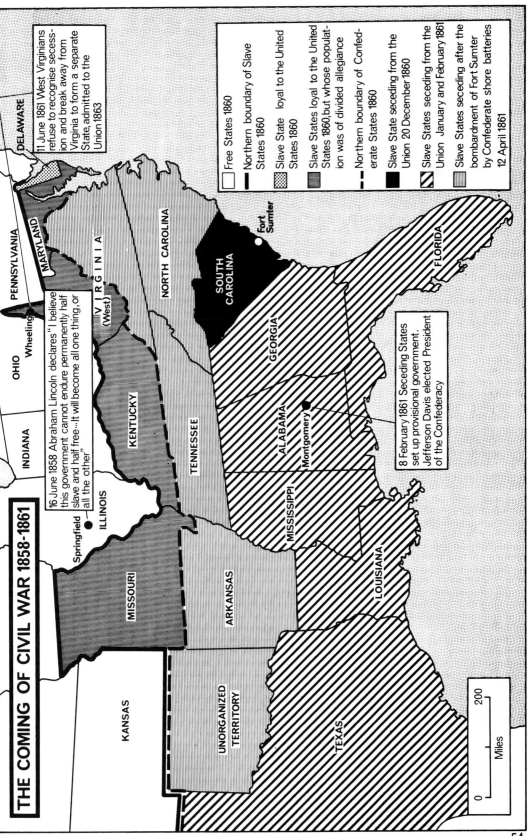

11 June 1861 West Virginians refuse to recognise secession and break away from Virginia to form a separate State, admitted to the Union 1863

16 June 1858 Abraham Lincoln declares "I believe this government cannot endure permanently half slave and half free...It will become all one thing, or all the other"

8 February 1861 Seceding States set up provisional government. Jefferson Davis elected President of the Confederacy

☐	Free States 1860
▮	Northern boundary of Slave States 1860
▦	Slave State loyal to the United States 1860
▤	Slave States loyal to the United States 1860, but whose population was of divided allegiance
┆	Northern boundary of Confederate States 1860
■	Slave State seceding from the Union 20 December 1860
▨	Slave States seceding from the Union January and February 1861
▥	Slave States seceding after the bombardment of Fort Sumter by Confederate shore batteries 12 April 1861

DELAWARE

PENNSYLVANIA

MARYLAND

OHIO
Wheeling

VIRGINIA

VIRGINIA (West)

NORTH CAROLINA

Fort Sumter

SOUTH CAROLINA

INDIANA

KENTUCKY

TENNESSEE

GEORGIA

FLORIDA

ILLINOIS
Springfield

MISSOURI

ARKANSAS

ALABAMA

MISSISSIPPI

Montgomery

LOUISIANA

KANSAS

UNORGANIZED TERRITORY

TEXAS

0   200
Miles

F

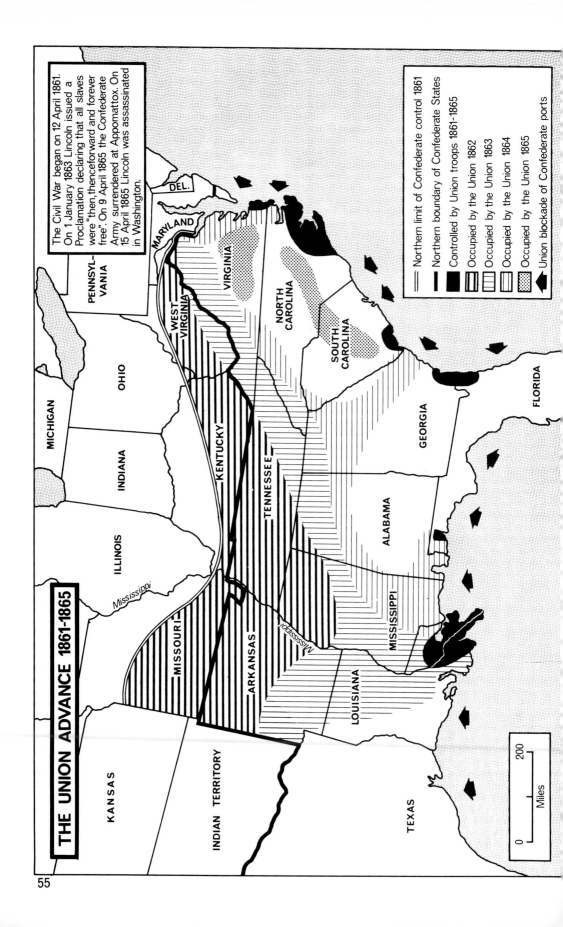

THE UNION ADVANCE 1861-1865

The Civil War began on 12 April 1861. On 1 January 1863 Lincoln issued a Proclamation declaring that all slaves were "then, thenceforward and forever free." On 9 April 1865 the Confederate Army surrendered at Appomattox. On 15 April 1865 Lincoln was assassinated in Washington.

Northern limit of Confederate control 1861

Northern boundary of Confederate States

Controlled by Union troops 1861-1865

Occupied by the Union 1862

Occupied by the Union 1863

Occupied by the Union 1864

Occupied by the Union 1865

Union blockade of Confederate ports

MICHIGAN

OHIO

PENNSYL-VANIA

DEL.

MARYLAND

WEST VIRGINIA

VIRGINIA

NORTH CAROLINA

SOUTH CAROLINA

ILLINOIS

INDIANA

KENTUCKY

TENNESSEE

GEORGIA

ALABAMA

KANSAS

MISSOURI

ARKANSAS

MISSISSIPPI

LOUISIANA

INDIAN TERRITORY

TEXAS

FLORIDA

Mississippi

Mississippi

0   200

Miles

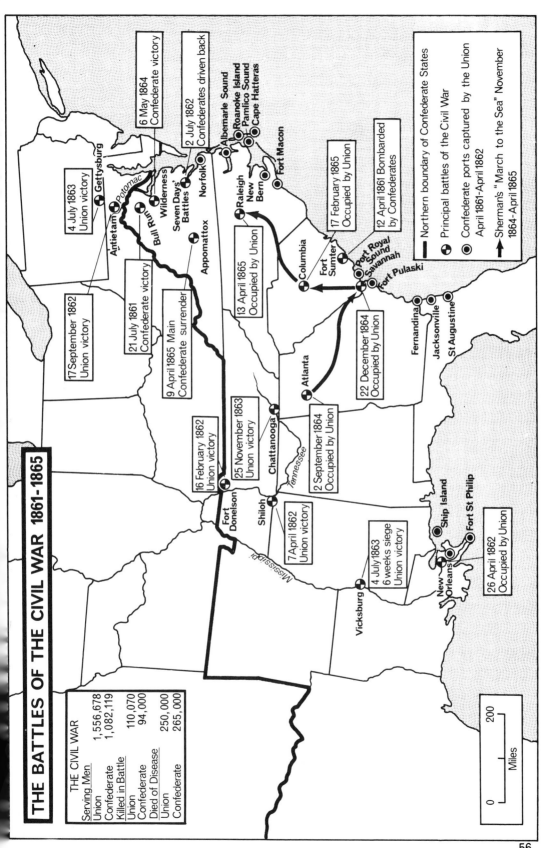

THE BATTLES OF THE CIVIL WAR 1861-1865

THE CIVIL WAR	
Serving Men	
Union	1,556,678
Confederate	1,082,119
Killed in Battle	
Union	110,070
Confederate	94,000
Died of Disease	
Union	250,000
Confederate	265,000

4 July 1863
Gettysburg
Union victory

17 September 1862
Union victory

Antietam

Potomac

Bull Run

21 July 1861
Confederate victory

Wilderness

Seven Days'
Battles

6 May 1864
Confederate victory

Confederates driven back
2 July 1862

Albemarle Sound
Roanoke Island
Pamlico Sound
Cape Hatteras

Fort Macon

Norfolk

Appomattox

9 April 1865 Main
Confederate surrender

Raleigh
New
Bern

Columbia

13 April 1865
Occupied by Union

Fort
Sumter

17 February 1865
Occupied by Union

12 April 1861 Bombarded
by Confederates

Port Royal
Sound
Savannah
Fort Pulaski

Fernandina
Jacksonville
St Augustine

Atlanta

22 December 1864
Occupied by Union

Chattanooga

25 November 1863
Union victory

2 September 1864
Occupied by Union

16 February 1862
Union victory

Fort
Donelson

Shiloh

7 April 1862
Union victory

Tennessee

Vicksburg

4 July 1863
6 weeks siege
Union victory

Ship Island
Fort St Philip

New
Orleans

26 April 1862
Occupied by Union

Mississippi

—— Northern boundary of Confederate States
● Principal battles of the Civil War
◉ Confederate ports captured by the Union
    April 1861-April 1862
→ Sherman's "March to the Sea" November
    1864-April 1865

0   200
Miles

56

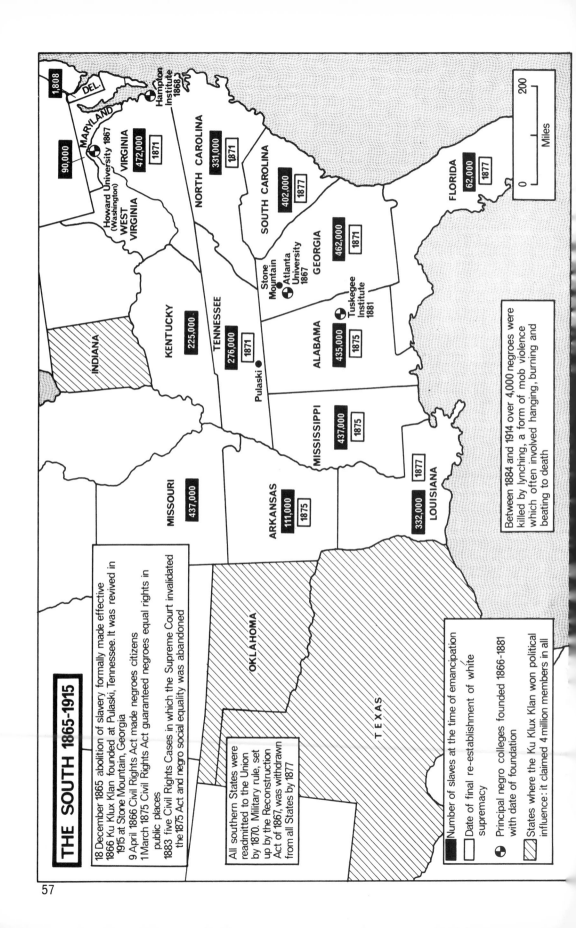

THE SOUTH 1865-1915

18 December 1865 abolition of slavery formally made effective
1866 Ku Klux Klan founded at Pulaski, Tennessee. It was revived in 1915 at Stone Mountain, Georgia
9 April 1866 Civil Rights Act made negroes citizens
1 March 1875 Civil Rights Act guaranteed negroes equal rights in public places
1883 five Civil Rights Cases in which the Supreme Court invalidated the 1875 Act and negro social equality was abandoned

All southern States were readmitted to the Union by 1870. Military rule, set up by the Reconstruction Act of 1867, was withdrawn from all States by 1877

Between 1884 and 1914 over 4,000 negroes were killed by lynching, a form of mob violence which often involved hanging, burning and beating to death

■ Number of slaves at the time of emancipation

□ Date of final re-establishment of white supremacy

☯ Principal negro colleges founded 1866-1881 with date of foundation

▨ States where the Ku Klux Klan won political influence: it claimed 4 million members in all

1,808
DEL.
Hampton Institute 1868
90,000
MARYLAND
Howard University (Washington) 1867
WEST VIRGINIA
VIRGINIA
472,000
1871
NORTH CAROLINA
331,000
1871
SOUTH CAROLINA
402,000
1877
Stone Mountain
Atlanta University 1867
GEORGIA
462,000
1871
Tuskegee Institute 1881
KENTUCKY
225,000
TENNESSEE
276,000
1871
Pulaski
ALABAMA
435,000
1875
MISSOURI
437,000
MISSISSIPPI
437,000
1875
ARKANSAS
111,000
1875
LOUISIANA
332,000
1877
FLORIDA
62,000
1877
INDIANA
OKLAHOMA
TEXAS

0   200
Miles

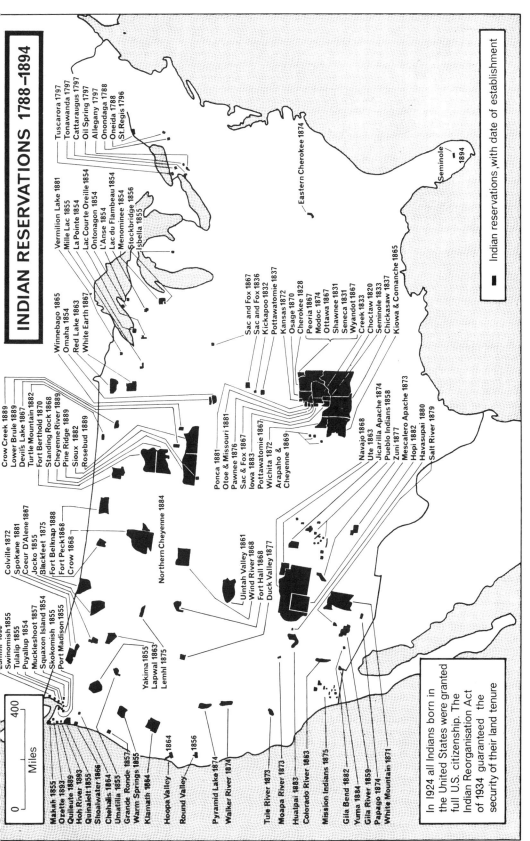

INDIAN RESERVATIONS 1788–1894

Tuscarora 1797
Tonawanda 1797
Cattaraugus 1797
Oil Spring 1797
Allegany 1797
Onondaga 1788
Oneida 1788
St. Regis 1796

Eastern Cherokee 1874

Seminole 1894

■ Indian reservations, with date of establishment

Vermilion Lake 1881
Mille Lac 1855
La Pointe 1854
Lac Courte Oreille 1854
Ontonagon 1854
L'Anse 1854
Lac du Flambeau 1854
Menominee 1854
Stockbridge 1856
Isbella 1855

Winnebago 1865
Omaha 1854
Red Lake 1863
White Earth 1867

Sac and Fox 1867
Sac and Fox 1836
Kickapoo 1832
Pottawatomie 1837
Kansas 1872
Osage 1870
Cherokee 1828
Peoria 1867
Modoc 1874
Ottawa 1867
Shawnee 1831
Seneca 1831
Wyandot 1867
Creek 1833
Choctaw 1820
Seminole 1833
Chickasaw 1837
Kiowa & Comanche 1865

Crow Creek 1889
Lower Brule 1889
Devils Lake 1867
Turtle Mountain 1882
Fort Berthold 1870
Standing Rock 1868
Cheyenne River 1889
Pine Ridge 1889
Sioux 1882
Rosebud 1889

Ponca 1881
Otoe & Missouri 1881
Pawnee 1876
Sac & Fox 1867
Iowa 1883
Pottawatomie 1867
Wichita 1872
Arapaho &
Cheyenne 1869

Navajo 1868
Ute 1863
Jicarilla Apache 1874
Pueblo Indians 1858
Zuni 1877
Mescalero Apache 1873
Hopi 1882
Havasupai 1880
Salt River 1879

Colville 1872
Spokane 1881
Coeur D'Alene 1867
Jocko 1855
Blackfeet 1875
Fort Belknap 1888
Fort Peck 1868
Crow 1868

Northern Cheyenne 1884

Uintah Valley 1861
Wind River 1868
Fort Hall 1868
Duck Valley 1877

Yakima 1855
Lapwal 1863
Lemhi 1875

Swinomish 1855
Tulalip 1855
Puyallup 1854
Muckleshoot 1857
Squaxon Island 1854
Skokomish 1855
Port Madison 1855

Makah 1855
Ozette 1893
Quileute 1889
Hoh River 1893
Quinaielt 1855
Shoalwater 1866
Chehalis 1864
Umatilla 1855
Grande Ronde 1857
Warm Springs 1855
Klamath 1864

1864
1856

Hoopa Valley
Round Valley

Pyramid Lake 1874
Walker River 1874

Tule River 1873
Moapa River 1873
Hualpai 1883
Colorado River 1863
Mission Indians 1875

Gila Bend 1882
Yuma 1884
Gila River 1859
Papago 1874
White Mountain 1871

In 1924 all Indians born in
the United States were granted
full U.S. citizenship. The
Indian Reorganisation Act
of 1934 guaranteed the
security of their land tenure

0   400
Miles

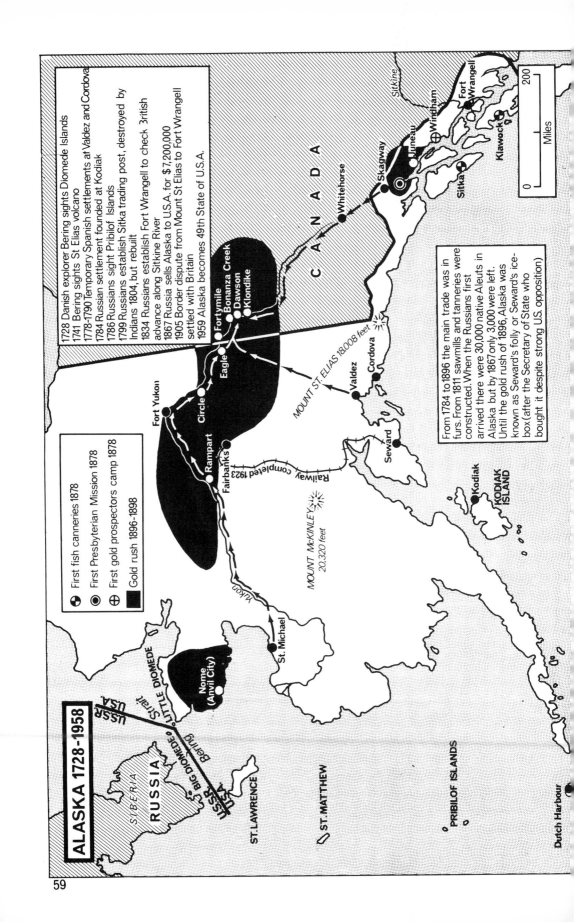

ALASKA 1728-1958

1728 Danish explorer Bering sights Diomede Islands
1741 Bering sights St Elias volcano
1778-1790 Temporary Spanish settlements at Valdez and Cordova
1784 Russian settlement founded at Kodiak
1786 Russians sight Pribilof Islands
1799 Russians establish Sitka trading post, destroyed by Indians 1804, but rebuilt
1834 Russians establish Fort Wrangell to check British advance along Sitkine River
1867 Russia sells Alaska to U.S.A. for $7,200,000
1905 Border dispute from Mount St Elias to Fort Wrangell settled with Britain
1959 Alaska becomes 49th State of U.S.A.

Legend:
- ◐ First fish canneries 1878
- ◉ First Presbyterian Mission 1878
- ⊕ First gold prospectors camp 1878
- ■ Gold rush 1896-1898

From 1784 to 1896 the main trade was in furs. From 1811 sawmills and tanneries were constructed. When the Russians first arrived there were 30,000 native Aleuts in Alaska but by 1867 only 3,000 were left. Until the gold rush of 1896, Alaska was known as Seward's folly or Seward's icebox (after the Secretary of State who bought it despite strong U.S. opposition)

Miles 0 ——— 200

RUSSIA
SIBERIA
USSR / USA
Bering Strait
BIG DIOMEDE
LITTLE DIOMEDE

Nome (Anvil City)
St. Michael
ST. LAWRENCE
ST. MATTHEW
PRIBILOF ISLANDS
Dutch Harbour
KODIAK ISLAND
Kodiak

MOUNT McKINLEY 20,320 feet
Railway completed 1923
Yukon
Fairbanks
Rampart
Circle
Fort Yukon
Eagle
Fortymile
Bonanza Creek
Dawson
Klondike
Seward
Valdez
Cordova
MOUNT ST. ELIAS 18,008 feet

C A N A D A

Whitehorse
Skagway
Juneau
Wrigham
Fort Wrangell
Sitka
Klawock
Sitkine

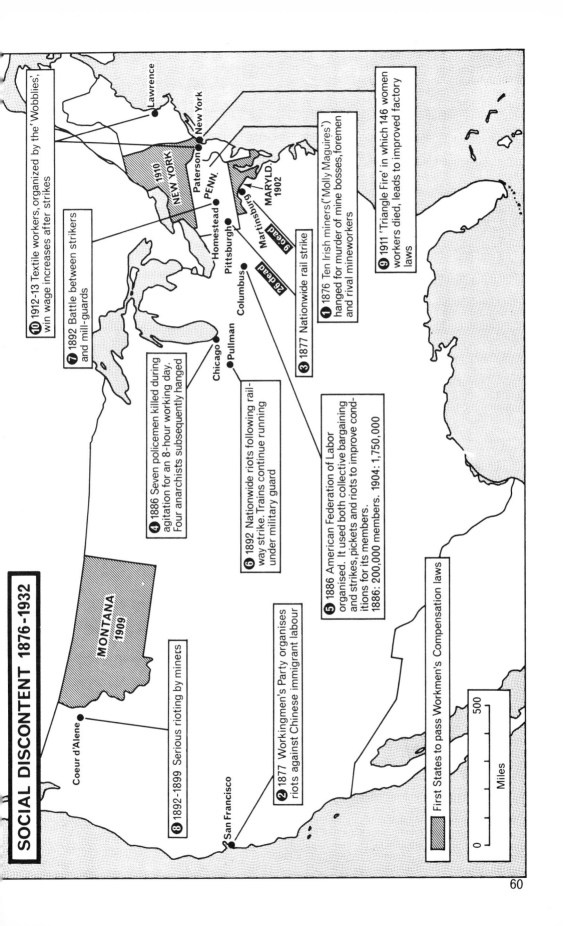

SOCIAL DISCONTENT 1876-1932

10 1912-13 Textile workers, organized by the 'Wobblies', win wage increases after strikes

7 1892 Battle between strikers and mill-guards

1 1876 Ten Irish miners ('Molly Maguires') hanged for murder of mine bosses, foremen and rival mineworkers

9 1911 'Triangle Fire' in which 146 women workers died, leads to improved factory laws

3 1877 Nationwide rail strike

4 1886 Seven policemen killed during agitation for an 8-hour working day. Four anarchists subsequently hanged

6 1892 Nationwide riots following rail-way strike. Trains continue running under military guard

5 1886 American Federation of Labor organised. It used both collective bargaining and strikes, pickets and riots to improve conditions for its members. 1886: 200,000 members. 1904: 1,750,000

8 1892-1899 Serious rioting by miners

2 1877 Workingmen's Party organises riots against Chinese immigrant labour

First States to pass Workmen's Compensation laws

Lawrence

New York

Paterson

PENN.

NEW YORK 1910

MARYLD. 1902

Martinsburg

1909

1892

Homestead

Pittsburgh

Columbus

Chicago

Pullman

San Francisco

Coeur d'Alene

MONTANA 1909

Miles

0 500

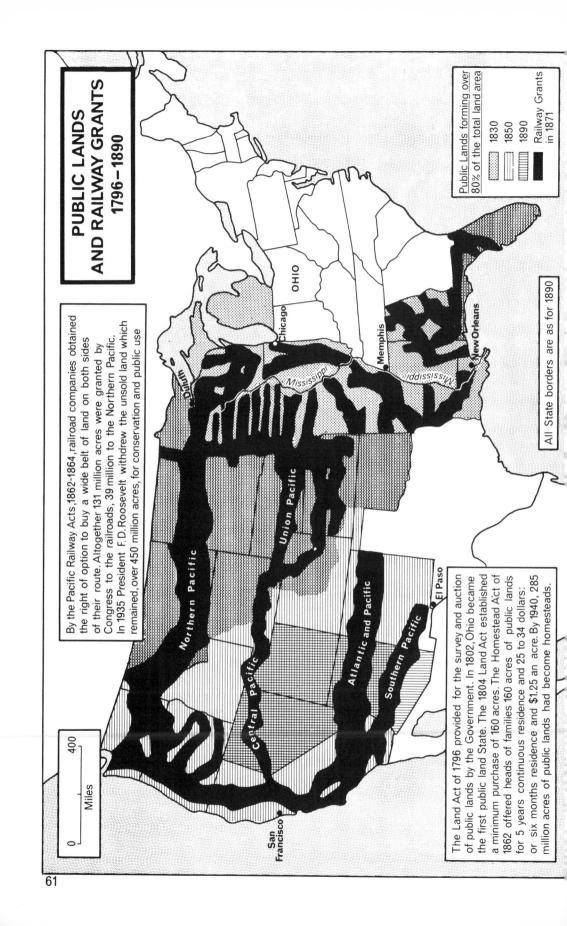

PUBLIC LANDS AND RAILWAY GRANTS 1796–1890

Public Lands forming over 80% of the total land area

- 1830
- 1850
- 1890
- Railway Grants in 1871

All State borders are as for 1890

By the Pacific Railway Acts,1862-1864,railroad companies obtained the right of option to buy a wide belt of land on both sides of their route. Altogether 131 million acres were granted by Congress to the railroads, 39 million to the Northern Pacific. In 1935 President F.D.Roosevelt withdrew the unsold land which remained, over 450 million acres, for conservation and public use

The Land Act of 1796 provided for the survey and auction of public lands by the Government. In 1802,Ohio became the first public land State. The 1804 Land Act established a minimum purchase of 160 acres. The Homestead Act of 1862 offered heads of families 160 acres of public lands for 5 years continuous residence and 25 to 34 dollars; or six months residence and $1.25 an acre.By 1940, 285 million acres of public lands had become homesteads.

Northern Pacific

Union Pacific

Central Pacific

Atlantic and Pacific

Southern Pacific

San Francisco

El Paso

Duluth

Chicago

Memphis

New Orleans

OHIO

Mississippi

Mississippi

0 400 Miles

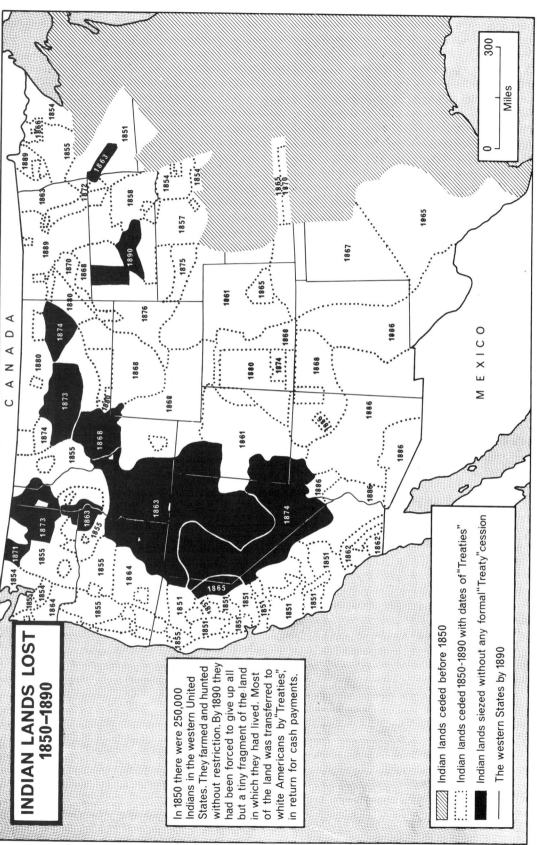

INDIAN LANDS LOST 1850–1890

In 1850 there were 250,000 Indians in the western United States. They farmed and hunted without restriction. By 1890 they had been forced to give up all but a tiny fragment of the land in which they had lived. Most of the land was transferred to white Americans by "Treaties", in return for cash payments.

Indian lands ceded before 1850

Indian lands ceded 1850–1890 with dates of "Treaties"

Indian lands siezed without any formal "Treaty" cession

The western States by 1890

CANADA

MEXICO

0   300
Miles

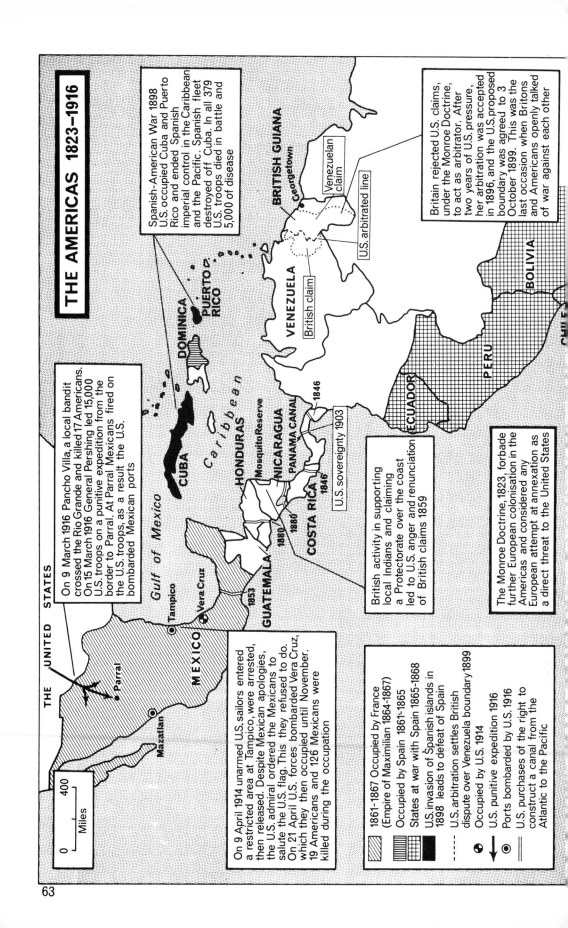

THE AMERICAS 1823–1916

THE UNITED STATES

Gulf of Mexico

On 9 March 1916 Pancho Villa, a local bandit crossed the Rio Grande and killed 17 Americans. On 15 March 1916 General Pershing led 15,000 U.S. troops on a punitive expedition from the border to Parral. At Parral Mexicans fired on the U.S. troops, as a result the U.S. bombarded Mexican ports

Spanish-American War 1898 U.S. occupied Cuba and Puerto Rico and ended Spanish imperial control in the Caribbean and the Pacific. Spanish fleet destroyed off Cuba. In all 379 U.S. troops died in battle and 5,000 of disease

Britain rejected U.S. claims, under the Monroe Doctrine, to act as arbitrator. After two years of U.S. pressure, her arbitration was accepted in 1896, and the U.S.proposed boundary was agreed to 3 October 1899. This was the last occasion when Britons and Americans openly talked of war against each other

BRITISH GUIANA
Georgetown

Venezuelan claim

U.S. arbitrated line

DOMINICA

PUERTO RICO

VENEZUELA
British claim

CUBA

Caribbean

HONDURAS
Mosquito Reserve

1846

NICARAGUA
PANAMA CANAL

1880
1860

COSTA RICA
1846

U.S. sovereignty 1903

ECUADOR

PERU

BOLIVIA

CHILE

GUATEMALA
1853

Tampico
Vera Cruz

MEXICO

Mazatlan

Parral

On 9 April 1914 unarmed U.S.sailors entered a restricted area at Tampico, were arrested, then released. Despite Mexican apologies, the U.S. admiral ordered the Mexicans to salute the U.S. flag.This they refused to do. On 21 April U.S. forces bombarded Vera Cruz, which they then occupied until November. 19 Americans and 126 Mexicans were killed during the occupation

British activity in supporting local Indians and claiming a Protectorate over the coast led to U.S. anger and renunciation of British claims 1859

The Monroe Doctrine,1823, forbade further European colonisation in the Americas and considered any European attempt at annexation as a direct threat to the United States

1861-1867 Occupied by France (Empire of Maximilian 1864-1867)

Occupied by Spain 1861-1865

States at war with Spain 1865-1868

U.S. invasion of Spanish islands in 1898 leads to defeat of Spain

U.S. arbitration settles British dispute over Venezuela boundary 1899

Occupied by U.S.1914

U.S. punitive expedition 1916

Ports bombarded by U.S.1916

U.S. purchases of the right to construct a canal from the Atlantic to the Pacific

0   400
Miles

63

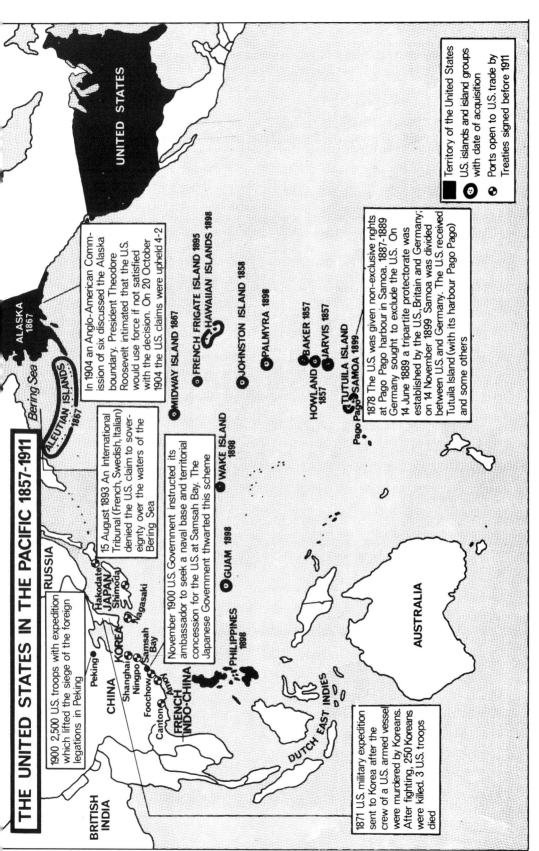

THE UNITED STATES IN THE PACIFIC 1857-1911

UNITED STATES

ALASKA 1867

Bering Sea

ALEUTIAN ISLANDS 1857

RUSSIA

BRITISH INDIA

CHINA
Peking
Shanghai
Ningpo
Foochow
Amoy
Canton

KOREA
Samsah Bay

JAPAN
Hakodate
Shimoda
Nagasaki

FRENCH INDO-CHINA

PHILIPPINES 1898

DUTCH EAST INDIES

AUSTRALIA

● GUAM 1898
● WAKE ISLAND 1898

● MIDWAY ISLAND 1867
● FRENCH FRIGATE ISLAND 1895
● HAWAIIAN ISLANDS 1898
● JOHNSTON ISLAND 1858
● PALMYRA 1898
● HOWLAND 1857
● BAKER 1857
● JARVIS 1857
● TUTUILA ISLAND
Pago Pago ● SAMOA 1899

1900 2,500 U.S. troops with expedition which lifted the siege of the foreign legations in Peking

15 August 1893 An International Tribunal (French, Swedish, Italian) denied the U.S. claim to sovereignty over the waters of the Bering Sea

November 1900 U.S. Government instructed its ambassador to seek a naval base and territorial concession for the U.S. at Samsah Bay. The Japanese Government thwarted this scheme

In 1904 an Anglo-American Commission of six discussed the Alaska boundary. President Theodore Roosevelt intimated that the U.S. would use force if not satisfied with the decision. On 20 October 1904 the U.S. claims were upheld 4-2

1878 The U.S. was given non-exclusive rights at Pago Pago harbour in Samoa. 1887-1889 Germany sought to exclude the U.S. On 14 June 1889 a tripartite protectorate was established by the U.S., Britain and Germany; on 14 November 1899 Samoa was divided between U.S. and Germany. The U.S. received Tutuila Island (with its harbour Pago Pago) and some others

1871 U.S. military expedition sent to Korea after the crew of a U.S. armed vessel were murdered by Koreans. After fighting, 250 Koreans were killed. 3 U.S. troops died

■ Territory of the United States
◉ U.S. islands and island groups with date of acquisition
● Ports open to U.S. trade by Treaties signed before 1911

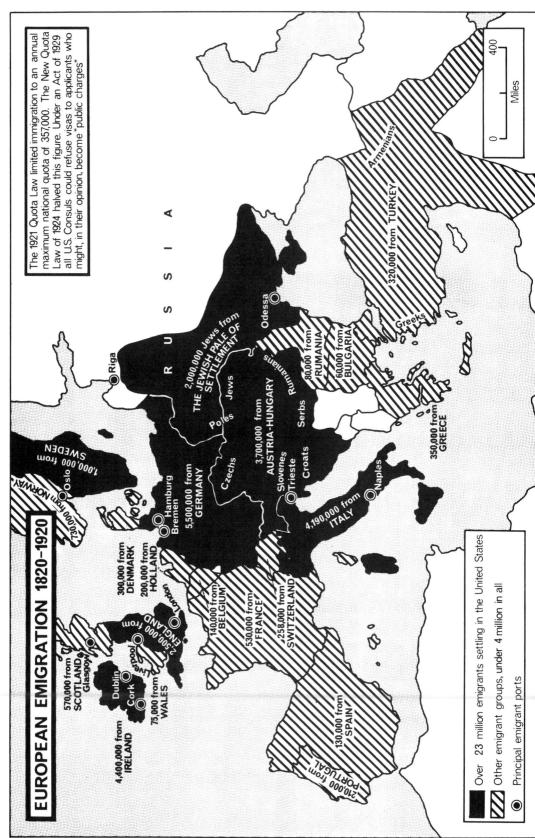

EUROPEAN EMIGRATION 1820–1920

The 1921 Quota Law limited immigration to an annual maximum national quota of 357,000. The New Quota Law of 1924 halved this figure. Under an Act of 1929 all U.S. Consuls could refuse visas to applicants who might, in their opinion, become "public charges"

1,000,000 from SWEDEN

730,000 from NORWAY
Oslo

Riga

R U S S I A

Odessa

THE JEWISH PALE OF SETTLEMENT
2,000,000 Jews from

Jews

Poles

Rumanians

80,000 from RUMANIA

60,000 from BULGARIA

Greeks

320,000 from TURKEY
Armenians

5,500,000 from GERMANY
Hamburg
Bremen

Czechs

AUSTRIA-HUNGARY
3,700,000 from

Slovenes
Trieste
Croats
Serbs

350,000 from GREECE

300,000 from DENMARK

200,000 from HOLLAND

570,000 from SCOTLAND
Glasgow

2,500,000 from ENGLAND
Liverpool
London

Dublin
Cork

75,000 from WALES

4,400,000 from IRELAND

140,000 from BELGIUM

530,000 from FRANCE

258,000 from SWITZERLAND

4,190,000 from ITALY
Naples

130,000 from SPAIN

210,000 from PORTUGAL

Miles
0   400

Over 23 million emigrants settling in the United States

Other emigrant groups, under 4 million in all

Principal emigrant ports

65

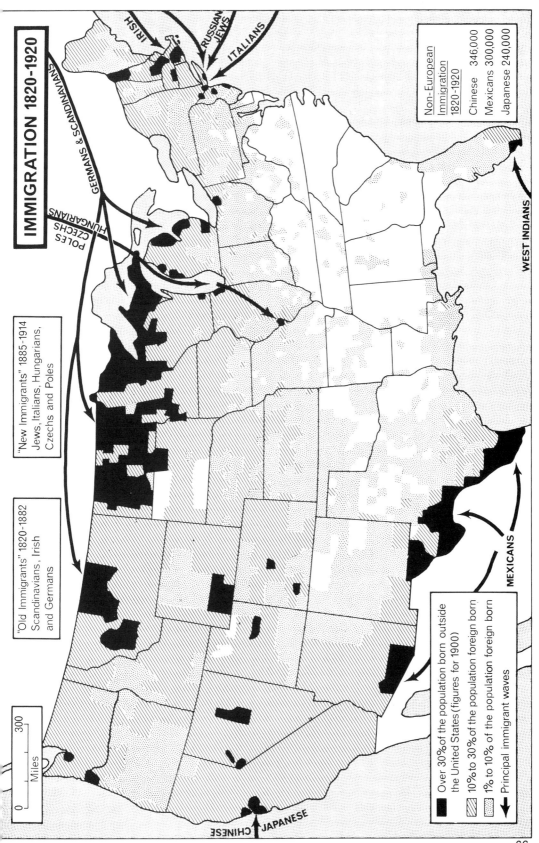

IMMIGRATION 1820-1920

"Old Immigrants" 1820-1882
Scandinavians, Irish and Germans

"New Immigrants" 1885-1914
Jews, Italians, Hungarians, Czechs and Poles

Non-European
Immigration
1820-1920

Chinese   346,000
Mexicans   300,000
Japanese   240,000

IRISH

RUSSIAN JEWS

ITALIANS

GERMANS & SCANDINAVIANS

POLES
CZECHS
HUNGARIANS

WEST INDIANS

MEXICANS

JAPANESE

CHINESE

Over 30% of the population born outside the United States (figures for 1900)

10% to 30% of the population foreign born

1% to 10% of the population foreign born

Principal immigrant waves

0   300
Miles

G

66

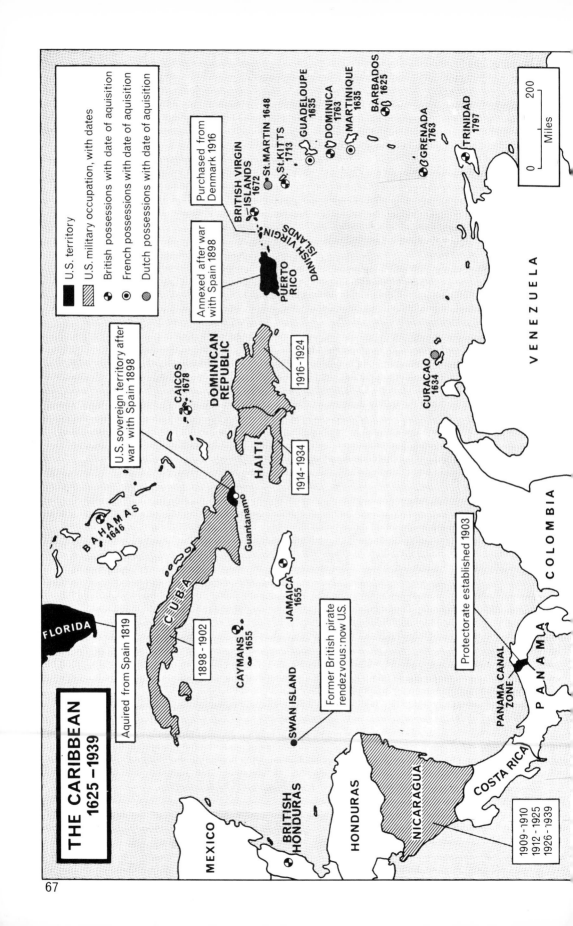

THE CARIBBEAN 1625–1939

Legend:
- U.S. territory
- U.S. military occupation, with dates
- British possessions with date of aquisition
- French possessions with date of aquisition
- Dutch possessions with date of aquisition

Purchased from Denmark 1916

Annexed after war with Spain 1898

BRITISH VIRGIN ISLANDS 1672

St. MARTIN 1648
St. KITTS 1713
GUADELOUPE 1635
DOMINICA 1763
MARTINIQUE 1635
BARBADOS 1625
GRENADA 1763
TRINIDAD 1797

DANISH VIRGIN ISLANDS

PUERTO RICO

200
0   Miles

U.S. sovereign territory after war with Spain 1898

CAICOS 1678

DOMINICAN REPUBLIC

1916–1924

1914–1934

HAITI

CURACAO 1634

BAHAMAS 1646

CUBA

Guantanamo

FLORIDA

Aquired from Spain 1819

1898–1902

CAYMANS 1655

JAMAICA 1655

Former British pirate rendezvous: now U.S.

SWAN ISLAND

MEXICO

BRITISH HONDURAS

HONDURAS

NICARAGUA

Protectorate established 1903

PANAMA CANAL ZONE

PANAMA

COSTA RICA

COLOMBIA

VENEZUELA

1909–1910
1912–1925
1926–1939

67

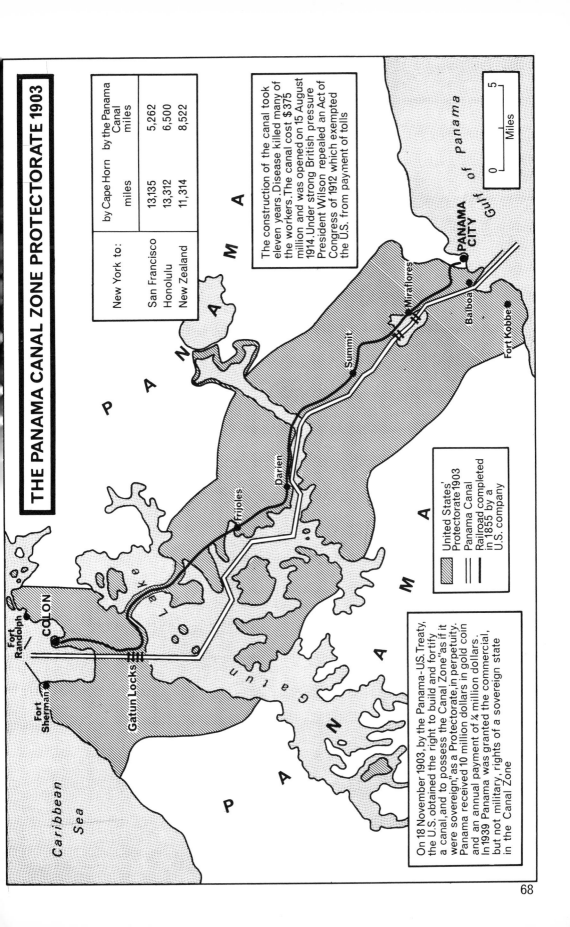

THE PANAMA CANAL ZONE PROTECTORATE 1903

New York to:	by Cape Horn miles	by the Panama Canal miles
San Francisco	13,135	5,262
Honolulu	13,312	6,500
New Zealand	11,314	8,522

The construction of the canal took eleven years. Disease killed many of the workers. The canal cost $375 million and was opened on 15 August 1914. Under strong British pressure President Wilson repealed an Act of Congress of 1912 which exempted the U.S. from payment of tolls

United States' Protectorate 1903

Panama Canal

Railroad completed in 1855 by a U.S. company

On 18 November 1903, by the Panama-U.S. Treaty, the U.S. obtained the right to build and fortify a canal, and to possess the Canal Zone "as if it were sovereign", as a Protectorate, in perpetuity. Panama received 10 million dollars in gold coin and an annual payment of ¼ million dollars. In 1939 Panama was granted the commercial, but not military, rights of a sovereign state in the Canal Zone

Caribbean Sea

Fort Sherman
Fort Randolph
COLON
Gatun Locks

Frijoles

Darien

Summit

Miraflores
Balboa
Fort Kobbe

PANAMA CITY

Gulf of Panama

P A N A M A

0 5
Miles

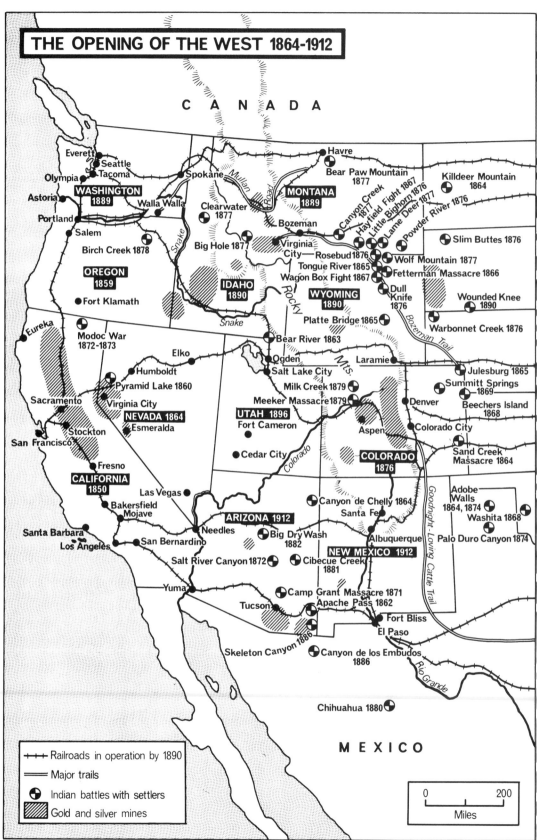

THE OPENING OF THE WEST 1864-1912

CANADA

Everett
Seattle
Olympia
Tacoma
Astoria
WASHINGTON 1889
Walla Walla
Portland
Salem
Birch Creek 1878
OREGON 1859
Fort Klamath

Spokane
Mullan Road

Havre
Bear Paw Mountain 1877
Killdeer Mountain 1864
MONTANA 1889
Canyon Creek 1877
Hayfield Fight 1867
Little Bighorn 1876
Lame Deer 1877
Powder River 1876
Clearwater 1877
Bozeman
Big Hole 1877
Virginia City
Slim Buttes 1876
Rosebud 1876
Tongue River 1865
Wolf Mountain 1877
Wagon Box Fight 1867
Fetterman Massacre 1866
IDAHO 1890
WYOMING 1890
Dull Knife 1876
Wounded Knee 1890
Platte Bridge 1865
Warbonnet Creek 1876

Eureka
Modoc War 1872-1873
Elko
Humboldt
Pyramid Lake 1860
Sacramento
Virginia City
Stockton
NEVADA 1864
Esmeralda
San Francisco
Fresno
CALIFORNIA 1850
Bakersfield
Mojave
Santa Barbara
Los Angeles
San Bernardino
Needles

Snake
Snake
Rocky
Bear River 1863
Ogden
Salt Lake City
Milk Creek 1879
Meeker Massacre 1879
UTAH 1896
Fort Cameron
Cedar City
Colorado
Las Vegas

Mts.
Laramie
Julesburg 1865
Summitt Springs 1869
Denver
Beechers Island 1868
Aspen
Colorado City
COLORADO 1876
Sand Creek Massacre 1864
Canyon de Chelly 1864
Santa Fe
ARIZONA 1912
Big Dry Wash 1882
Salt River Canyon 1872
Cibecue Creek 1881
Yuma
Camp Grant Massacre 1871
Apache Pass 1862
Tucson
Skeleton Canyon 1886
Canyon de los Embudos 1886
Adobe Walls 1864, 1874
Washita 1868
Palo Duro Canyon 1874
Albuquerque
NEW MEXICO 1912
Fort Bliss
El Paso
Goodnight-Loving Cattle Trail
Bozeman Trail

Chihuahua 1880

MEXICO

Rio Grande

+++	Railroads in operation by 1890
===	Major trails
⊕	Indian battles with settlers
▨	Gold and silver mines

0   200
Miles

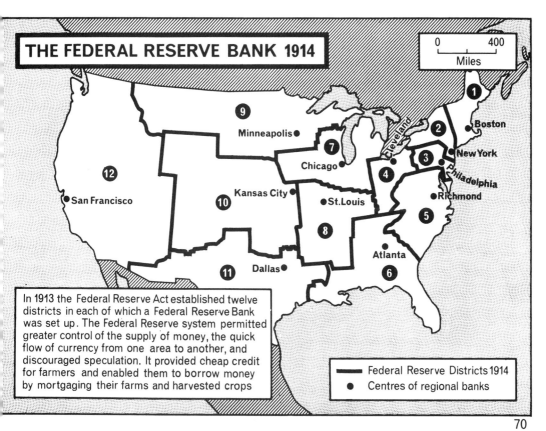

THE FEDERAL RESERVE BANK 1914

0   400
Miles

❶ Boston
❷
❸
❹
❺
❻
❼ Chicago
❽
❾ Minneapolis
❿ Kansas City
⓫ Dallas
⓬ San Francisco

Cleveland
New York
Philadelphia
Richmond
St. Louis
Atlanta

In 1913 the Federal Reserve Act established twelve districts in each of which a Federal Reserve Bank was set up. The Federal Reserve system permitted greater control of the supply of money, the quick flow of currency from one area to another, and discouraged speculation. It provided cheap credit for farmers and enabled them to borrow money by mortgaging their farms and harvested crops

—— Federal Reserve Districts 1914
● Centres of regional banks

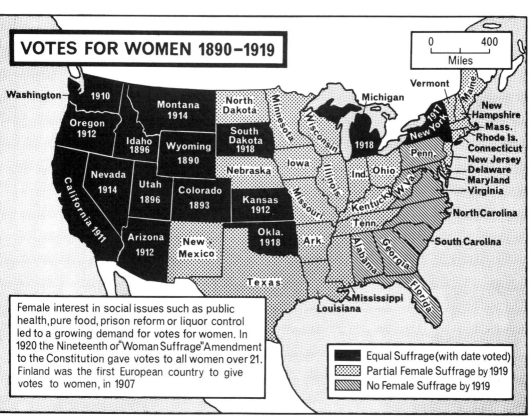

VOTES FOR WOMEN 1890–1919

0   400
Miles

Washington 1910
Oregon 1912
Montana 1914
North Dakota
Minnesota
Michigan
Vermont
Maine
New Hampshire
Mass.
Rhode Is.
New York 1917
Idaho 1896
Wyoming 1890
South Dakota 1918
Wisconsin
Iowa
1918
Penn.
Connecticut
New Jersey
Delaware
Maryland
Virginia
Nevada 1914
Utah 1896
Colorado 1893
Nebraska
Illinois
Ind.
Ohio
W.Va.
California 1911
Arizona 1912
New Mexico
Kansas 1912
Missouri
Kentucky
Tenn.
North Carolina
Okla. 1918
Ark
Alabama
Georgia
South Carolina
Texas
Mississippi
Louisiana
Florida

Female interest in social issues such as public health, pure food, prison reform or liquor control led to a growing demand for votes for women. In 1920 the Nineteenth or "Woman Suffrage" Amendment to the Constitution gave votes to all women over 21. Finland was the first European country to give votes to women, in 1907

■ Equal Suffrage (with date voted)
▦ Partial Female Suffrage by 1919
▨ No Female Suffrage by 1919

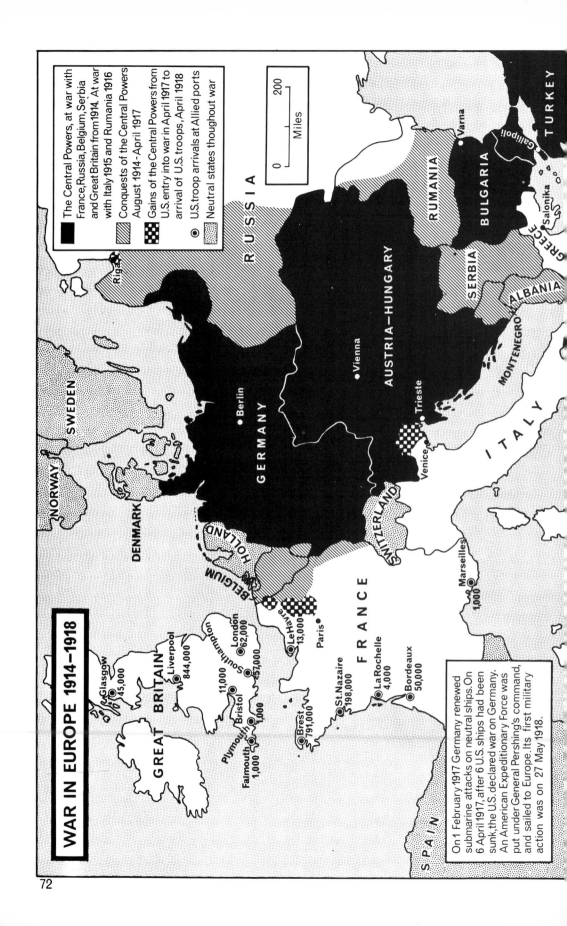

WAR IN EUROPE 1914-1918

Legend:

- ■ The Central Powers, at war with France, Russia, Belgium, Serbia and Great Britain from 1914. At war with Italy 1915 and Rumania 1916
- ▨ Conquests of the Central Powers August 1914 - April 1917
- ▦ Gains of the Central Powers from U.S. entry into war in April 1917 to arrival of U.S. troops, April 1918
- ⊙ U.S. troop arrivals at Allied ports
- ▨ Neutral states thoughout war

0 ___ 200

Miles

TURKEY

Gallipoli

RUSSIA

Varna

RUMANIA

BULGARIA

SERBIA

AUSTRIA–HUNGARY

Vienna

GREECE

Salonika

ALBANIA

MONTENEGRO

Riga

SWEDEN

NORWAY

Berlin

GERMANY

Trieste

ITALY

DENMARK

Venice

HOLLAND

BELGIUM

SWITZERLAND

Glasgow
45,000

Liverpool
844,000

GREAT BRITAIN

11,000

London
62,000

Southampton
57,000

Bristol
1,000

Plymouth

Falmouth
1,000

Le Havre
13,000

Paris

FRANCE

Brest
791,000

St. Nazaire
198,000

La Rochelle
4,000

Bordeaux
50,000

Marseilles
1,000

SPAIN

On 1 February 1917 Germany renewed submarine attacks on neutral ships. On 6 April 1917, after 6 U.S. ships had been sunk, the U.S. declared war on Germany. An American Expeditionary Force was put under General Pershing's command, and sailed to Europe. Its first military action was on 27 May 1918.

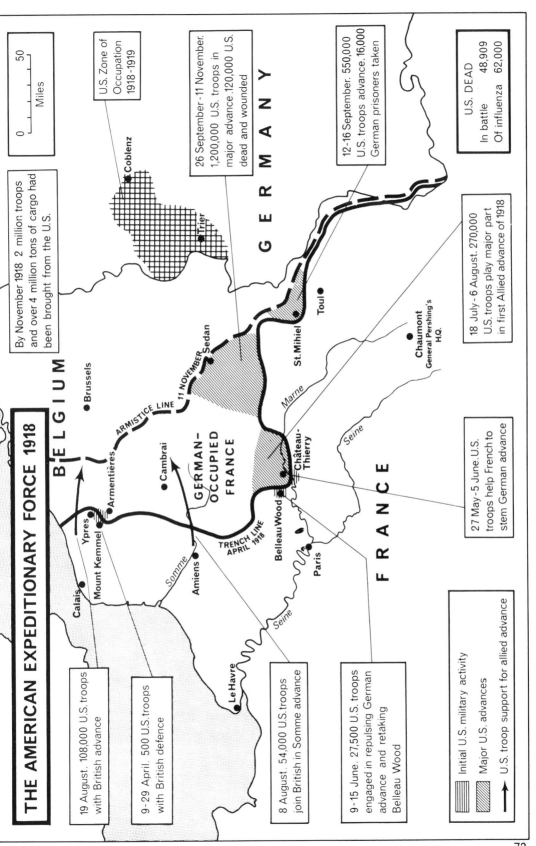

THE AMERICAN EXPEDITIONARY FORCE 1918

U.S. Zone of Occupation 1918-1919

26 September - 11 November. 1,200,000 U.S. troops in major advance.120,000 U.S. dead and wounded

12-16 September. 550,000 U.S. troops advance.16,000 German prisoners taken

U.S. DEAD

In battle   48,909
Of influenza   62,000

By November 1918 2 million troops and over 4 million tons of cargo had been brought from the U.S.

18 July - 6 August. 270,000 U.S. troops play major part in first Allied advance of 1918

GERMANY

BELGIUM

• Brussels

• Coblenz

• Trier

• Toul

ARMISTICE LINE 11 NOVEMBER

Sedan

St. Mihiel

Chaumont
General Pershing's H.Q.

Marne

Seine

GERMAN-OCCUPIED FRANCE

Château-Thierry

27 May - 5 June. U.S. troops help French to stem German advance

• Cambrai

Armentières

Ypres

Mount Kemmel •

• Calais

Somme

Amiens •

Seine

TRENCH LINE APRIL 1918

Belleau Wood

• Paris

FRANCE

Le Havre •

19 August. 108,000 U.S. troops with British advance

9 - 29 April. 500 U.S. troops with British defence

8 August. 54,000 U.S. troops join British in Somme advance

9 - 15 June. 27,500 U.S. troops engaged in repulsing German advance and retaking Belleau Wood

Initial U.S. military activity

Major U.S. advances

U.S. troop support for allied advance

0   50
Miles

73

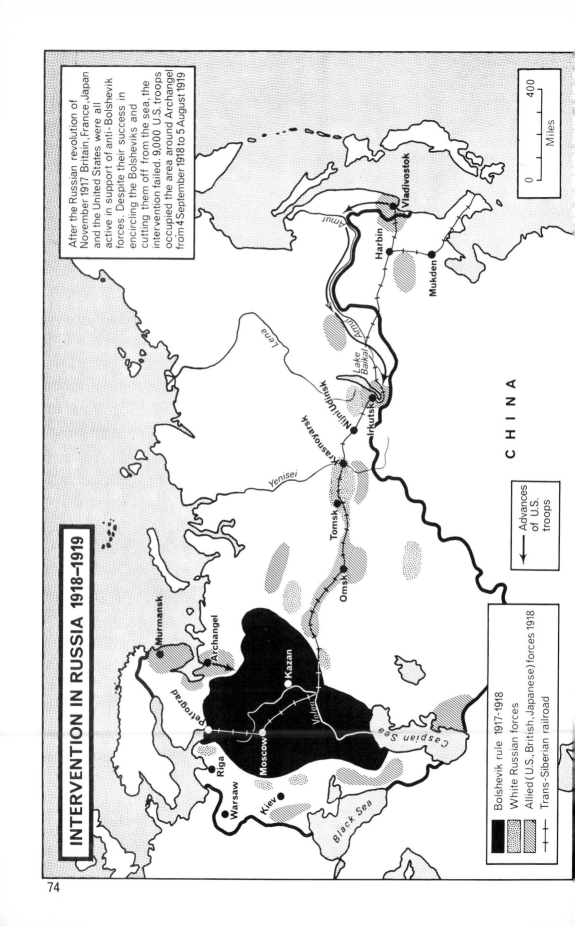

INTERVENTION IN RUSSIA 1918–1919

After the Russian revolution of November 1917 Britain, France, Japan and the United States were all active in support of anti-Bolshevik forces. Despite their success in encircling the Bolsheviks and cutting them off from the sea, the intervention failed. 9,000 U.S. troops occupied the area around Archangel from 4 September 1918 to 5 August 1919

Murmansk
Archangel
Petrograd
Riga
Warsaw
Kiev
Moscow
Kazan
Omsk
Tomsk
Krasnoyarsk
Nijni Udinsk
Irkutsk
Harbin
Mukden
Vladivostok

Volga
Caspian Sea
Black Sea
Yenisei
Lena
Lake Baikal
Amur

CHINA

Miles
0   400

Advances
of U.S.
troops

Bolshevik rule 1917-1918
White Russian forces
Allied (U.S., British, Japanese) forces 1918
Trans-Siberian railroad

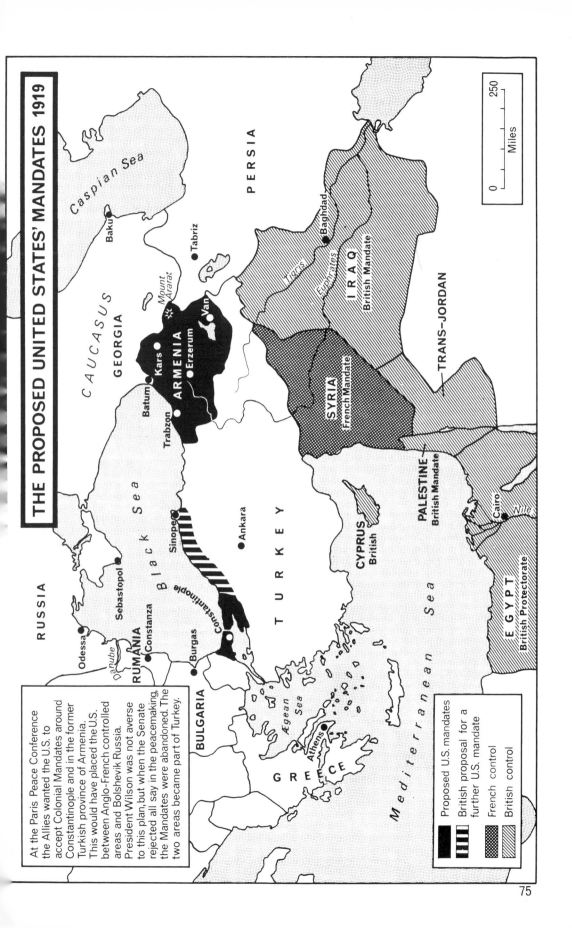

THE PROPOSED UNITED STATES' MANDATES 1919

At the Paris Peace Conference the Allies wanted the U.S. to accept Colonial Mandates around Constantinople and in the former Turkish province of Armenia. This would have placed the U.S. between Anglo-French controlled areas and Bolshevik Russia. President Wilson was not averse to this plan, but when the Senate rejected all say in the peacemaking, the Mandates were abandoned. The two areas became part of Turkey.

Legend:
- Proposed U.S. mandates
- British proposal for a further U.S. mandate
- French control
- British control

Labels on map:

RUSSIA

Caspian Sea

Baku

PERSIA

Tabriz

Mount Ararat

CAUCASUS

GEORGIA

ARMENIA

Kars • Erzerum • Van

Batum

Trabzon

Black Sea

Odessa

Sebastopol

RUMANIA

Constanza

Danube

Burgas

BULGARIA

Sinope

Constantinople

Ankara

TURKEY

GREECE

Athens

Aegean Sea

Mediterranean Sea

CYPRUS British

PALESTINE British Mandate

SYRIA French Mandate

IRAQ British Mandate

Tigris

Euphrates

Baghdad

TRANS-JORDAN

EGYPT British Protectorate

Cairo

Nile

0   250

Miles

75

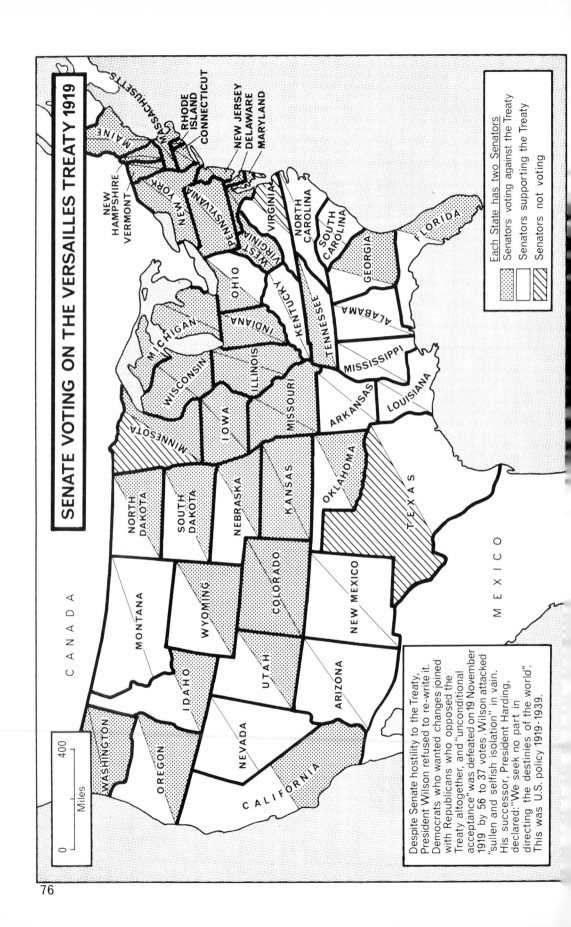

SENATE VOTING ON THE VERSAILLES TREATY 1919

Despite Senate hostility to the Treaty, President Wilson refused to re-write it. Democrats who wanted changes joined with Republicans who opposed the Treaty altogether, and "unconditional acceptance" was defeated on 19 November 1919 by 56 to 37 votes. Wilson attacked "sullen and selfish isolation" in vain. His successor, President Harding, declared: "We seek no part in directing the destinies of the world". This was U.S. policy 1919-1939.

Each State has two Senators

Senators voting against the Treaty

Senators supporting the Treaty

Senators not voting

Miles
0   400

CANADA

MEXICO

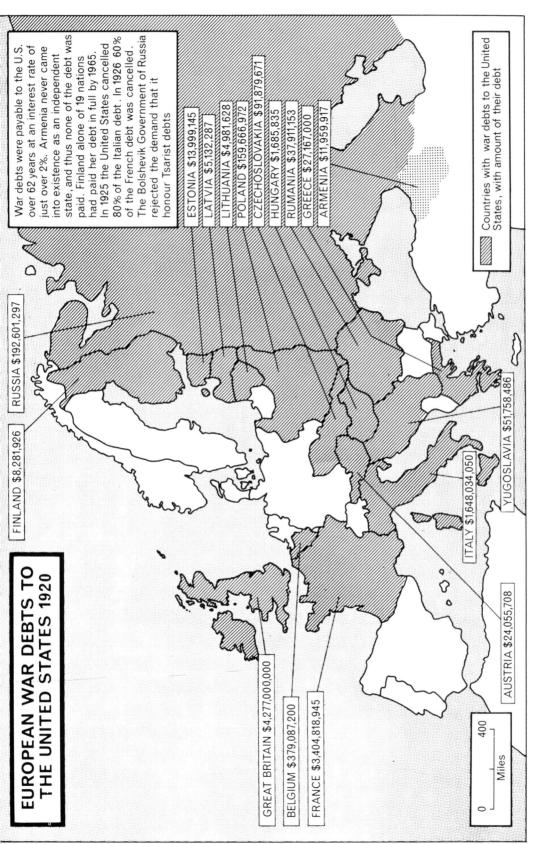

EUROPEAN WAR DEBTS TO THE UNITED STATES 1920

War debts were payable to the U.S. over 62 years at an interest rate of just over 2%. Armenia never came into existence as an independent state, and thus none of the debt was paid. Finland alone of 19 nations had paid her debt in full by 1965. In 1925 the United States cancelled 80% of the Italian debt. In 1926 60% of the French debt was cancelled. The Bolshevik Government of Russia rejected the demand that it honour Tsarist debts

ESTONIA $13,999,145
LATVIA $5,132,287
LITHUANIA $4,981,628
POLAND $159,666,972
CZECHOSLOVAKIA $91,879,671
HUNGARY $1,685,835
RUMANIA $37,911,153
GREECE $27,167,000
ARMENIA $11,959,917

FINLAND $8,281,926
RUSSIA $192,601,297

ITALY $1,648,034,050
YUGOSLAVIA $51,758,486

AUSTRIA $24,055,708

GREAT BRITAIN $4,277,000,000
BELGIUM $379,087,200
FRANCE $3,404,818,945

Countries with war debts to the United States, with amount of their debt

0   400
Miles

77

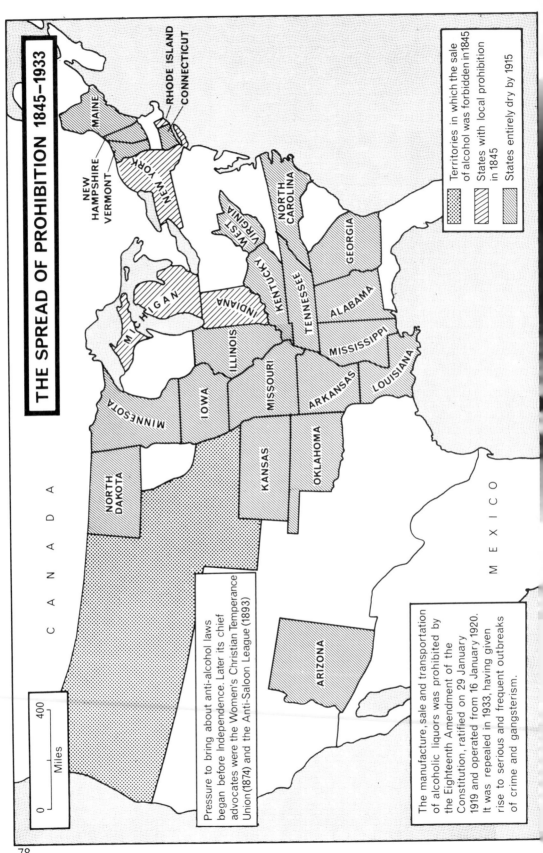

THE SPREAD OF PROHIBITION 1845–1933

CANADA

MEXICO

NORTH DAKOTA
MINNESOTA
MICHIGAN
IOWA
ILLINOIS
INDIANA
MISSOURI
KANSAS
OKLAHOMA
ARKANSAS
LOUISIANA
MISSISSIPPI
ALABAMA
TENNESSEE
KENTUCKY
WEST VIRGINIA
GEORGIA
NORTH CAROLINA
ARIZONA
MAINE
NEW HAMPSHIRE
VERMONT
NEW YORK
RHODE ISLAND
CONNECTICUT

Territories in which the sale of alcohol was forbidden in 1845

States with local prohibition in 1845

States entirely dry by 1915

Miles
0   400

Pressure to bring about anti-alcohol laws began before Independence. Later its chief advocates were the Women's Christian Temperance Union (1874) and the Anti-Saloon League (1893)

The manufacture, sale and transportation of alcoholic liquors was prohibited by the Eighteenth Amendment of the Constitution, ratified on 29 January 1919 and operated from 16 January 1920. It was repealed in 1933, having given rise to serious and frequent outbreaks of crime and gangsterism.

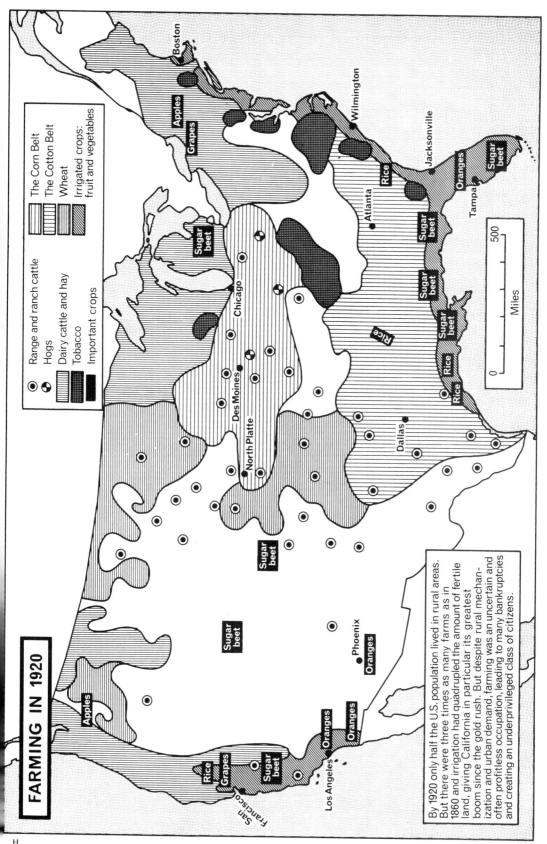

FARMING IN 1920

Legend:

- ⊚ Range and ranch cattle
- ⊙ Hogs
- (horizontal lines) Dairy cattle and hay
- (dark) Tobacco
- (black) Important crops

- The Corn Belt
- The Cotton Belt
- Wheat
- Irrigated crops: fruit and vegetables

Labeled places: Boston, Wilmington, Jacksonville, Tampa, Atlanta, Chicago, Des Moines, North Platte, Dallas, Phoenix, Los Angeles, San Francisco

Crop labels: Apples, Grapes, Rice, Oranges, Sugar beet

0 ____ 500 Miles

By 1920 only half the U.S. population lived in rural areas. But there were three times as many farms as in 1860 and irrigation had quadrupled the amount of fertile land, giving California in particular its greatest boom since the gold rush. But despite rural mechanization and urban demand, farming was an uncertain and often profitless occupation, leading to many bankruptcies and creating an underprivileged class of citizens.

H

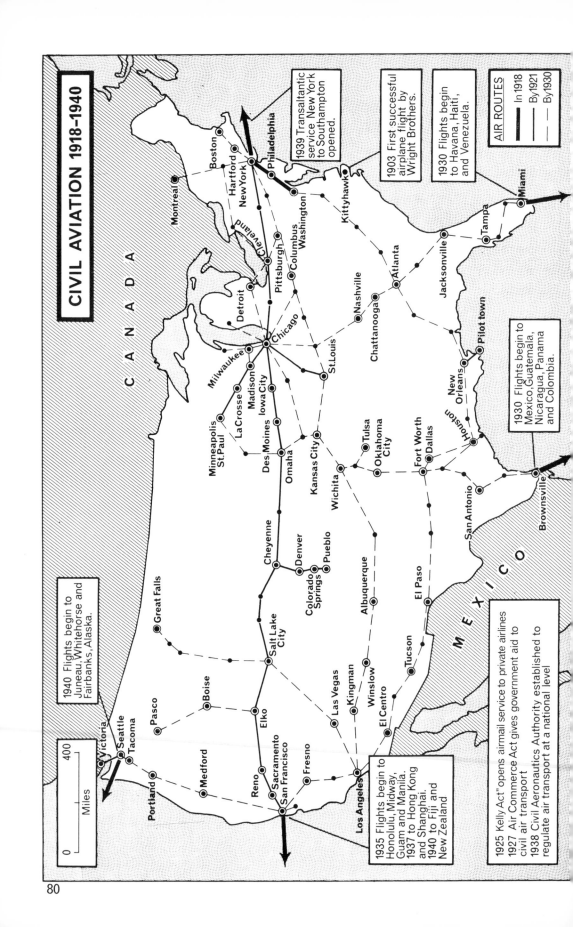

CIVIL AVIATION 1918-1940

AIR ROUTES
— In 1918
— By 1921
--- By 1930

1939 Transatlantic service New York to Southampton opened.

1903 First successful airplane flight by Wright Brothers.

1930 Flights begin to Havana, Haiti, and Venezuela.

1930 Flights begin to Mexico, Guatemala, Nicaragua, Panama and Colombia.

1940 Flights begin to Juneau, Whitehorse and Fairbanks, Alaska.

1935 Flights begin to Honolulu, Midway, Guam and Manila. 1937 to Hong Kong and Shanghai. 1940 to Fiji and New Zealand

1925 Kelly Act" opens airmail service to private airlines
1927 Air Commerce Act gives government aid to civil air transport
1938 Civil Aeronautics Authority established to regulate air transport at a national level

CANADA

MEXICO

Miles
0   400

Montreal
Boston
Hartford
New York
Philadelphia
Cleveland
Washington
Columbus
Pittsburgh
Kittyhawk
Detroit
Chicago
Milwaukee
Nashville
Atlanta
Jacksonville
Tampa
Miami
Chattanooga
St.Louis
Minneapolis St.Paul
La Crosse
Madison
Iowa City
Des Moines
Omaha
Kansas City
Wichita
Tulsa
Oklahoma City
Fort Worth
Dallas
New Orleans
Pilot town
Houston
San Antonio
Brownsville
Cheyenne
Denver
Pueblo
Colorado Springs
Albuquerque
El Paso
Tucson
Winslow
Kingman
El Centro
Las Vegas
Salt Lake City
Great Falls
Boise
Pasco
Elko
Reno
Sacramento
San Francisco
Fresno
Los Angeles
Medford
Portland
Seattle
Tacoma
Victoria

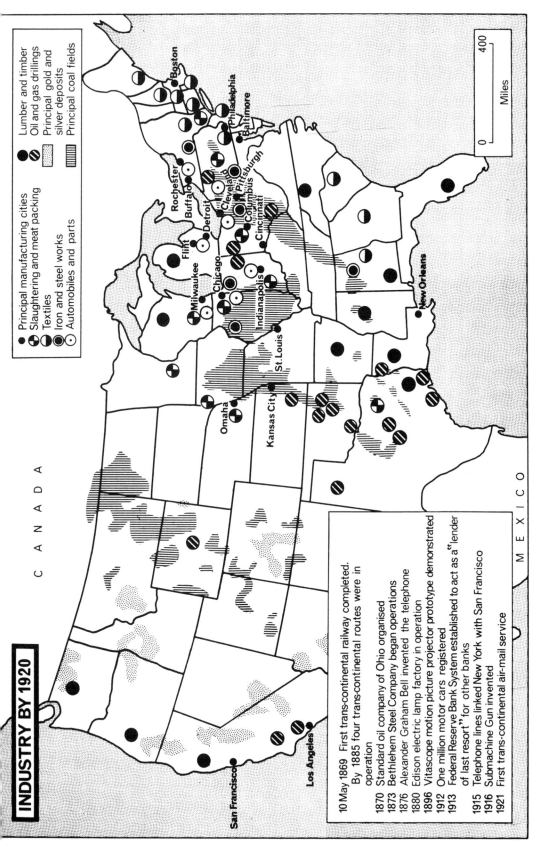

INDUSTRY BY 1920

CANADA

MEXICO

Key:
- Principal manufacturing cities
- Slaughtering and meat packing
- Textiles
- Iron and steel works
- Automobiles and parts
- Lumber and timber
- Oil and gas drillings
- Principal gold and silver deposits
- Principal coal fields

0 — 400 Miles

Cities labelled:
Boston, Philadelphia, Baltimore, Rochester, Buffalo, Detroit, Cleveland, Pittsburgh, Columbus, Cincinnati, Flint, Milwaukee, Chicago, Indianapolis, St. Louis, Omaha, Kansas City, New Orleans, San Francisco, Los Angeles

10 May 1869 First trans-continental railway completed. By 1885 four trans-continental routes were in operation
1870 Standard oil company of Ohio organised
1873 Bethlehem Steel Company began operations
1876 Alexander Graham Bell invented the telephone
1880 Edison electric lamp factory in operation
1896 Vitascope motion picture projector prototype demonstrated
1912 One million motor cars registered
1913 Federal Reserve Bank System established to act as a "lender of last resort" for other banks
1915 Telephone lines linked New York with San Francisco
1916 Submachine Gun invented
1921 First trans-continental air-mail service

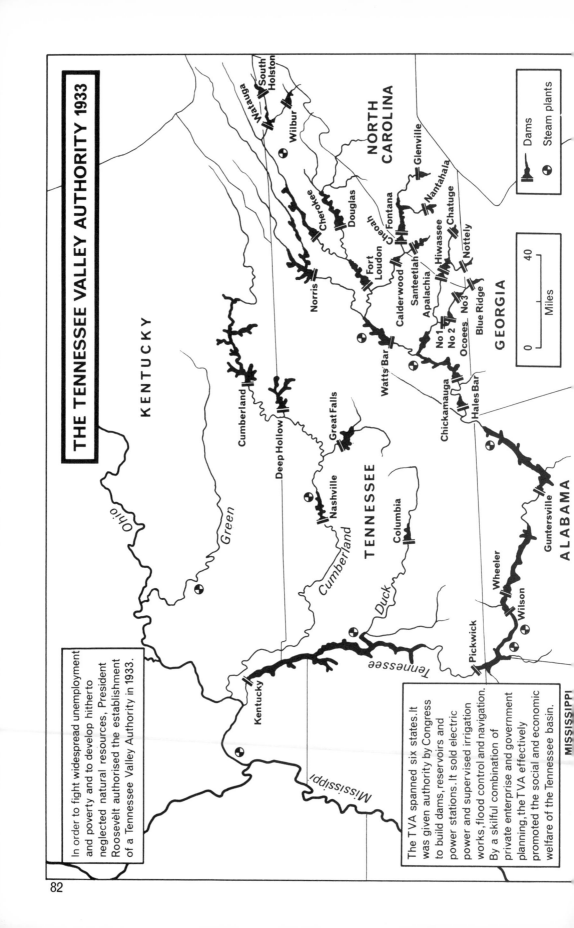

THE TENNESSEE VALLEY AUTHORITY 1933

In order to fight widespread unemployment and poverty and to develop hitherto neglected natural resources, President Roosevelt authorised the establishment of a Tennessee Valley Authority in 1933.

The TVA spanned six states. It was given authority by Congress to build dams, reservoirs and power stations. It sold electric power and supervised irrigation works, flood control and navigation. By a skilful combination of private enterprise and government planning, the TVA effectively promoted the social and economic welfare of the Tennessee basin.

Dams
Steam plants

0   40
Miles

KENTUCKY

TENNESSEE

NORTH CAROLINA

GEORGIA

ALABAMA

MISSISSIPPI

Ohio
Green
Cumberland
Duck
Tennessee
Mississippi

Watauga
South Holston
Wilbur
Cherokee
Douglas
Norris
Fort Loudon
Cheoah
Glenville
Fontana
Nantahala
Calderwood
Santeetlah
Apalachia
Chatuge
Hiwassee
Nottely
No 1
No 2
Ocoees
No 3
Blue Ridge
Watts' Bar
Chickamauga
Hales Bar
Cumberland
Deep Hollow
Great Falls
Nashville
Columbia
Wheeler
Guntersville
Wilson
Pickwick
Kentucky

THE UNITED STATES 1914-1945

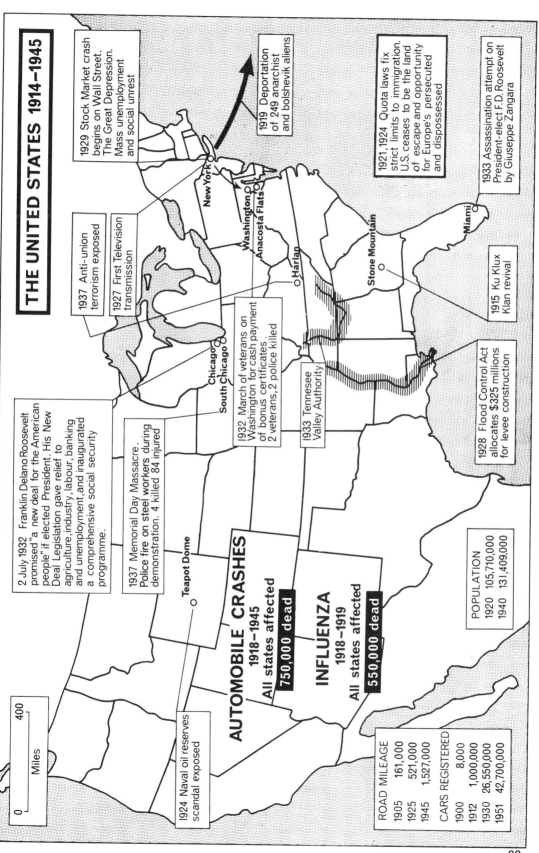

1929 Stock Market crash begins on Wall Street. The Great Depression. Mass unemployment and social unrest

1919 Deportation of 249 anarchist and bolshevik aliens

1921,1924 Quota laws fix strict limits to immigration. U.S. ceases to be the land of escape and opportunity for Europe's persecuted and dispossessed

1933 Assassination attempt on President-elect F.D. Roosevelt by Giuseppe Zangara

1937 Anti-union terrorism exposed

1927 First Television transmission

1915 Ku Klux Klan revival

2 July 1932 Franklin Delano Roosevelt promised "a new deal for the American people" if elected President. His New Deal Legislation gave relief to agriculture, industry, labour, banking and unemployment, and inaugurated a comprehensive social security programme.

1937 Memorial Day Massacre. Police fire on steel workers during demonstration. 4 killed 84 injured

1932 March of veterans on Washington for cash payment of bonus certificates. 2 veterans, 2 police killed

1933 Tennessee Valley Authority

1928 Flood Control Act allocates $325 millions for levee construction

1924 Naval oil reserves scandal exposed

AUTOMOBILE CRASHES
1918-1945
All states affected
750,000 dead

INFLUENZA
1918-1919
All states affected
550,000 dead

New York
Washington
Anacosta Flats
Harlan
Stone Mountain
Miami
Chicago
South Chicago
Teapot Dome

0   400
Miles

POPULATION	
1920	105,710,000
1940	131,409,000

ROAD MILEAGE	
1905	161,000
1925	521,000
1945	1,527,000

CARS REGISTERED	
1900	8,000
1912	1,000,000
1930	26,550,000
1951	42,700,000

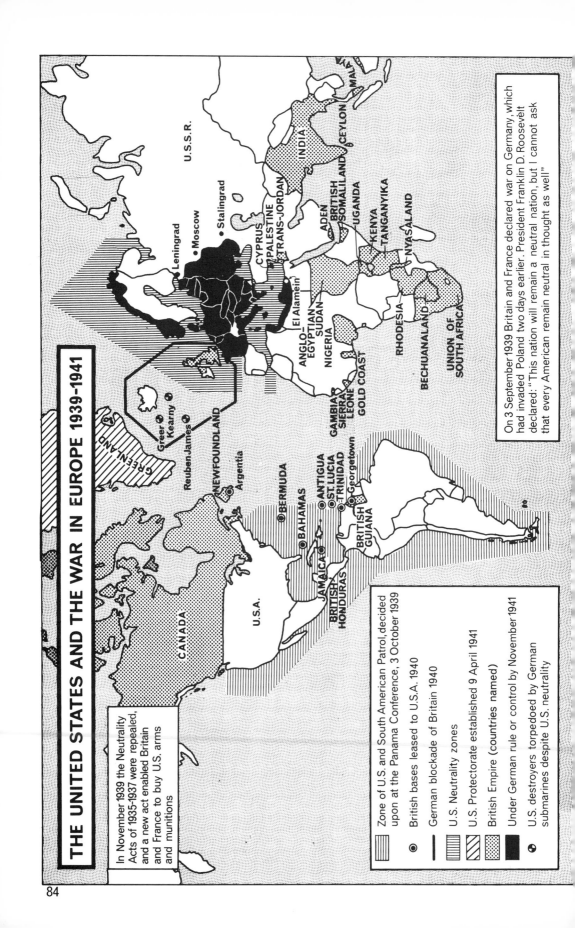

THE UNITED STATES AND THE WAR IN EUROPE 1939-1941

In November 1939 the Neutrality Acts of 1935-1937 were repealed, and a new act enabled Britain and France to buy U.S. arms and munitions

On 3 September 1939 Britain and France declared war on Germany, which had invaded Poland two days earlier. President Franklin D. Roosevelt declared: "This nation will remain a neutral nation, but I cannot ask that every American remain neutral in thought as well"

U.S.S.R.

Leningrad
Moscow
Stalingrad

CYPRUS
PALESTINE
TRANS-JORDAN

INDIA

ADEN
BRITISH
SOMALILAND
CEYLON

UGANDA

El Alamein
ANGLO-
EGYPTIAN
SUDAN
NIGERIA

KENYA
TANGANYIKA

NYASALAND

RHODESIA

BECHUANALAND

UNION OF
SOUTH AFRICA

GAMBIA
SIERRA
LEONE
GOLD COAST

GREENLAND

Green
Kearny
Reuben James
NEWFOUNDLAND
Argentia

BERMUDA
BAHAMAS
JAMAICA
BRITISH
HONDURAS
ANTIGUA
ST LUCIA
TRINIDAD
Georgetown
BRITISH
GUIANA

CANADA

U.S.A.

	Zone of U.S. and South American Patrol, decided upon at the Panama Conference, 3 October 1939
⊚	British bases leased to U.S.A. 1940
—	German blockade of Britain 1940
	U.S. Neutrality zones
	U.S. Protectorate established 9 April 1941
	British Empire (countries named)
	Under German rule or control by November 1941
◑	U.S. destroyers torpedoed by German submarines despite U.S. neutrality

84

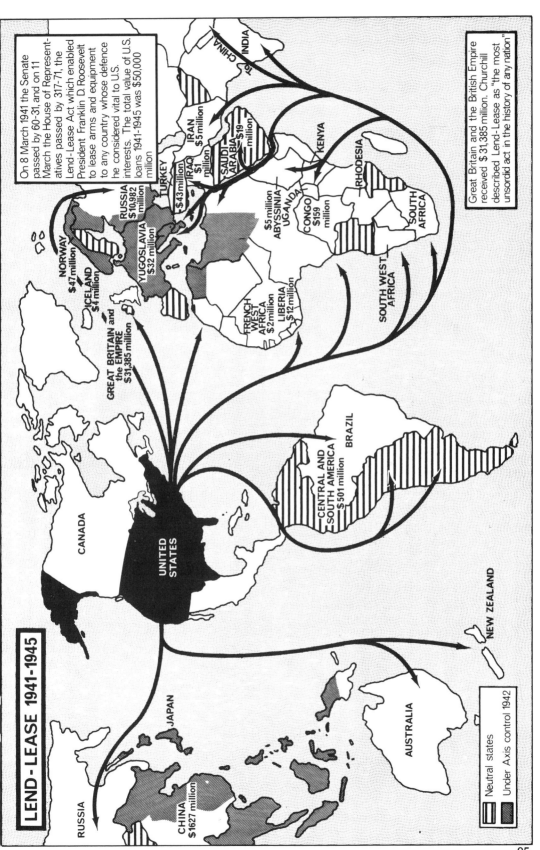

LEND-LEASE 1941-1945

On 8 March 1941 the Senate passed by 60-31, and on 11 March the House of Representatives passed by 317-71, the Lend-Lease Act which enabled President Franklin D. Roosevelt to lease arms and equipment to any country whose defence he considered vital to U.S. interests. The total value of U.S. loans 1941-1945 was $50,000 million

Great Britain and the British Empire received $ 31,385 million. Churchill described Lend-Lease as "the most unsordid act in the history of any nation"

RUSSIA $10,982 million

TURKEY $43million

IRAQ $1 million

IRAN $5 million

SAUDI ARABIA $19 million

KENYA

RHODESIA

SOUTH AFRICA

UGANDA $5 million

ABYSSINIA

CONGO $159 million

SOUTH WEST AFRICA

NORWAY $47million

ICELAND $4 million

YUGOSLAVIA $32 million

FRENCH WEST AFRICA $2 million

LIBERIA $12million

GREAT BRITAIN and the EMPIRE $31,385 million

CANADA

UNITED STATES

CENTRAL AND SOUTH AMERICA $501 million

BRAZIL

NEW ZEALAND

JAPAN

RUSSIA

CHINA $1627 million

AUSTRALIA

to CHINA

INDIA

Neutral states

Under Axis control 1942

85

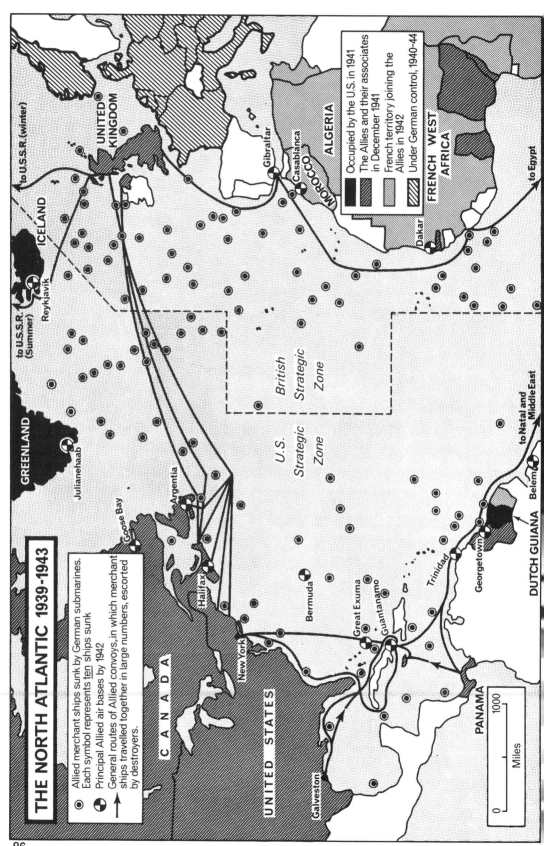

THE NORTH ATLANTIC 1939-1943

◉ Allied merchant ships sunk by German submarines.
Each symbol represents <u>ten</u> ships sunk

⊕ Principal Allied air bases by 1942

↑ General routes of Allied convoys, in which merchant ships travelled together in large numbers, escorted by destroyers.

Legend box (top right):

Occupied by the U.S. in 1941

The Allies and their associates in December 1941

French territory joining the Allies in 1942

Under German control, 1940-44

GREENLAND

ICELAND

to U.S.S.R. (Summer)

to U.S.S.R. (winter)

Reykjavik

Julianehaab

UNITED KINGDOM

Gibraltar

Casablanca

MOROCCO

ALGERIA

FRENCH WEST AFRICA

Dakar

to Egypt

CANADA

Goose Bay

Argentia

Halifax

UNITED STATES

New York

Galveston

Bermuda

Great Exuma

Guantanamo

PANAMA

Trinidad

Georgetown

DUTCH GUIANA

Belem

to Natal and Middle East

British Strategic Zone

U.S. Strategic Zone

Miles

0   1000

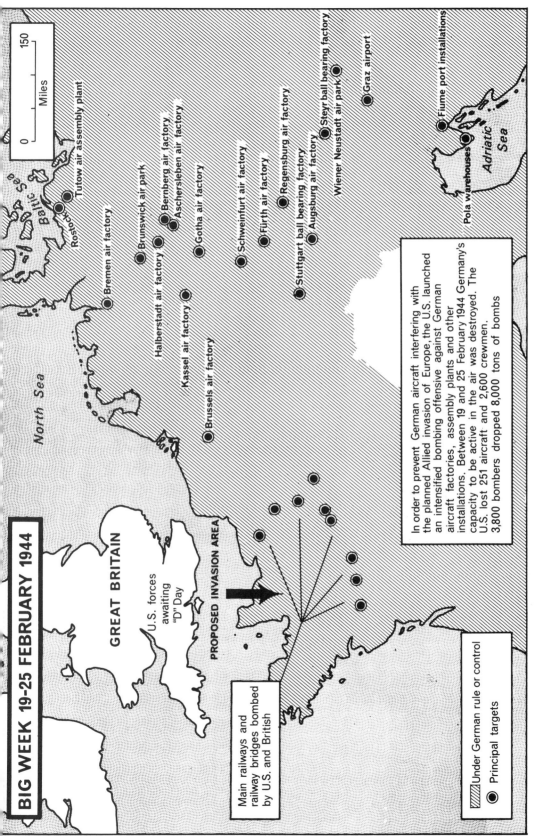

BIG WEEK 19-25 FEBRUARY 1944

0 ——— 150
Miles

Baltic Sea

North Sea

GREAT BRITAIN

U.S. forces awaiting "D" Day

PROPOSED INVASION AREA

Main railways and railway bridges bombed by U.S. and British

Rostock

Tutow air assembly plant

Bremen air factory

Brunswick air park

Bernberg air factory

Aschersleben air factory

Halberstadt air factory

Gotha air factory

Kassel air factory

Schweinfurt air factory

Fürth air factory

Regensburg air factory

Brussels air factory

Stuttgart ball bearing factory

Augsburg air factory

Wiener Neustadt air park

Steyr ball bearing factory

Graz airport

Fiume port installations

Pola warehouses

Adriatic Sea

In order to prevent German aircraft interfering with the planned Allied invasion of Europe, the U.S. launched an intensified bombing offensive against German aircraft factories, assembly plants and other installations. Between 19 and 25 February 1944 Germany's capacity to be active in the air was destroyed. The U.S. lost 251 aircraft and 2,600 crewmen. 3,800 bombers dropped 8,000 tons of bombs

▨ Under German rule or control
● Principal targets

87

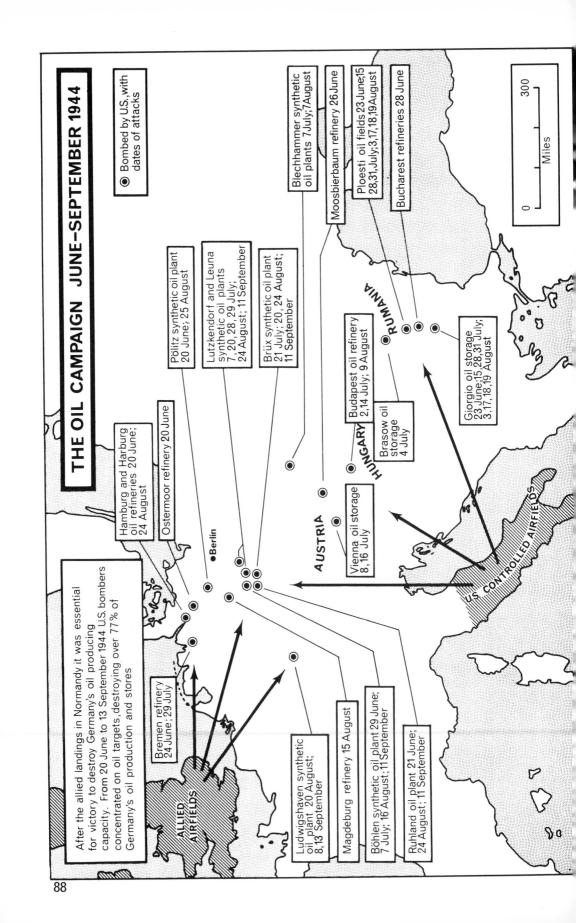

THE OIL CAMPAIGN JUNE–SEPTEMBER 1944

⦿ Bombed by U.S., with dates of attacks

After the allied landings in Normandy it was essential for victory to destroy Germany's oil producing capacity. From 20 June to 13 September 1944 U.S. bombers concentrated on oil targets, destroying over 77% of Germany's oil production and stores

Pölitz synthetic oil plant 20 June; 25 August

Lutzkendorf and Leuna synthetic oil plants 7, 20, 28, 29 July; 24 August; 11 September

Brüx synthetic oil plant 21 July; 20, 24 August; 11 September

Blechhammer synthetic oil plants 7 July; 7 August

Moosbierbaum refinery 26 June

Ploesti oil fields 23 June;15 28,31,July;3,17,18,19August

Bucharest refineries 28 June

Hamburg and Harburg oil refineries 20 June; 24 August

Ostermoor refinery 20 June

•Berlin

Budapest oil refinery 2,14 July; 9 August

Brasow oil storage 4 July

Giorgio oil storage 23 June;15,28,31 July; 3, 17, 18,19 August

RUMANIA

HUNGARY

AUSTRIA

Vienna oil storage 8,16 July

U.S. CONTROLLED AIRFIELDS

ALLIED AIRFIELDS

Bremen refinery 24 June; 29 July

Ludwigshaven synthetic oil plant 20 August; 8,13 September

Magdeburg refinery 15 August

Böhlen synthetic oil plant 29 June; 7 July; 16 August; 11 September

Ruhland oil plant 21 June; 24 August; 11 September

0   300
Miles

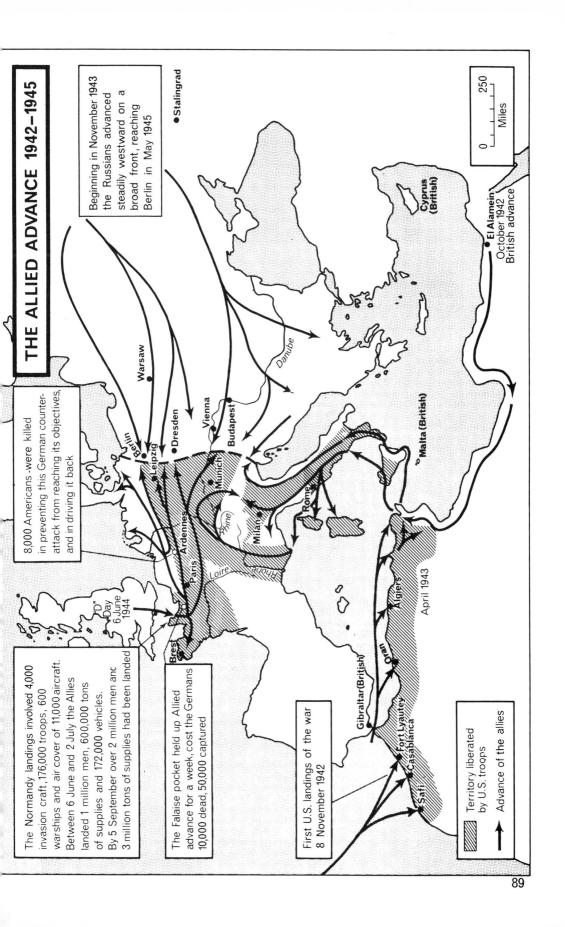

THE ALLIED ADVANCE 1942–1945

Beginning in November 1943 the Russians advanced steadily westward on a broad front, reaching Berlin in May 1945

8,000 Americans were killed in preventing this German counter-attack from reaching its objectives, and in driving it back

The Normandy landings involved 4,000 invasion craft, 176,000 troops, 600 warships and air cover of 11,000 aircraft. Between 6 June and 2 July the Allies landed 1 million men, 600,000 tons of supplies and 172,000 vehicles. By 5 September over 2 million men anc 3 million tons of supplies had been landed

The Falaise pocket held up Allied advance for a week, cost the Germans 10,000 dead, 50,000 captured

First U.S. landings of the war 8 November 1942

Territory liberated by U.S. troops

Advance of the allies

0   250
Miles

• Stalingrad

Cyprus (British)

El Alamein
October 1942
British advance

Warsaw •

• Dresden
Leipzig
Vienna •
Berlin
Budapest •

Danube

Munich

Ardennes
Paris
Rhine
Loire
Rhône

Milan •
Rome •

Malta (British)

April 1943

Brest

"D" Day 6 June 1944

Gibraltar (British)

Oran
Algiers

Fort Lyautey
Casablanca
Safi

89

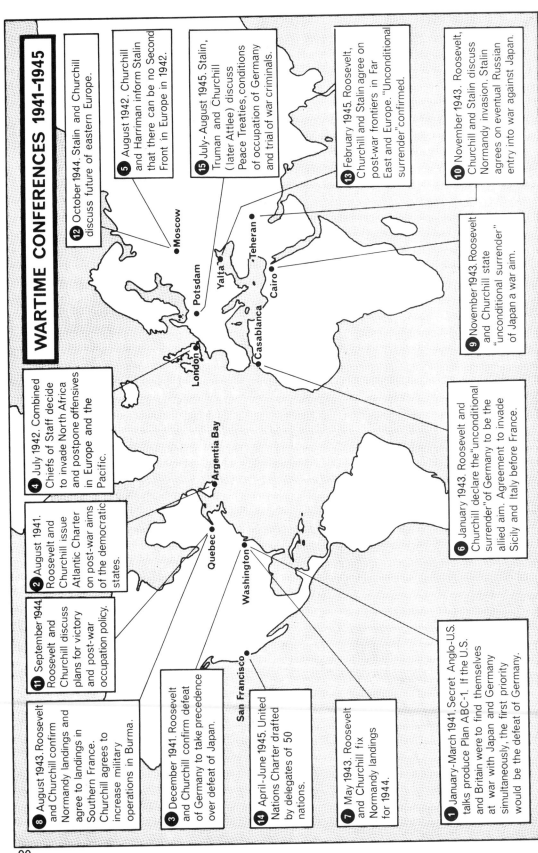

WARTIME CONFERENCES 1941-1945

12 October 1944. Stalin and Churchill discuss future of eastern Europe.

5 August 1942. Churchill and Harriman inform Stalin that there can be no Second Front in Europe in 1942.

15 July- August 1945. Stalin, Truman and Churchill (later Attlee) discuss Peace Treaties, conditions of occupation of Germany and trial of war criminals.

13 February 1945. Roosevelt, Churchill and Stalin agree on post-war frontiers in Far East and Europe. "Unconditional surrender" confirmed.

10 November 1943. Roosevelt, Churchill and Stalin discuss Normandy invasion. Stalin agrees on eventual Russian entry into war against Japan.

9 November 1943. Roosevelt and Churchill state "unconditional surrender" of Japan a war aim.

4 July 1942. Combined Chiefs of Staff decide to invade North Africa and postpone offensives in Europe and the Pacific.

2 August 1941. Roosevelt and Churchill issue Atlantic Charter on post-war aims of the democratic states.

11 September 1944. Roosevelt and Churchill discuss plans for victory and post-war occupation policy.

8 August 1943. Roosevelt and Churchill confirm Normandy landings and agree to landings in Southern France. Churchill agrees to increase military operations in Burma.

3 December 1941. Roosevelt and Churchill confirm defeat of Germany to take precedence over defeat of Japan.

14 April–June 1945. United Nations Charter drafted by delegates of 50 nations.

7 May 1943. Roosevelt and Churchill fix Normandy landings for 1944.

6 January 1943. Roosevelt and Churchill declare the "unconditional surrender" of Germany to be the allied aim. Agreement to invade Sicily and Italy before France.

1 January–March 1941. Secret Anglo-U.S. talks produce Plan ABC-1. If the U.S. and Britain were to find themselves at war with Japan and Germany simultaneously, the first priority would be the defeat of Germany.

●Moscow

●Teheran

Potsdam ●

Yalta ●

Cairo ●

Casablanca ●

London ●

●Argentia Bay

Quebec ●

Washington ●

San Francisco ●

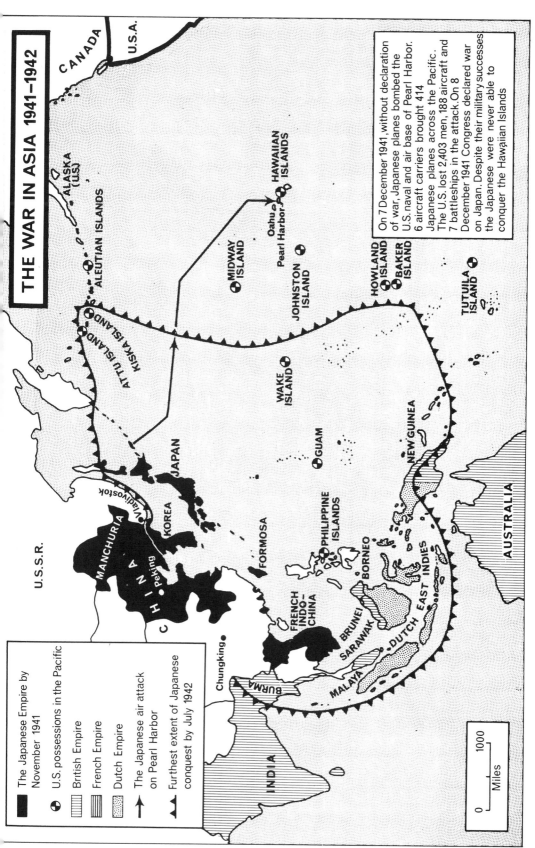

THE WAR IN ASIA 1941–1942

U.S.S.R.

CANADA

U.S.A.

ALASKA (U.S.)

ALEUTIAN ISLANDS

ATTU ISLAND

KISKA ISLAND

Vladivostok

KOREA

MANCHURIA

Peking

C H I N A

Chungking

JAPAN

FORMOSA

FRENCH INDO-CHINA

BURMA

INDIA

MALAYA

BRUNEI

SARAWAK

BORNEO

PHILIPPINE ISLANDS

DUTCH EAST INDIES

NEW GUINEA

GUAM

WAKE ISLAND

MIDWAY ISLAND

Oahu
Pearl Harbor

HAWAIIAN ISLANDS

JOHNSTON ISLAND

HOWLAND ISLAND
BAKER ISLAND

TUTUILA ISLAND

AUSTRALIA

On 7 December 1941, without declaration of war, Japanese planes bombed the U.S. naval and air base of Pearl Harbor. 6 aircraft carriers brought 414 Japanese planes across the Pacific. The U.S. lost 2,403 men, 188 aircraft and 7 battleships in the attack. On 8 December 1941 Congress declared war on Japan. Despite their military successes the Japanese were never able to conquer the Hawaiian Islands

The Japanese Empire by November 1941

U.S. possessions in the Pacific

British Empire

French Empire

Dutch Empire

The Japanese air attack on Pearl Harbor

Furthest extent of Japanese conquest by July 1942

0   1000
Miles

91

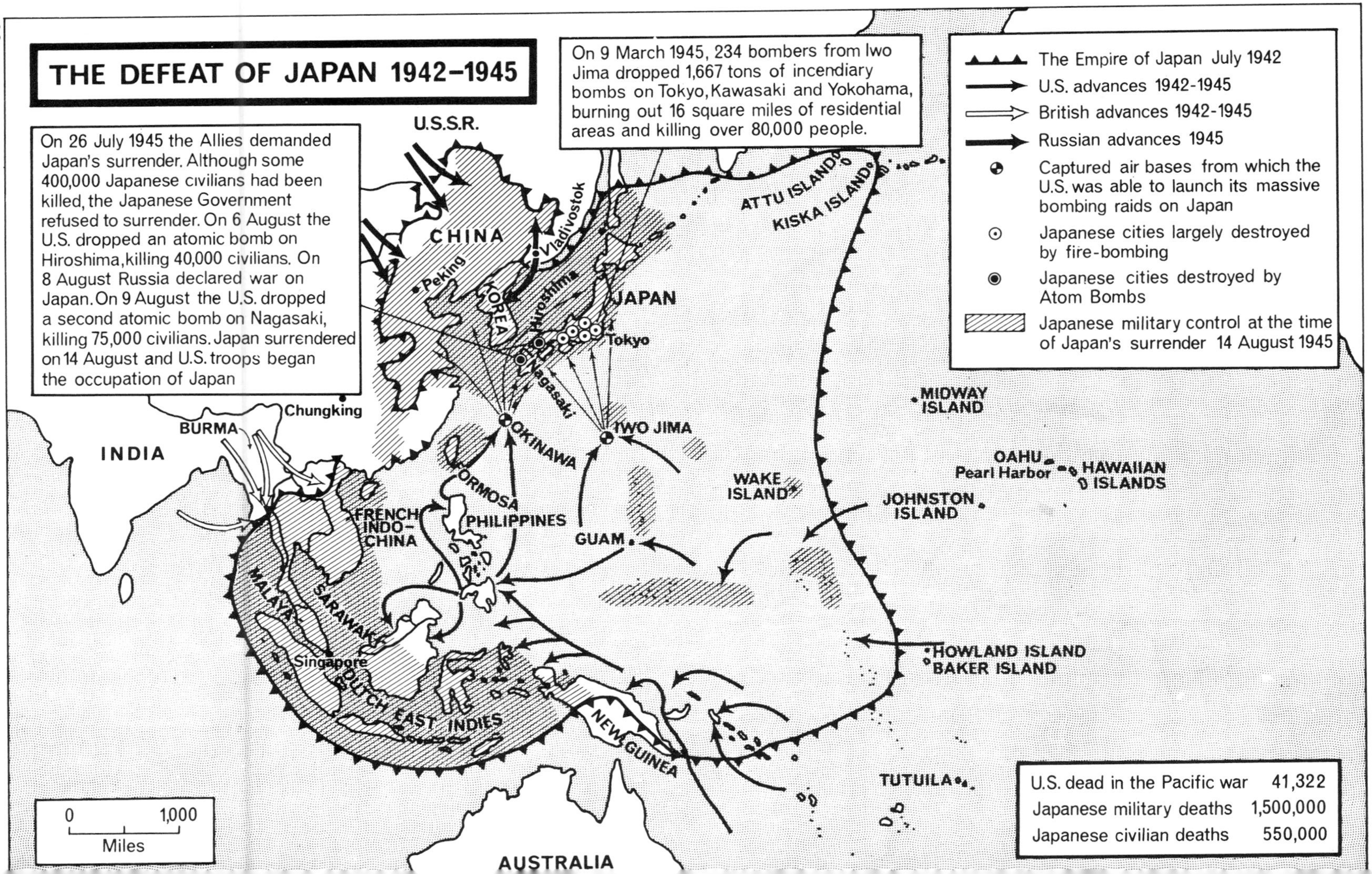
THE DEFEAT OF JAPAN 1942–1945
On 26 July 1945 the Allies demanded Japan's surrender. Although some 400,000 Japanese civilians had been killed, the Japanese Government refused to surrender. On 6 August the U.S. dropped an atomic bomb on Hiroshima, killing 40,000 civilians. On 8 August Russia declared war on Japan. On 9 August the U.S. dropped a second atomic bomb on Nagasaki, killing 75,000 civilians. Japan surrendered on 14 August and U.S. troops began the occupation of Japan
On 9 March 1945, 234 bombers from Iwo Jima dropped 1,667 tons of incendiary bombs on Tokyo, Kawasaki and Yokohama, burning out 16 square miles of residential areas and killing over 80,000 people.
The Empire of Japan July 1942
U.S. advances 1942-1945
British advances 1942-1945
Russian advances 1945
Captured air bases from which the U.S. was able to launch its massive bombing raids on Japan
Japanese cities largely destroyed by fire-bombing
Japanese cities destroyed by Atom Bombs
Japanese military control at the time of Japan's surrender 14 August 1945
U.S.S.R.
CHINA
Peking
Vladivostok
KOREA
Hiroshima
JAPAN
Tokyo
Nagasaki
ATTU ISLAND
KISKA ISLAND
OKINAWA
IWO JIMA
Chungking
BURMA
INDIA
FORMOSA
PHILIPPINES
GUAM
WAKE ISLAND
MIDWAY ISLAND
OAHU
Pearl Harbor
HAWAIIAN ISLANDS
JOHNSTON ISLAND
FRENCH INDO-CHINA
MALAYA
SARAWAK
Singapore
DUTCH EAST INDIES
NEW GUINEA
HOWLAND ISLAND
BAKER ISLAND
TUTUILA
AUSTRALIA
0 1,000
Miles
U.S. dead in the Pacific war 41,322
Japanese military deaths 1,500,000
Japanese civilian deaths 550,000

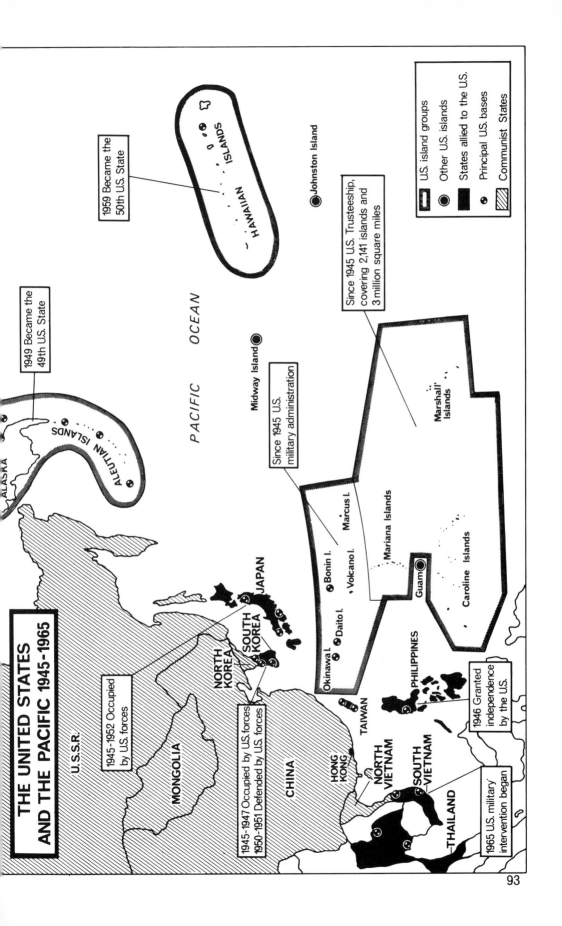

THE UNITED STATES
AND THE PACIFIC 1945-1965

U.S.S.R.

MONGOLIA

CHINA

HONG KONG

NORTH
VIETNAM

SOUTH
VIETNAM

THAILAND

1965 U.S. military
intervention began

NORTH KOREA

SOUTH KOREA

JAPAN

TAIWAN

PHILIPPINES

1946 Granted
independence
by the U.S.

ALASKA

ALEUTIAN ISLANDS

PACIFIC OCEAN

1949 Became the
49th U.S. State

1959 Became the
50th U.S. State

HAWAIIAN ISLANDS

Johnston Island

Midway Island

Since 1945 U.S.
military administration

Okinawa I.

Daito I.

Bonin I.

Volcano I.

Marcus I.

Mariana Islands

Guam

Caroline Islands

Marshall Islands

Since 1945 U.S. Trusteeship,
covering 2,141 islands and
3 million square miles

1945-1952 Occupied
by U.S. forces

1945-1947 Occupied by U.S. forces
1950-1951 Defended by U.S. forces

U.S. island groups

Other U.S. islands

States allied to the U.S.

Principal U.S. bases

Communist States

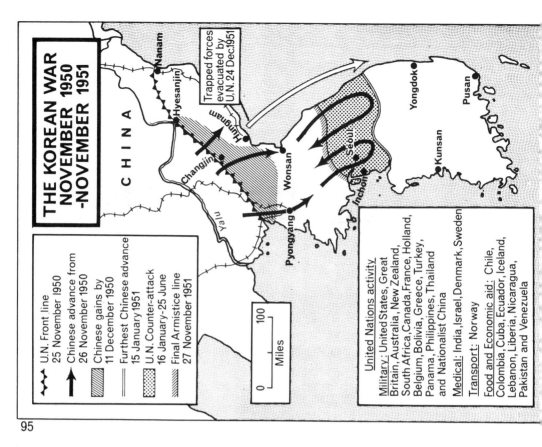

THE KOREAN WAR NOVEMBER 1950 -NOVEMBER 1951

CHINA

Nanam · Hyesanjin · Hungnam · Changjin · Wonsan · Seoul · Yongdok · Pusan · Kunsan · Inchon · Pyongyang · Yalu

Trapped forces evacuated by U.N. 24 Dec 1951

Legend:
- U.N. Front line 25 November 1950
- Chinese advance from 26 November 1950
- Chinese gains by 11 December 1950
- Furthest Chinese advance 15 January 1951
- U.N. Counter-attack 16 January-25 June
- Final Armistice line 27 November 1951

Scale: 0 — 100 Miles

United Nations activity

Military: United States, Great Britain, Australia, New Zealand, South Africa, Canada, France, Holland, Belgium, Bolivia, Greece, Turkey, Panama, Philippines, Thailand and Nationalist China

Medical: India, Israel, Denmark, Sweden

Transport: Norway

Food and Economic aid: Chile, Colombia, Cuba, Ecuador, Iceland, Lebanon, Liberia, Nicaragua, Pakistan and Venezuela

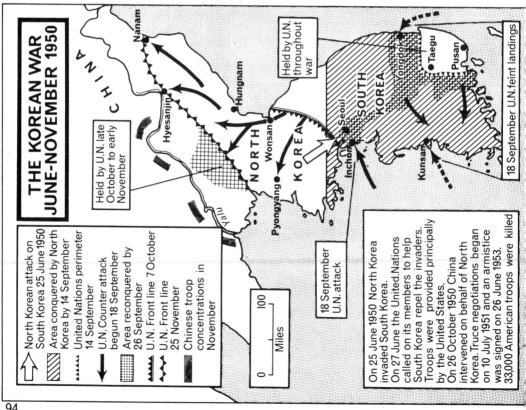

THE KOREAN WAR JUNE-NOVEMBER 1950

CHINA

Nanam · Hyesanjin · Hungnam · Wonsan · Pyongyang · NORTH KOREA · SOUTH KOREA · Seoul · Inchon · Kunsan · Yongdok · Taegu · Pusan · Yalu

Held by U.N. late October to early November

Held by U.N. throughout war

18 September U.N. attack

18 September U.N. feint landings

Legend:
- North Korean attack on South Korea 25 June 1950
- Area conquered by North Korea by 14 September
- United Nations perimeter 14 September
- U.N. Counter attack begun 18 September
- Area reconquered by 26 September
- U.N. Front line 7 October
- U.N. Front line 25 November
- Chinese troop concentrations in November

Scale: 0 — 100 Miles

On 25 June 1950 North Korea invaded South Korea. On 27 June the United Nations called on its members to help South Korea repel the invaders. Troops were provided principally by the United States. On 26 October 1950 China intervened on behalf of North Korea. Truce negotiations began on 10 July 1951 and an armistice was signed on 26 June 1953. 33,000 American troops were killed

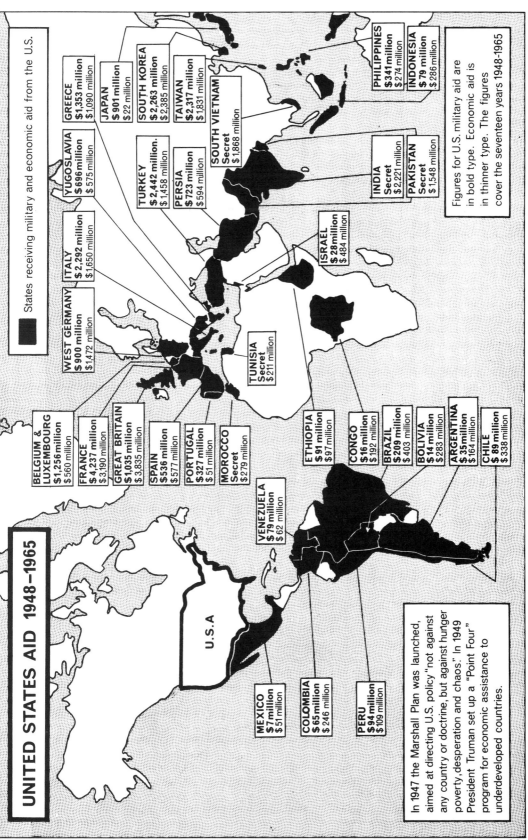

UNITED STATES AID 1948–1965

States receiving military and economic aid from the U.S.

Figures for U.S. military aid are in bold type. Economic aid is in thinner type. The figures cover the seventeen years 1948-1965.

In 1947 the Marshall Plan was launched, aimed at directing U.S. policy "not against any country or doctrine, but against hunger poverty, desperation and chaos." In 1949 President Truman set up a "Point Four" program for economic assistance to underdeveloped countries.

U.S.A

GREECE
$1,353 million
$ 1,090 million

JAPAN
$ 901 million
$ 22 million

SOUTH KOREA
$ 2,263 million
$ 2,385 million

TAIWAN
$ 2,317 million
$ 1,831 million

SOUTH VIETNAM
Secret
$ 1,868 million

PHILIPPINES
$341 million
$ 274 million

INDONESIA
$ 79 million
$ 286 million

YUGOSLAVIA
$ 696 million
$ 575 million

TURKEY
$ 2,442 million.
$ 1,458 million

PERSIA
$ 723 million
$ 594 million

INDIA
Secret
$ 2,221 million

PAKISTAN
Secret
$ 1,548 million

ITALY
$ 2,292 million
$ 1,650 million

ISRAEL
$ 28 million
$ 484 million

WEST GERMANY
$ 900 million
$ 1,472 million

TUNISIA
Secret
$ 211 million

**BELGIUM &
LUXEMBOURG**
$1,256 million
$ 560 million

FRANCE
$ 4,237 million
$ 3,190 million

GREAT BRITAIN
$1,035 million
$ 3,835 million

SPAIN
$ 536 million
$ 577 million

PORTUGAL
$ 327 million
$ 51 million

MOROCCO
Secret
$ 279 million

ETHIOPIA
$ 91 million
$ 97 million

CONGO
$ 16 million
$ 192 million

BRAZIL
$ 209 million
$ 403 million

BOLIVIA
$ 14 million
$ 283 million

ARGENTINA
$ 35 million
$ 164 million

CHILE
$ 89 million
$ 338 million

VENEZUELA
$ 79 million
$ 62 million

MEXICO
$7 million
$ 51 million

COLOMBIA
$ 65 million
$ 246 million

PERU
$ 94 million
$ 109 million

96

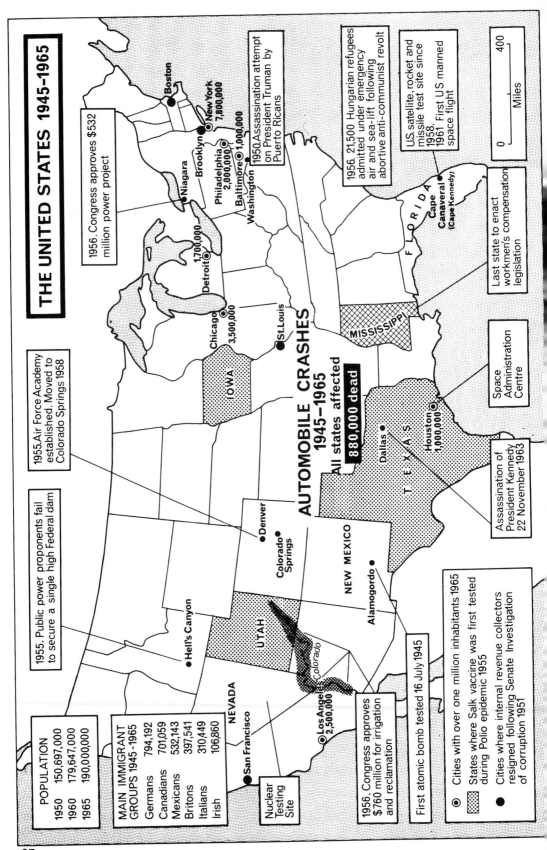

THE UNITED STATES 1945-1965

1956. Congress approves $532 million power project

1950.Assassination attempt on President Truman by Puerto Ricans

1956. 21,500 Hungarian refugees admitted under emergency air and sea-lift following abortive anti-communist revolt

US. satellite, rocket and missile test site since 1958. 1961 First US manned space flight

Last state to enact workmen's compensation legislation

Space Administration Centre

1955.Air Force Academy established. Moved to Colorado Springs 1958

1955. Public power proponents fail to secure a single high Federal dam

Assassination of President Kennedy 22 November 1963

First atomic bomb tested 16 July 1945

1956. Congress approves $760 million for irrigation and reclamation

Nuclear Testing Site

POPULATION

1950	150,697,000
1960	179,647,000
1965	190,000,000

MAIN IMMIGRANT GROUPS 1945-1965

Germans	794,192
Canadians	701,059
Mexicans	532,143
Britons	397,541
Italians	310,449
Irish	106,860

AUTOMOBILE CRASHES 1945-1965

All states affected

880,000 dead

Boston

New York 7,800,000

Brooklyn 2,000,000

Baltimore 1,000,000

Philadelphia 2,000,000

Washington

Niagara

FLORIDA

Cape Canaveral (Cape Kennedy)

MISSISSIPPI

Detroit 1,700,000

Chicago 3,500,000

St.Louis

IOWA

TEXAS

Houston 1,000,000

Dallas

NEW MEXICO

Alamogordo

Denver

Colorado Springs

Hell's Canyon

UTAH

Colorado

NEVADA

Los Angeles 2,500,000

San Francisco

◉ Cities with over one million inhabitants 1965

▦ States where Salk vaccine was first tested during Polio epidemic 1955

● Cities where internal revenue collectors resigned following Senate Investigation of corruption 1951

0		400
	Miles	

FROM LAKE SUPERIOR TO THE ATLANTIC 1959

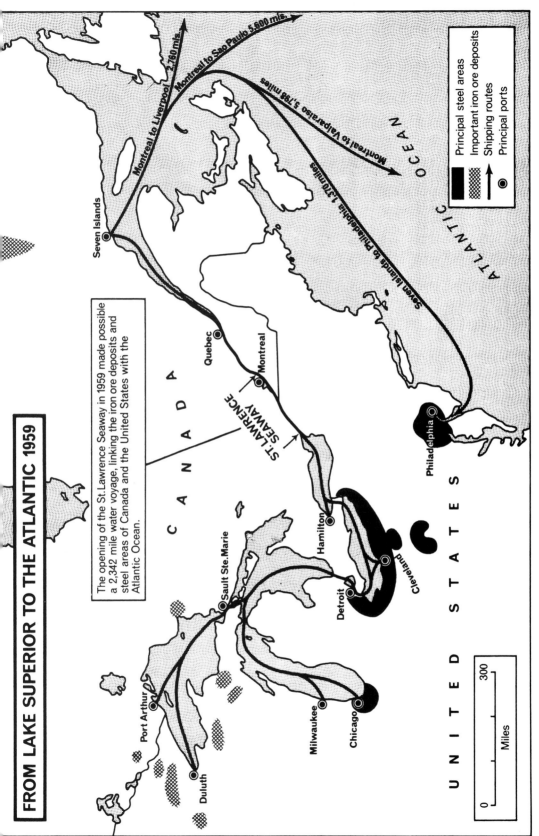

The opening of the St. Lawrence Seaway in 1959 made possible a 2,342 mile water voyage, linking the iron ore deposits and steel areas of Canada and the United States with the Atlantic Ocean.

Montreal to Liverpool 2,760 mls.

Montreal to Sao Paulo 5,800 mls.

Seven Islands to Valparaiso 5,788 miles

Seven Islands to Philadelphia 1,370 miles

ATLANTIC OCEAN

Seven Islands

CANADA

Quebec

Montreal

ST. LAWRENCE SEAWAY

Sault Ste. Marie

Port Arthur

Duluth

Milwaukee

Chicago

Detroit

Cleveland

Hamilton

Philadelphia

UNITED STATES

Legend:
- Principal steel areas
- Important iron ore deposits
- Shipping routes
- Principal ports

0   300

Miles

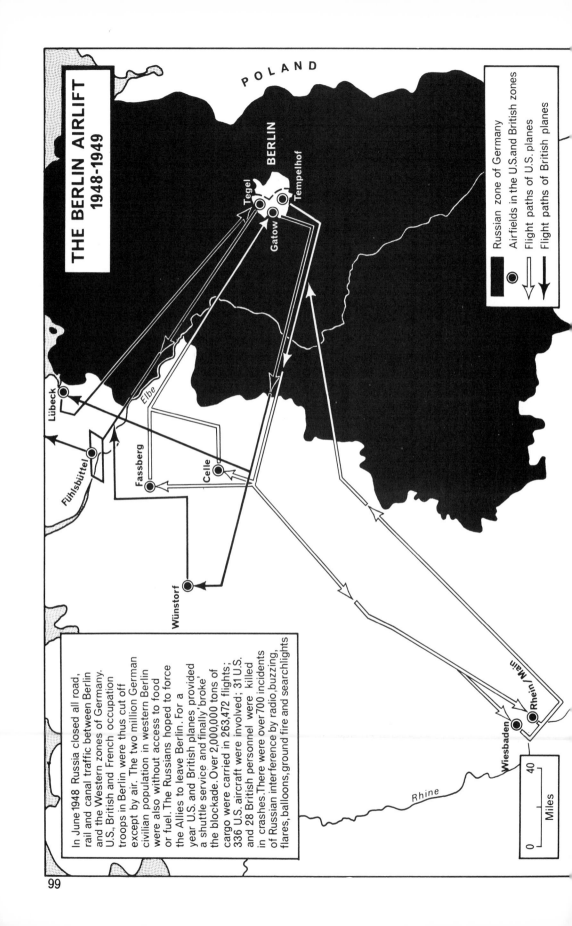

THE BERLIN AIRLIFT
1948-1949

POLAND

BERLIN

Tegel
Tempelhof
Gatow

Lübeck

Elbe

Fuhlsbüttel

Fassberg
Celle

Wünstorf

Rhein / Main

Wiesbaden

Rhine

■	Russian zone of Germany
⊙	Airfields in the U.S. and British zones
⇨	Flight paths of U.S. planes
➡	Flight paths of British planes

0   40
Miles

In June 1948 Russia closed all road, rail and canal traffic between Berlin and the Western zones of Germany. U.S., British and French occupation troops in Berlin were thus cut off except by air. The two million German civilian population in western Berlin were also without access to food or fuel. The Russians hoped to force the Allies to leave Berlin. For a year U.S. and British planes provided a shuttle service and finally 'broke' the blockade. Over 2,000,000 tons of cargo were carried in 263,472 flights; 336 U.S. aircraft were involved; 31 U.S. and 28 British personnel were killed in crashes. There were over 700 incidents of Russian interference by radio, buzzing, flares, balloons, ground fire and searchlights

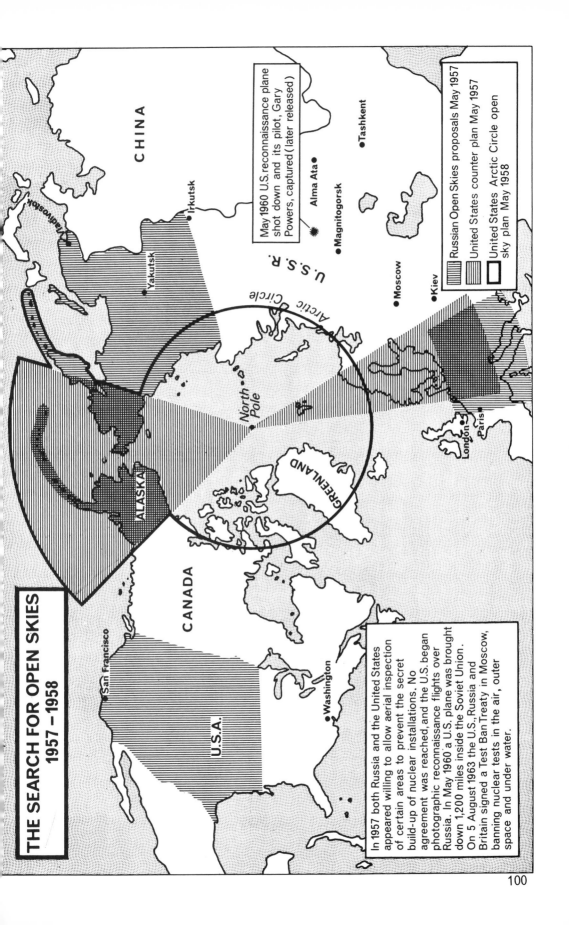

THE SEARCH FOR OPEN SKIES
1957 – 1958

CHINA

U.S.S.R.

May 1960 U.S. reconnaissance plane shot down and its pilot, Gary Powers, captured (later released)

• Irkutsk

• Yakutsk

Alma Ata ●

● Magnitogorsk

●Tashkent

● Moscow

●Kiev

Vladivostok

Arctic Circle

North Pole

GREENLAND

London

Paris

ALASKA

CANADA

U.S.A.

• San Francisco

●Washington

Russian Open Skies proposals May 1957

United States counter plan May 1957

United States Arctic Circle open sky plan May 1958

In 1957 both Russia and the United States appeared willing to allow aerial inspection of certain areas to prevent the secret build-up of nuclear installations. No agreement was reached, and the U.S. began photographic reconnaissance flights over Russia. In May 1960 a U.S. plane was brought down 1,200 miles inside the Soviet Union. On 5 August 1963 the U.S., Russia and Britain signed a Test Ban Treaty in Moscow, banning nuclear tests in the air, outer space and under water.

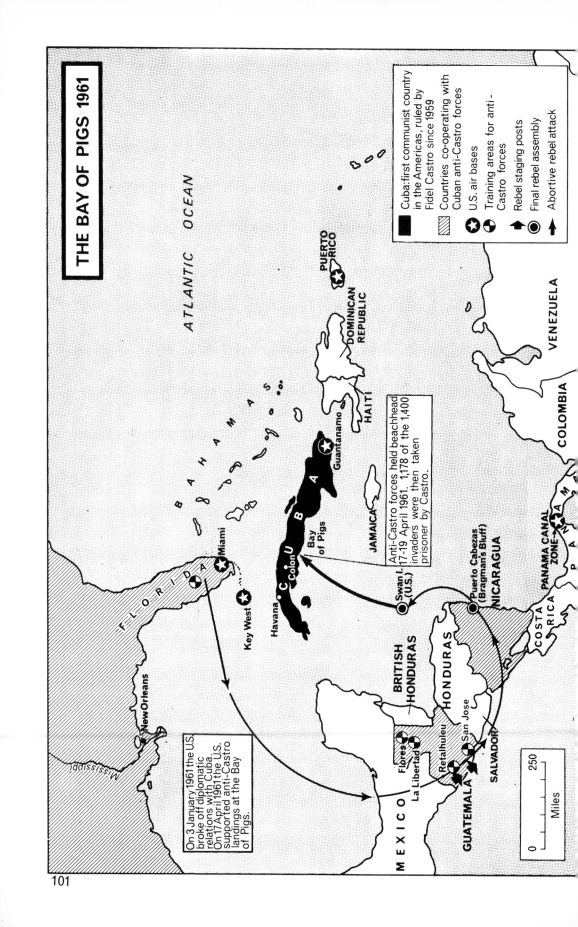

THE BAY OF PIGS 1961

ATLANTIC OCEAN

Cuba: first communist country in the Americas, ruled by Fidel Castro since 1959

Countries co-operating with Cuban anti-Castro forces

U.S. air bases

Training areas for anti-Castro forces

Rebel staging posts

Final rebel assembly

Abortive rebel attack

PUERTO RICO

DOMINICAN REPUBLIC

HAITI

Guantanamo

B A H A M A S

JAMAICA

Miami

Key West

Havana · C U B A
Colon ·
Bay of Pigs

Anti-Castro forces held beachhead 17-19 April 1961. 1,178 of the 1,400 invaders were then taken prisoner by Castro.

Swan I. (U.S.)

FLORIDA

New Orleans

Mississippi

On 3 January 1961 the U.S. broke off diplomatic relations with Cuba. On 17 April 1961 the U.S. supported anti-Castro landings at the Bay of Pigs.

M E X I C O

BRITISH HONDURAS

HONDURAS

Flores
La Libertad

Retalhuleu
· San Jose

GUATEMALA

SALVADOR

Puerto Cabezas (Bragman's Bluff)

NICARAGUA

COSTA RICA

PANAMA CANAL ZONE
P A N A M A

VENEZUELA

COLOMBIA

0   250
|————————|
Miles

THE CUBAN MISSILE CRISIS 1962

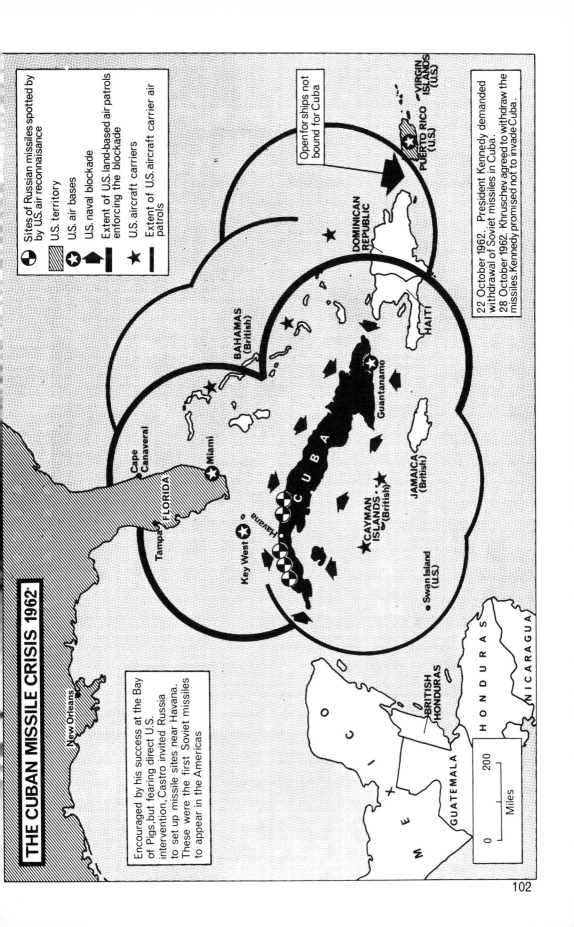

Legend:
- Sites of Russian missiles spotted by U.S. air reconnaissance
- U.S. territory
- U.S. air bases
- U.S. naval blockade
- Extent of U.S. land-based air patrols enforcing the blockade
- U.S. aircraft carriers
- Extent of U.S. aircraft carrier air patrols

Open for ships not bound for Cuba

New Orleans

FLORIDA
Tampa
Cape Canaveral
Miami
Key West
Havana
CUBA
Guantanamo
BAHAMAS (British)
CAYMAN ISLANDS (British)
JAMAICA (British)
Swan Island (U.S.)
HAITI
DOMINICAN REPUBLIC
PUERTO RICO (U.S.)
VIRGIN ISLANDS (U.S.)

MEXICO
GUATEMALA
BRITISH HONDURAS
HONDURAS
NICARAGUA

0   200
Miles

Encouraged by his success at the Bay of Pigs, but fearing direct U.S. intervention, Castro invited Russia to set up missile sites near Havana. These were the first Soviet missiles to appear in the Americas

22 October 1962. President Kennedy demanded withdrawal of Soviet missiles in Cuba.
28 October 1962. Khruschev agreed to withdraw the missiles. Kennedy promised not to invade Cuba.

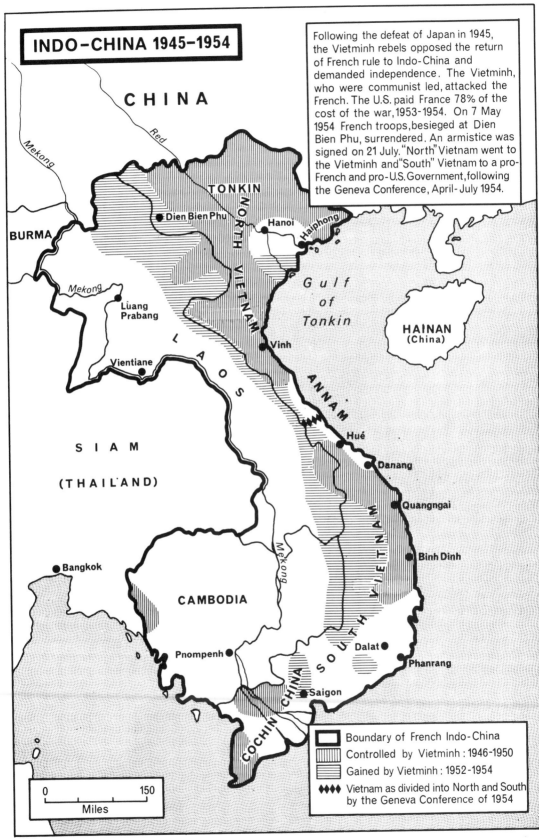

INDO-CHINA 1945-1954

Following the defeat of Japan in 1945, the Vietminh rebels opposed the return of French rule to Indo-China and demanded independence. The Vietminh, who were communist led, attacked the French. The U.S. paid France 78% of the cost of the war, 1953-1954. On 7 May 1954 French troops, besieged at Dien Bien Phu, surrendered. An armistice was signed on 21 July. "North" Vietnam went to the Vietminh and "South" Vietnam to a pro-French and pro-U.S. Government, following the Geneva Conference, April-July 1954.

CHINA

Red

Mekong

TONKIN

• Dien Bien Phu

Hanoi • Haiphong

BURMA

NORTH VIETNAM

Mekong

Luang Prabang

Gulf
of
Tonkin

HAINAN
(China)

L A O S

Vientiane •

• Vinh

ANNAM

Hué •

Danang •

S I A M

(THAILAND)

Quangngai •

SOUTH VIETNAM

• Binh Dinh

Mekong

• Bangkok

CAMBODIA

COCHIN CHINA

Dalat •

Pnompenh •

Phanrang •

Saigon •

	Boundary of French Indo-China
	Controlled by Vietminh : 1946-1950
	Gained by Vietminh : 1952-1954
♦♦♦♦	Vietnam as divided into North and South by the Geneva Conference of 1954

0   150
Miles

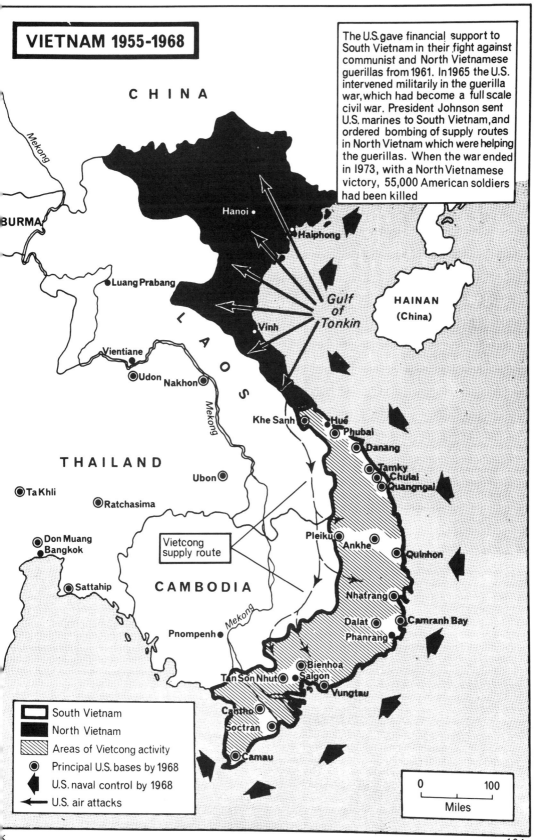

VIETNAM 1955-1968

CHINA

The U.S. gave financial support to South Vietnam in their fight against communist and North Vietnamese guerillas from 1961. In 1965 the U.S. intervened militarily in the guerilla war, which had become a full scale civil war. President Johnson sent U.S. marines to South Vietnam, and ordered bombing of supply routes in North Vietnam which were helping the guerillas. When the war ended in 1973, with a North Vietnamese victory, 55,000 American soldiers had been killed

Mekong

BURMA

Hanoi

Haiphong

Luang Prabang

LAOS

HAINAN
(China)

Vinh

Gulf
of
Tonkin

Vientiane

Udon   Nakhon

Mekong

THAILAND

Khe Sanh   Hué
Phubai

Danang

Ubon

Tamky
Chulai
Quangngai

Ta Khli

Ratchasima

Don Muang
Bangkok

Vietcong
supply route

Pleiku   Ankhe

Quinhon

Sattahip

CAMBODIA

Mekong

Nhatrang

Dalat   Camranh Bay
Phanrang

Pnompenh

Bienhoa
Tan Son Nhut   Salgon
Vungtau

Cantho
Soctran

Camau

☐ South Vietnam

■ North Vietnam

▨ Areas of Vietcong activity

◎ Principal U.S. bases by 1968

◆ U.S. naval control by 1968

← U.S. air attacks

0   100
Miles

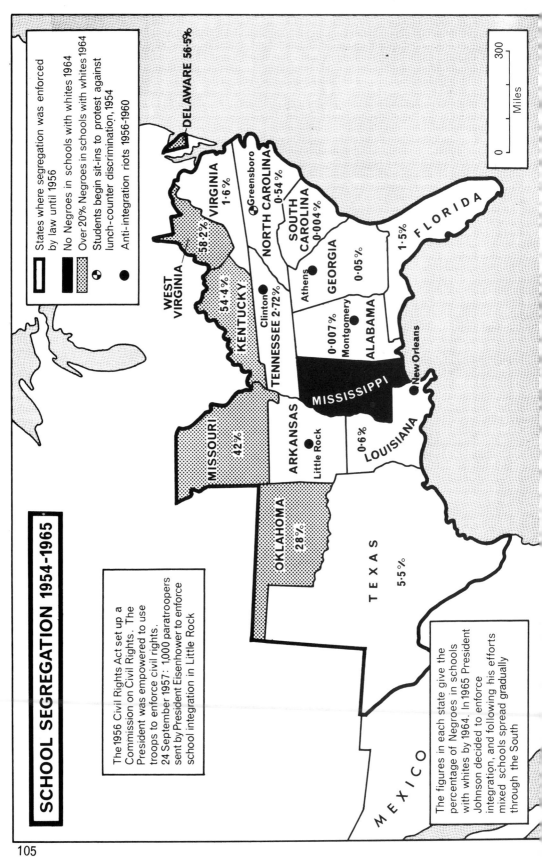

SCHOOL SEGREGATION 1954-1965

Legend:
- States where segregation was enforced by law until 1956
- No Negroes in schools with whites 1964
- Over 20% Negroes in schools with whites 1964
- Students begin sit-ins to protest against lunch-counter discrimination, 1954
- Anti-integration riots 1956-1960

The 1956 Civil Rights Act set up a Commission on Civil Rights. The President was empowered to use troops to enforce civil rights. 24 September 1957: 1,000 paratroopers sent by President Eisenhower to enforce school integration in Little Rock

The figures in each state give the percentage of Negroes in schools with whites by 1964. In 1965 President Johnson decided to enforce integration, and following his efforts mixed schools spread gradually through the South

DELAWARE 56·5%

VIRGINIA 1·6%

WEST VIRGINIA 58·2%

NORTH CAROLINA 0·54%

SOUTH CAROLINA 0·004%

Greensboro

KENTUCKY 54·4%

Clinton
TENNESSEE 2·72%

GEORGIA 0·05%

FLORIDA 1·5%

Athens

Montgomery
ALABAMA 0·007%

MISSISSIPPI

New Orleans

MISSOURI 42%

ARKANSAS
Little Rock

LOUISIANA 0·6%

OKLAHOMA 28%

TEXAS 5·5%

MEXICO

0   300
Miles

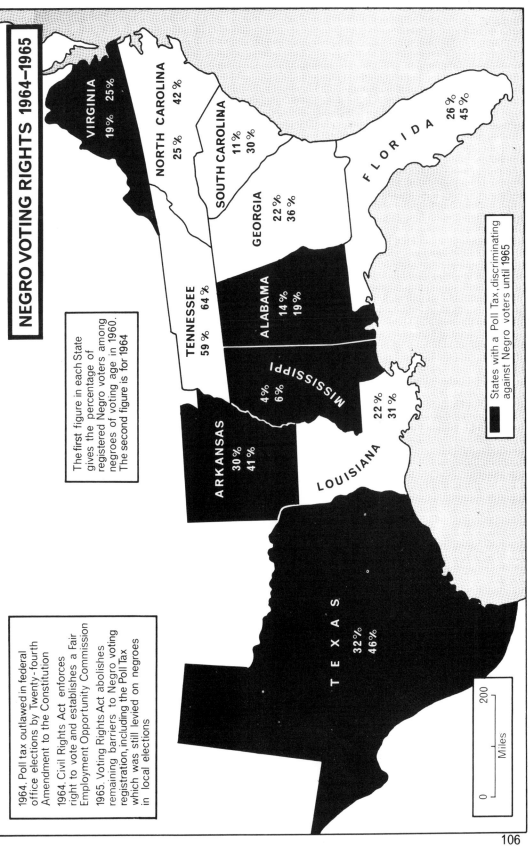

NEGRO VOTING RIGHTS 1964-1965

The first figure in each State gives the percentage of registered Negro voters among negroes of voting age in 1960. The second figure is for 1964

1964. Poll tax outlawed in federal office elections by Twenty-fourth Amendment to the Constitution

1964. Civil Rights Act enforces right to vote and establishes a Fair Employment Opportunity Commission

1965. Voting Rights Act abolishes remaining barriers to Negro voting registration, including the Poll Tax which was still levied on negroes in local elections

VIRGINIA 19% 25%

NORTH CAROLINA 42%
25%

SOUTH CAROLINA
11%
30%

FLORIDA 26% 45%

GEORGIA
22%
36%

TENNESSEE 64%
59%

ALABAMA
14%
19%

MISSISSIPPI
4%
6%

ARKANSAS
30%
41%

LOUISIANA
22%
31%

T E X A S
32%
46%

States with a Poll Tax, discriminating against Negro voters until 1965

0   200
Miles

106

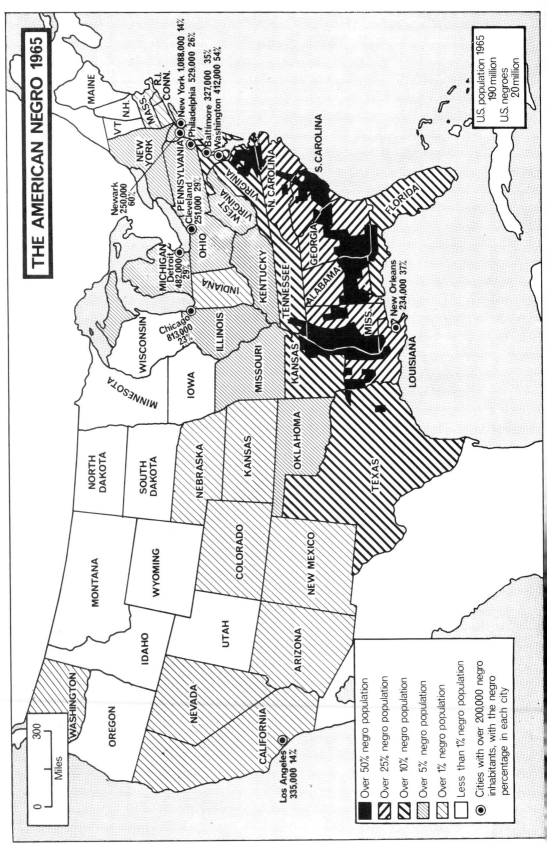

THE AMERICAN NEGRO 1965

U.S. population 1965 190 million
U.S. negroes 20 million

New York 1,088,000 14%
Philadelphia 529,000 26%
Baltimore 327,000 35%
Washington 412,000 54%
Newark 250,000 60%
Cleveland 251,000 29%
Detroit 482,000 29%
Chicago 813,000 23%
New Orleans 234,000 37%
Los Angeles 335,000 14%

MAINE
VT
N.H.
MASS.
R.I.
CONN.
NEW YORK
PENNSYLVANIA
WEST VIRGINIA
VIRGINIA
N. CAROLINA
S. CAROLINA
FLORIDA
GEORGIA
ALABAMA
MISS.
LOUISIANA
TENNESSEE
KENTUCKY
OHIO
INDIANA
MICHIGAN
WISCONSIN
MINNESOTA
IOWA
ILLINOIS
MISSOURI
KANSAS
OKLAHOMA
TEXAS
NEW MEXICO
ARIZONA
COLORADO
NEBRASKA
SOUTH DAKOTA
NORTH DAKOTA
WYOMING
UTAH
NEVADA
CALIFORNIA
IDAHO
MONTANA
OREGON
WASHINGTON

300
Miles
0

Over 50% negro population
Over 25% negro population
Over 10% negro population
Over 5% negro population
Over 1% negro population
Less than 1% negro population
Cities with over 200,000 negro inhabitants, with the negro percentage in each city

107

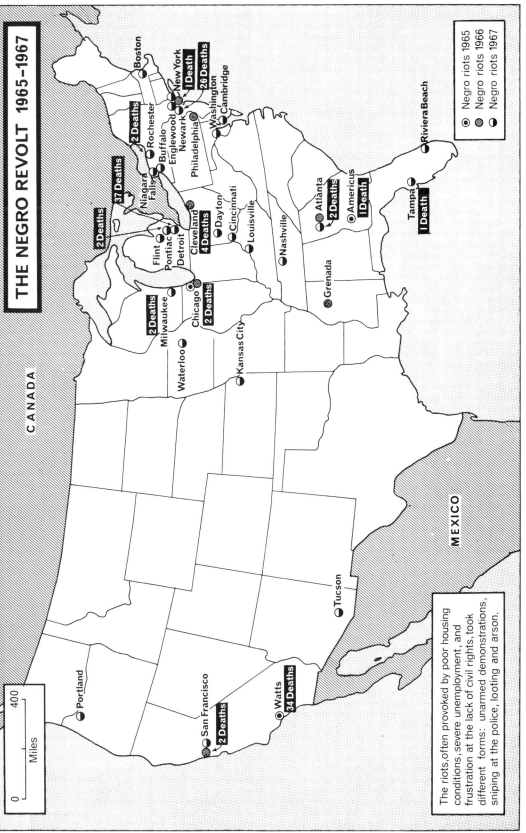

THE NEGRO REVOLT 1965-1967

CANADA

MEXICO

Legend:
- Negro riots 1965
- Negro riots 1966
- Negro riots 1967

Locations and deaths:
- Boston
- New York — 1 Death
- 26 Deaths
- 2 Deaths (Rochester)
- Buffalo
- Englewood
- Newark
- Washington
- Cambridge
- Philadelphia
- Riviera Beach
- 37 Deaths
- Niagara Falls
- 2 Deaths
- Cleveland — 4 Deaths
- Dayton
- Cincinnati
- Louisville
- Atlanta — 2 Deaths
- Americus — 1 Death
- Tampa — 1 Death
- Flint
- Pontiac
- Detroit
- Nashville
- 2 Deaths (Chicago)
- 2 Deaths (Milwaukee)
- Waterloo
- Kansas City
- Grenada
- Tucson
- Portland
- San Francisco — 2 Deaths
- Watts — 34 Deaths

0 400
Miles

The riots, often provoked by poor housing conditions, severe unemployment, and frustration at the lack of civil rights, took different forms: unarmed demonstrations, sniping at the police, looting and arson.

108

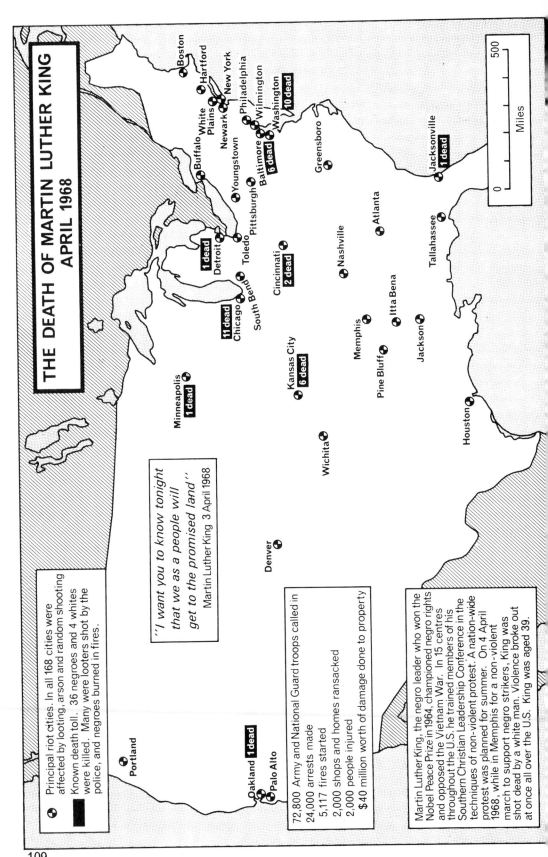

THE DEATH OF MARTIN LUTHER KING
APRIL 1968

Boston
Hartford
Buffalo White New York
Plains
Newark Philadelphia
Youngstown Baltimore Wilmington
Pittsburgh Washington **10 dead**
6 dead
Greensboro
Jacksonville **1 dead**

Detroit **1 dead**
Toledo
Cincinnati **2 dead**
South Bend
Chicago **11 dead**
Nashville
Atlanta
Itta Bena
Memphis
Kansas City Jackson
6 dead Pine Bluff
Tallahassee

Minneapolis **1 dead**

Houston

Wichita

*"I want you to know tonight
that we as a people will
get to the promised land"*
Martin Luther King 3 April 1968

Denver

Portland

Oakland **1 dead**
Palo Alto

- Principal riot cities. In all 168 cities were
  affected by looting, arson and random shooting

  Known death toll. 36 negroes and 4 whites
  were killed. Many were looters shot by the
  police, and negroes burned in fires.

72,800 Army and National Guard troops called in
24,000 arrests made
5,117 fires started
2,000 shops and homes ransacked
2,000 people injured
$40 million worth of damage done to property

Martin Luther King, the negro leader who won the
Nobel Peace Prize in 1964, championed negro rights
and opposed the U.S. he trained members of his
Southern Christian Leadership Conference in the
techniques of non-violent protest. A nation-wide
protest was planned for summer. On 4 April
1968, while in Memphis for a non-violent
march to support negro strikers, King was
shot dead by a white man. Violence broke out
at once all over the U.S. King was aged 39.

0   500
Miles

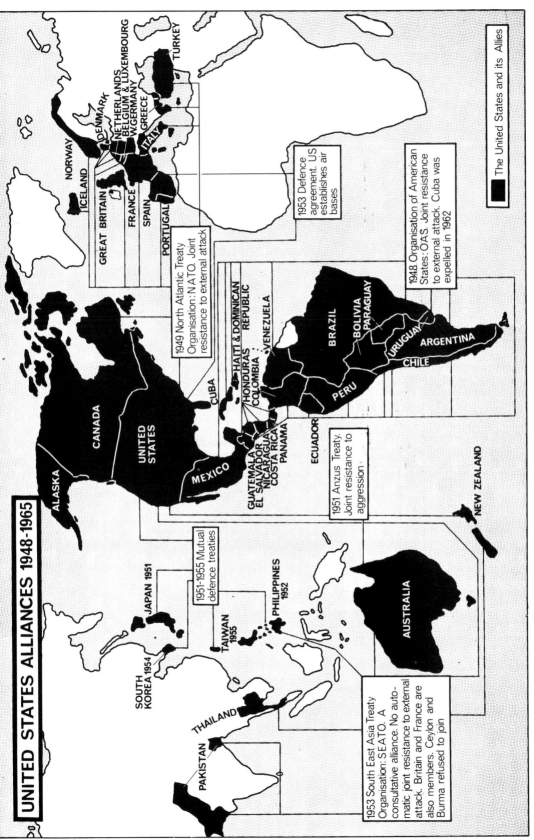

UNITED STATES ALLIANCES 1948-1965

ALASKA

CANADA

UNITED STATES

MEXICO

GUATEMALA
EL SALVADOR
NICARAGUA
COSTA RICA
PANAMA

CUBA

HAITI & DOMINICAN REPUBLIC
HONDURAS
COLOMBIA
VENEZUELA

ECUADOR

PERU

BRAZIL

BOLIVIA
PARAGUAY

CHILE

URUGUAY

ARGENTINA

ICELAND
NORWAY
GREAT BRITAIN
DENMARK
NETHERLANDS
BELGIUM & LUXEMBOURG
W.GERMANY
GREECE
FRANCE
ITALY
SPAIN
PORTUGAL
TURKEY

PAKISTAN

THAILAND

SOUTH KOREA 1954

JAPAN 1951

TAIWAN 1955

PHILIPPINES 1952

AUSTRALIA

NEW ZEALAND

The United States and its Allies

1953 Defence agreement. US establishes air bases

1949 North Atlantic Treaty Organisation: NATO. Joint resistance to external attack

1948 Organisation of American States: OAS. Joint resistance to external attack. Cuba was expelled in 1962

1951 Anzus Treaty. Joint resistance to aggression

1951-1955 Mutual defence treaties

1953 South East Asia Treaty Organisation: SEATO. A consultative alliance. No auto-matic joint resistance to external attack. Britain and France are also members. Ceylon and Burma refused to join

110

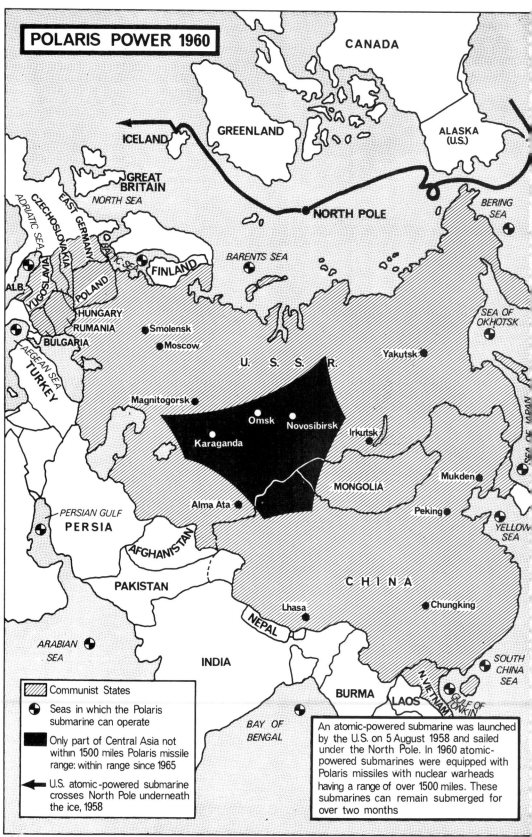

POLARIS POWER 1960

CANADA

GREENLAND

ALASKA (U.S.)

ICELAND

NORTH POLE

GREAT BRITAIN

NORTH SEA

BERING SEA

BARENTS SEA

ADRIATIC SEA

CZECHOSLOVAKIA

EAST GERMANY

FINLAND

ALB.

YUGOSLAVIA

POLAND

HUNGARY

RUMANIA

BULGARIA

AEGEAN SEA

TURKEY

Smolensk

Moscow

U. S. S. R.

Yakutsk

SEA OF OKHOTSK

Magnitogorsk

Omsk

Novosibirsk

Irkutsk

SEA OF JAPAN

Karaganda

Mukden

MONGOLIA

PERSIAN GULF

PERSIA

Alma Ata

Peking

YELLOW SEA

AFGHANISTAN

C H I N A

PAKISTAN

Lhasa

Chungking

NEPAL

ARABIAN SEA

INDIA

BURMA

LAOS

SOUTH CHINA SEA

N.VIETNAM

GULF OF TONKIN

BAY OF BENGAL

Communist States

Seas in which the Polaris submarine can operate

Only part of Central Asia not within 1500 miles Polaris missile range: within range since 1965

U.S. atomic-powered submarine crosses North Pole underneath the ice, 1958

An atomic-powered submarine was launched by the U.S. on 5 August 1958 and sailed under the North Pole. In 1960 atomic-powered submarines were equipped with Polaris missiles with nuclear warheads having a range of over 1500 miles. These submarines can remain submerged for over two months

AMERICAN PREPAREDNESS 1960

S.VIETNAM
Tan Son Nhut
Bienhoa
Chulai
Camranh Bay
Nhatrang
Ankhe
Danang
Ubon
Ratchasima
Sattahip
Bangkok
Ta Khli
Udon **THAILAND**
Nakhon

7

Langley Point
Subic Bay
Clark
PHILIPPINES

Tainan
Taipei
TAIWAN
Kadena Naha
OKINAWA

Andersen
Agana
Apra
Harbour
Iwo Jima
JAPAN
Yokosuka
Misawa

7

S.KOREA
Kunsan
Sasebo
Iwakuni
Osan
Kimpo
Yokota
Tachikawa
Atsugi

CHINA

MONGOLIA

U.S.S.R.

PAKISTAN
Peshawar

**SAUDI
ARABIA**
Dhahran

TURKEY
Incirlik
Ankara
Cigli
Iraklion
GREECE
6
Wheelus
Naples
ITALY
Aviano
Ramstein
W.GERMANY
Wiesbaden
Villefranche
New Amsterdam
FRANCE
SPAIN
Zaragoza
HOLLAND
London
High
Wycombe
Prestwick
LIBYA
**UNITED
KINGDOM**
Torrejon
Moron
Rota
Kentra
MOROCCO

Shemya

7

**NORTH
POLE**

ICELAND
Keflavik Airport

Thule

GREENLAND
Sondrestrom

Lajes Field
AZORES

Adak

ALASKA
Eielson
Elmendorf
Kodiak

DISTANT EARLY WARNING LINE

2
Goose
Argentia

Midway

Johnston

HAWAIIAN IS.
Pearl Harbor
Hickam
Wheeler
Bellows

1

MID-CANADA LINE
CANADA
PINETREE LINE

UNITED STATES

Kindley
Bermuda

U.S. NAVAL SPACE
SURVEILLANCE SYSTEM

Ramey
Roosevelt
Roads
PUERTO RICO

CUBA
Guantanamo Bay

PANAMA
Coco Solo

Legend

▨	Communist States
⊕	Major U.S. bases
⸙	Ballistic Missile Early Warning System
•••••	Radar coverage
═══	Other warning lines
●	U.S. Fleets with numbers

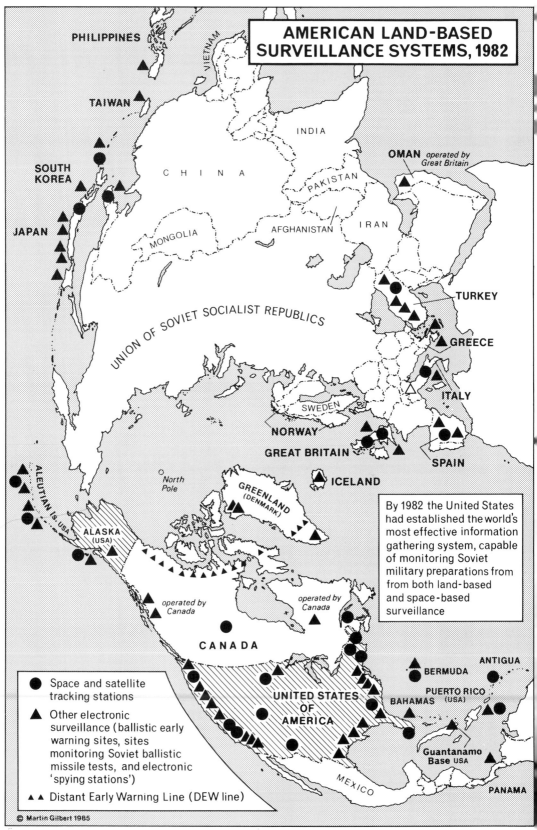

AMERICAN LAND-BASED SURVEILLANCE SYSTEMS, 1982

PHILIPPINES

VIETNAM

TAIWAN

INDIA

OMAN *operated by Great Britain*

SOUTH KOREA

CHINA

PAKISTAN

JAPAN

MONGOLIA

AFGHANISTAN

IRAN

TURKEY

UNION OF SOVIET SOCIALIST REPUBLICS

GREECE

ITALY

SWEDEN

NORWAY

GREAT BRITAIN

SPAIN

North Pole

ICELAND

ALEUTIAN Is. USA

GREENLAND (DENMARK)

ALASKA (USA)

By 1982 the United States had established the world's most effective information gathering system, capable of monitoring Soviet military preparations from from both land-based and space-based surveillance

operated by Canada

operated by Canada

CANADA

ANTIGUA

BERMUDA

PUERTO RICO (USA)

BAHAMAS

UNITED STATES OF AMERICA

Guantanamo Base USA

MEXICO

PANAMA

● Space and satellite tracking stations

▲ Other electronic surveillance (ballistic early warning sites, sites monitoring Soviet ballistic missile tests, and electronic 'spying stations')

▲▲ Distant Early Warning Line (DEW line)

© Martin Gilbert 1985

THE UNITED STATES AND THE SOVIET UNION IN OUTER SPACE

Between 1957 and 1981 a total of 2,725 satellites were launched, most of them by the United States and the Soviet Union. Some of the principal satellites in orbit in 1981 are shown here. In March 1981 the US National Aeronautics and Space Administration (NASA) launched its Columbia Orbiter, the first re-usable space vehicle (44 missions planned by the end of 1985, nine of them military)

SATELLITES

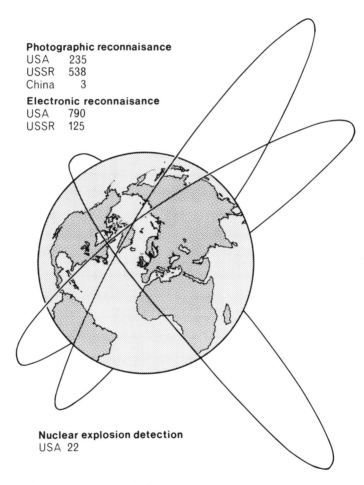

Early Warning
USA 22
USSR 25

Communications
USA 118
USSR 366
NATO   5
UK   4
France 2

Photographic reconnaisance
USA 235
USSR 538
China 3

Electronic reconnaisance
USA 790
USSR 125

Navigation
USA 39
USSR 25

Nuclear explosion detection
USA 22

Ocean surveillance
USA 18
USSR 32

Interception - destruction
USSR 33

In January 1985, at Geneva, the United States and the Soviet Union agreed to begin talks aimed at an agreement over the restriction of warfare in outer space. The United States was involved in the development of anti-satellite missiles and anti-missile lasers, and the Soviet Union in anti-satellite satellites

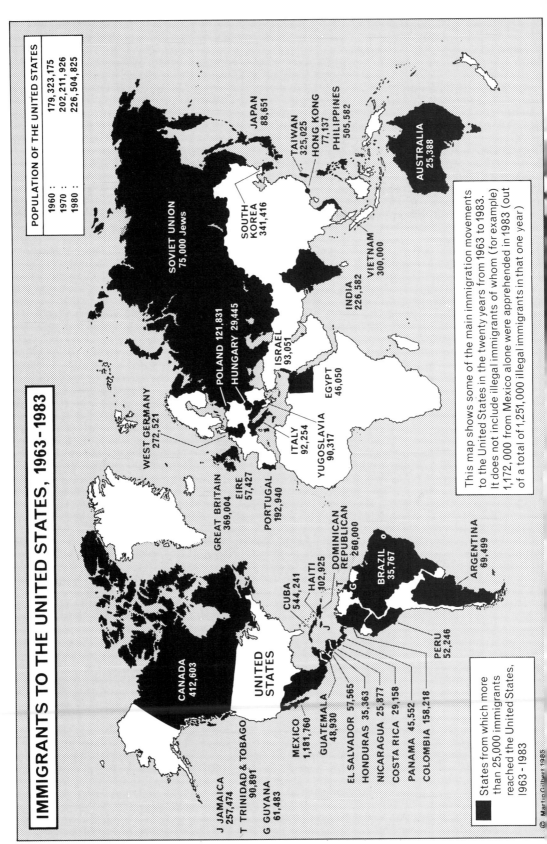

IMMIGRANTS TO THE UNITED STATES, 1963 - 1983

POPULATION OF THE UNITED STATES

1960 : 179,323,175
1970 : 202,211,926
1980 : 226,504,825

SOVIET UNION
75,000 Jews

JAPAN 88,651

TAIWAN 325,025

HONG KONG 77,137

PHILIPPINES 505,582

SOUTH KOREA 341,416

AUSTRALIA 25,388

VIETNAM 300,000

INDIA 226,582

POLAND 121,831

HUNGARY 29,445

ISRAEL 93,051

EGYPT 46,050

WEST GERMANY 272,521

ITALY 92,254

YUGOSLAVIA 90,317

GREAT BRITAIN 369,004

EIRE 57,427

PORTUGAL 192,940

DOMINICAN REPUBLICAN 260,000

ARGENTINA 69,499

BRAZIL 35,767

CUBA 544,241

HAITI 102,925

PERU 52,246

CANADA 412,603

UNITED STATES

MEXICO 1,181,760

GUATEMALA 48,930

EL SALVADOR 57,565

HONDURAS 35,363

NICARAGUA 25,877

COSTA RICA 29,158

PANAMA 45,552

COLOMBIA 158,218

J JAMAICA 257,474

T TRINIDAD & TOBAGO 90,891

G GUYANA 61,483

This map shows some of the main immigration movements to the United States in the twenty years from 1963 to 1983. It does not include illegal immigrants of whom (for example) 1,172,000 from Mexico alone were apprehended in 1983 (out of a total of 1,251,000 illegal immigrants in that one year)

■ States from which more than 25,000 immigrants reached the United States, 1963 - 1983

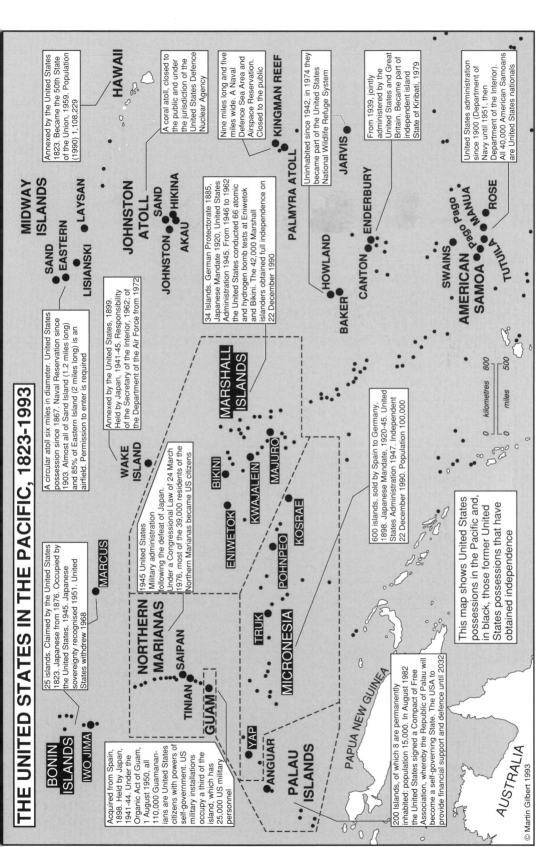

THE UNITED STATES IN THE PACIFIC, 1823-1993

HAWAII

Annexed by the United States 1823. Became the 50th State of the Union, 1959. Population (1990) 1,108,229

MIDWAY ISLANDS

A circular atoll six miles in diameter. United States possession since 1867. Naval Reservation since 1903. Almost all of Sand Island (1.2 miles long) and 85% of Eastern Island (2 miles long) is an airfield. Permission to enter is required

SAND • EASTERN
LISIANSKI • • LAYSAN

JOHNSTON ATOLL

A coral atoll, closed to the public and under the jurisdiction of the United States Defence Nuclear Agency

SAND • HIKINA
JOHNSTON • • AKAU

KINGMAN REEF

Nine miles long and five miles wide. A Naval Defence Sea Area and Airspace Reservation. Closed to the public

PALMYRA ATOLL

Uninhabited since 1942, in 1974 they became part of the United States National Wildlife Refuge System

JARVIS

From 1939, jointly administered by the United States and Great Britain. Became part of independent island State of Kiribati, 1979

HOWLAND
• BAKER

CANTON • • ENDERBURY

AMERICAN SAMOA

United States administration since 1900 (Department of Navy until 1951, then Department of the Interior). All 40,000 American Samoans are United States nationals

SWAINS •
• MANUA
Pago Pago
• • ROSE
TUTUILA

Annexed by the United States, 1899. Held by Japan, 1941-45. Responsibility of the Secretary of the Interior, 1962; of the Department of the Air Force from 1972

WAKE ISLAND

MARCUS

BONIN ISLANDS

25 Islands. Claimed by the United States 1823. Japanese from 1876. Occupied by the United States, 1945. Japanese sovereignty recognised 1951. United States withdrew 1968

• • •
IWO JIMA

1945 United States Military administration following the defeat of Japan. Under a Congressional Law of 24 March 1976, most of the 39,000 residents of the Northern Marianas became US citizens

MARSHALL ISLANDS

34 Islands. German Protectorate 1885, Japanese Mandate 1920, United States Administration 1945. From 1946 to 1962 the United States conducted 66 atomic and hydrogen bomb tests at Eniwetok and Bikini. The 42,000 Marshall islanders obtained full independence on 22 December 1990

BIKINI
ENIWETOK •
• KWAJALEIN
• • MAJURO

• POHNPEO • KOSRAE

600 islands, sold by Spain to Germany, 1898. Japanese Mandate, 1920-45. United States Administration 1947. Independent 22 December 1990. Population 100,000

NORTHERN MARIANAS

SAIPAN
TINIAN •
GUAM

Acquired from Spain, 1898. Held by Japan, 1941-44. Under the Organic Act of Guam, 1 August 1950, all 110,000 Guamananians are United States citizens with powers of self-government. US military installations occupy a third of the island, which has 25,000 US military personnel

• YAP
• TRUK
MICRONESIA

• ANGUAR

PALAU ISLANDS

200 Islands, of which 8 are permanently inhabited: population 15,000. In August 1982 the United States signed a Compact of Free Association, whereby the Republic of Palau will become a self-governing State. The USA to provide financial support and defence until 2032

This map shows United States possessions in the Pacific and, in black, those former United States possessions that have obtained independence

PAPUA NEW GUINEA

0   800
|——————|
kilometres
0   500
|—————|
miles

AUSTRALIA

© Martin Gilbert 1993

116

GREAT POWER CONFRONTATION AND CONCILIATION, 1972-1986

① Beginning in 1972, during the period known as Detente, the United States and the Soviet Union sought means to reduce the arms race and to end the Cold War. At the same time, a series of conflicts set back the process, as did the abuse of human rights in the Soviet Union

① Moscow, 22-30 May 1972: President Nixon visits Moscow, where he and Communist Party Chairman Leonid Brezhnev sign the first Strategic Arms Limitation Treaty (SALT) between the United States and the Soviet Union

② Vladivostok, 23 November 1974: President Gerald Ford and Leonid Brezhnev reaffirm significance to USA and USSR of limitation of strategic offensive arms, and initiate arms limitation. "A cap has been put on the arms race for a period of ten years" (US Secretary of State, Henry Kissinger)

③ Baikonur-Cape Canaveral, 15 July 1975: Soyuz and Apollo spacecraft launched for Soviet-United States link-up in space

④ Helsinki, 1 August 1975: Brezhnev, Ford and other leaders (Harold Wilson for Britain) guarantee East and West European borders, and pledge observance of human rights, including right of free movement of peoples

⑤ Vienna, 18 June 1979: US President Carter and Brezhnev, in signing Strategic Arms Limitations Treaty (SALT II), advocate further reduction of nuclear weapons. "God will not forgive us if we fail" (Brezhnev)

⑥ AFGHANISTAN, 27 December 1979: Soviet forces invade, to support Marxist regime

⑦ New York, 8 January 1980: Soviet Union vetoes United Nations Security Council resolution, condemning the Soviet invasion of Afghanistan

⑧ Moscow, 19 July 1980: Olympic Games boycotted by the United States and sixty-five other nations, in protest against Soviet invasion of Afghanistan

⑨ Washington, 8 March 1983: President Reagan calls the Soviet Union an "evil empire"

⑩ SAKHALIN, 30 August 1983: a Soviet fighter tracks a civilian (Korean) airliner for two hours after it strayed into Soviet air space, then shoots it down. All 269 passengers including 61 Americans are killed

⑪ Geneva, 21 November 1985: US President Ronald Reagan and Soviet Communist Party Chairman Mikhail Gorbachev sign six bilateral agreements on scientific and cultural exchanges, resumption of civil aviation ties, establishment of consulates in New York and Kiev, and environmental protection. Reagan called the meeting a "fresh start"

⑫ Moscow, 30 August 1986: Nicholas Daniloff, an American journalist, detained on espionage charges. A month later he was released and allowed to leave the Soviet Union

⑬ Rejkyavik, 11 October 1986: Reagan and Gorbachev agree to further arms limitation, and phased reduction of nuclear testing, but Reagan rejects call to abandon United States strategic defense initiative (Star Wars). Gorbachev promises progress on emigration and human rights

SOVIET UNION

Moscow

Kiev

Helsinki

Vienna

Geneva

Moscow
22-30 May 1972
19 July-3 August 1980
30 August 1986

Helsinki
1 August 1975

Rejkyavik
11 October 1986

Geneva
21 November 1985

Vienna
18 June 1979

Atlantic Ocean

UNITED STATES

New York
8 January 1980

Washington
8 March 1983

Cape Canaveral
15 July 1975

Pacific Ocean

SOVIET UNION

Baikonur

Vladivostok
23 November 1974

AFGHANISTAN
27 December 1979

SAKHALIN
30 August 1983

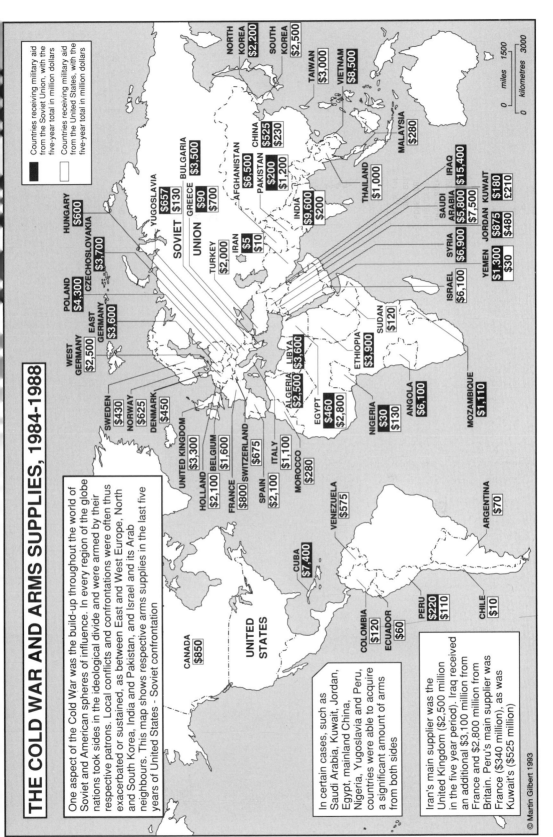

THE COLD WAR AND ARMS SUPPLIES, 1984-1988

One aspect of the Cold War was the build-up throughout the world of Soviet and American spheres of influence. In every region of the globe nations took sides in the ideological divide and were armed by their respective patrons. Local conflicts and confrontations were often thus exacerbated or sustained, as between East and West Europe, North and South Korea, India and Pakistan, and Israel and its Arab neighbours. This map shows respective arms supplies in the last five years of United States - Soviet confrontation

In certain cases, such as Saudi Arabia, Kuwait, Jordan, Egypt, mainland China, Nigeria, Yugoslavia and Peru, countries were able to acquire a significant amount of arms from both sides

Iran's main supplier was the United Kingdom ($2,500 million in the five year period). Iraq received an additional $3,100 million from France and $2,800 million from Britain. Peru's main supplier was France ($340 million), as was Kuwait's ($525 million)

Countries receiving military aid from the Soviet Union, with the five-year total in million dollars

Countries receiving military aid from the United States, with the five-year total in million dollars

NORTH KOREA	$2,200
SOUTH KOREA	$2,500
TAIWAN	$3,000
VIETNAM	$8,500
MALAYSIA	$280
CHINA	$525 / $230
AFGHANISTAN	$6,500
PAKISTAN	$200 / $1,200
THAILAND	$1,000
IRAQ	$15,400
KUWAIT	$180 / £210
SAUDI ARABIA	$5,800 / $7,500
JORDAN	$875 / $480
SYRIA	$6,900
YEMEN	$1,300 / $30
ISRAEL	$6,100
INDIA	$9,600 / $200
IRAN	$5 / $10
TURKEY	$2,000
GREECE	$90 / $700
BULGARIA	$3,500
YUGOSLAVIA	$657 / $130
HUNGARY	$600
CZECHOSLOVAKIA	$3,700
POLAND	$4,300
EAST GERMANY	$3,600
WEST GERMANY	$2,500
SWEDEN	$430
NORWAY	$625
DENMARK	$450
UNITED KINGDOM	$3,300
HOLLAND	$2,100
BELGIUM	$1,600
FRANCE	$800
SWITZERLAND	$675
SPAIN	$2,100
ITALY	$1,100
MOROCCO	$280
ALGERIA	$2,500
LIBYA	$3,600
EGYPT	$460 / $2,800
SUDAN	$120
ETHIOPIA	$3,900
NIGERIA	$30 / $130
ANGOLA	$6,100
MOZAMBIQUE	$1,110
CANADA	$850
CUBA	$7,400
VENEZUELA	$575
COLOMBIA	$120
ECUADOR	$60
PERU	$220 / $110
CHILE	$10
ARGENTINA	$70

SOVIET UNION

UNITED STATES

0   miles   1500

0   kilometres   3000

© Martin Gilbert 1993

118

THE END OF THE COLD WAR, 1987-1993

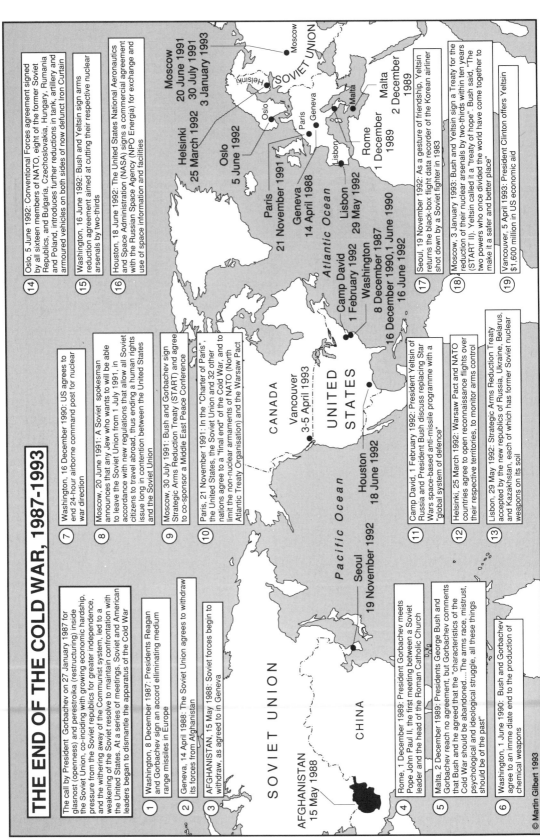

The call by President Gorbachev on 27 January 1987 for glasnost (openness) and perestroika (restructuring) inside the Soviet Union, co-inciding with growing economic hardship, pressure from the Soviet republics for greater independence, and the withering away of the Communist system, led to a weakening of the Soviet resolve to maintain confrontation with the United States. At a series of meetings, Soviet and American leaders began to dismantle the apparatus of the Cold War

(1) Washington, 8 December 1987: Presidents Reagan and Gorbachev sign an accord elliminating medium range missiles in Europe

(2) Geneva, 14 April 1988: The Soviet Union agrees to withdraw its forces from Afghanistan

(3) AFGHANISTAN, 15 May 1988: Soviet forces begin to withdraw, as agreed to in Geneva

(4) Rome, 1 December 1989: President Gorbachev meets Pope John Paul II, the first meeting between a Soviet leader and the head of the Roman Catholic Church

(5) Malta, 2 December 1989: Presidents George Bush and Gorbachev reach no agreement, but Gorbachev comments that Bush and he agreed that the "characteristics of the Cold War should be abandoned....The arms race, mistrust, psychological and ideological struggle, all these things should be of the past"

(6) Washington, 1 June 1990: Bush and Gorbachev agree to an imme diate end to the production of chemical weapons

(7) Washington, 16 December 1990: US agrees to end 24-hour airborne command post for nuclear war direction

(8) Moscow, 20 June 1991: A Soviet spokesman announces that any Jew who wants to will be able to leave the Soviet Union from 1 July 1991, in accordance with new regulations that allow all Soviet citizens to travel abroad, thus ending a human rights issue long in contention between the United States and the Soviet Union

(9) Moscow, 30 July 1991: Bush and Gorbachev sign Strategic Arms Reduction Treaty (START) and agree to co-sponsor a Middle East Peace Conference

(10) Paris, 21 November 1991: In the "Charter of Paris", the United States, the Soviet Union and 32 other nations agree to a "final end" of the Cold War, and to limit the non-nuclear armaments of NATO (North Atlantic Treaty Organisation) and the Warsaw Pact

(11) Camp David, 1 February 1992: President Yeltsin of Russia and President Bush discuss replacing Star Wars space-based anti-missile programme with a "global system of defence"

(12) Helsinki, 25 March 1992: Warsaw Pact and NATO countries agree to open reconnaissance flights over their respective territories, to monitor arms control

(13) Lisbon, 29 May 1992: Strategic Arms Reduction Treaty accepted by the new republics of Russia, Ukraine, Belarus, and Kazakhstan, each of which has former Soviet nuclear weapons on its soil

(14) Oslo, 5 June 1992: Conventional Forces agreement signed by all sixteen members of NATO, eight of the former Soviet Republics, and Bulgaria, Czechoslovakia, Hungary, Rumania and Poland, introduces further reductions in tank, artillery and armoured vehicles on both sides of now defunct Iron Curtain

(15) Washington, 16 June 1992: Bush and Yeltsin sign arms reduction agreement aimed at cutting their respective nuclear arsenals by two-thirds

(16) Houston, 18 June 1992: The United States National Aeronautics and Space Administration (NASA) signs a commercial agreement with the Russian Space Agency (NPO Energia) for exchange and use of space information and facilities

(17) Seoul, 19 November 1992: As a gesture of friendship, Yeltsin returns the black-box flight data recorder of the Korean airliner shot down by a Soviet fighter in 1983

(18) Moscow, 3 January 1993: Bush and Yeltsin sign a Treaty for the reduction of their nuclear arsenals by two-thirds within ten years (START II). Yeltsin called it a "treaty of hope". Bush said, "The two powers who once divided the world have come together to make it a safer and better place"

(19) Vancouver, 5 April 1993: President Clinton offers Yeltsin $1,600 million in US economic aid

© Martin Gilbert 1993

MILITARY, ECONOMIC AND HUMANITARIAN MISSIONS, 1975-1993

Under Presidents Gerald Ford (1974-77), Jimmy Carter (1977-81), Ronald Reagan (1981-89), George Bush (1989-92) and Bill Clinton (1993-) the United States took an active part in global peacekeeping, and in the provision of aid. With the decline of the Cold War in the late 1980s, such action was increasingly undertaken as part of an overall United Nations commitment, as against Iraq during the Gulf War; or in conjunction with the European Community, with economic aid to the former Soviet Union, and the distribution of food in Somalia

COMMONWEALTH OF INDEPENDENT STATES

February 10, 1992 Operation "Provide Hope": fifty four flights bring 17,000 tons of US food and medical aid to the former Soviet Union

March 31, 1993 Operation "Deny Flight": US warplanes join a NATO force warning the Serbs not to overfly Bosnia

September 6, 1990 Operation "Desert Shield" begins: US forces lead United Nations coalition to protect possible Iraqi invasion of Saudi Arabia, after Iraq invades Kuwait

January 17-February 28, 1991 Operation "Desert Storm": United Nations coalition forces, commanded by Norman Schwartzkopf, and including predominant US participation, drive Iraqi forces out of Kuwait. 148 US troops killed

May 15, 1975 Rescue of US merchant ship *Mayaguez* seized by Cambodian forces. 38 Marines killed

CAMBODIA

April 25, 1980 Desert raid to rescue hostages fails when a helicopter and a cargo plane collide. 8 US servicemen killed

February 28, 1993 Operation "Provide Promise": US drops food and medical supplies to Muslim enclaves besieged by Serb forces in Bosnia: 21,850 meals were dropped on the first night

April 13, 1991 Operation "Provide Comfort": US helps to protect and to feed safe havens set up for Kurds in northern Iraq

May 17, 1987 37 US soldiers killed on frigate *Stark* by Iraqi missiles. Iraq apologises on following day

July 3, 1988 US peace-keeping force cruiser *Vincennes* accidentally shoots down an Iranian civilian aircraft, killing all 290 on board

Persian Gulf

• Teheran

IRAQ

Beirut • KUWAIT

Bengazi

SOMALIA

Tripoli

April 15, 1986 Air strike at Libyan air base, 30 Libyan dead, also 2 US airmen killed

December 19, 1992 Operation "Renew Hope": 18,000 US troops land to protect United Nations food convoys and help distribution in famine areas. President-elect Bill Clinton accepts this commitment

BOSNIA

• Rhein-Main

April 18, 1983 During US peacekeeping task, terrorist bomb kills 17 US nationals

April 15, 1986 Air strike on barracks which included Colonel Gaddafi's home. 100 Libyan dead

LIBERIA

October 23, 1983 Terrorist bomb kills 260 US Marines

October 25, 1983 Operation "Urgent Fury": after a left-wing military coup, 1,900 US troops overcome 800 Cuban soldiers on the island within five days. 42 US troops killed. US deputy commander Norman Schwarzkopf says 160 Grenadians and 71 Cubans killed

August 5, 1990 Operation "Sharp Edge": 2,335 US Marines airlift 2,600 foreigners (including 330 US citizens) to safety during civil war

Atlantic Ocean

UNITED STATES

CUBA

GRENADA

PANAMA

Pacific Ocean

0   kilometres   3,000
0   miles   2,000

December 20, 1989 Operation "Just Cause": 24,500 US troops overthrow the government of military dictator General Noriega. 22 US troops killed

© Martin Gilbert 1993

120

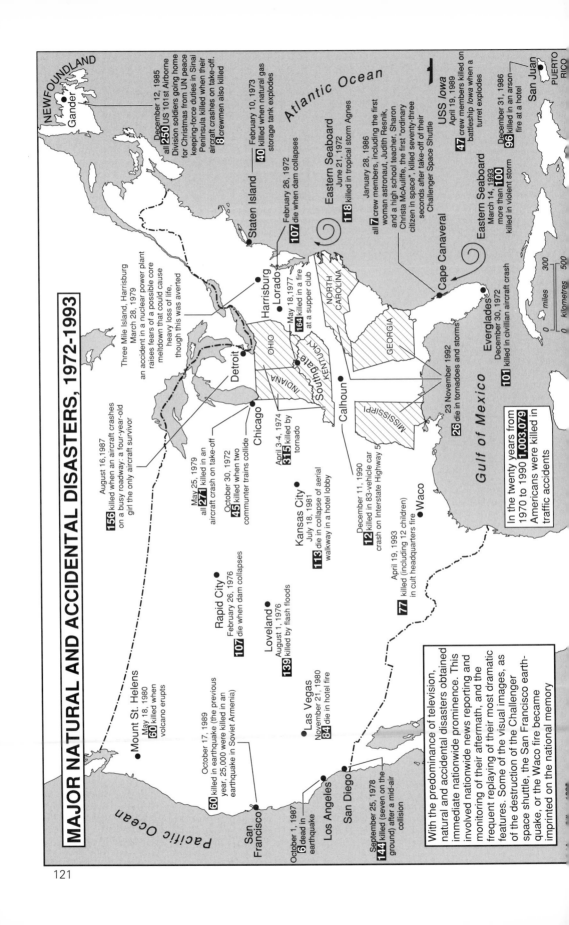

MAJOR NATURAL AND ACCIDENTAL DISASTERS, 1972-1993

NEWFOUNDLAND
Gander

December 12, 1985
250 US 101st Airborne Division soldiers going home for Christmas from UN peace keeping-force duties in Sinai Peninsula killed when their aircraft crashes on take-off. **8** crewmen also killed

Atlantic Ocean

Staten Island — February 10, 1973
40 killed when natural gas storage tank explodes

February 26, 1972
107 die when dam collapses

Eastern Seaboard — June 21, 1972
118 killed in tropical storm Agnes

January 28, 1986
all **7** crew members, including the first woman astronaut, Judith Resnik, and a high school teacher, Sharon Christa McAuliffe, the first "ordinary citizen in space", killed seventy-three seconds after take-off of their Challenger Space Shuttle

USS *Iowa*
April 19, 1989
47 crew members killed on battleship *Iowa* when a turret explodes

December 31, 1986
96 killed in an arson fire at a hotel

San Juan
PUERTO RICO

Cape Canaveral

Eastern Seaboard
March 14, 1993
more than **100** killed in violent storm

0   miles   300
0   kilometres   500

Three Mile Island, Harrisburg March 28, 1979
an accident in a nuclear power plant raises fears of a possible core meltdown that could cause heavy loss of life, though this was averted

Harrisburg
Lorado
May 18, 1977
164 killed in a fire at a supper club

NORTH CAROLINA
OHIO
INDIANA
KENTUCKY
Southgate
GEORGIA
MISSISSIPPI

Detroit

August 16, 1987
156 killed when an aircraft crashes on a busy roadway: a four-year-old girl the only aircraft survivor

May 25, 1979
all **271** killed in an aircraft crash on take-off

October 30, 1972
45 killed when two commuter trains collide

Chicago

April 3-4, 1974
315 killed by tornado

Kansas City
July 18, 1981
113 die in collapse of aerial walkway in a hotel lobby

December 11, 1990
12 killed in 83-vehicle car crash on Interstate Highway 5

April 19, 1993
77 killed (including 12 children) in cult headquarters fire

Calhoun
Waco

23 November 1992
26 die in tornadoes and storms

Gulf of Mexico

Everglades
December 30, 1972
101 killed in civillian aircraft crash

Rapid City
February 26, 1976
107 die when dam collapses

Loveland
August 1, 1976
139 killed by flash floods

Las Vegas
November 21, 1980
84 die in hotel fire

Mount St. Helens
May 18, 1980
60 killed when volcano erupts

October 17, 1989
60 killed in earthquake (the previous year, 25,000 were killed in an earthquake in Soviet Armenia)

San Francisco

October 1, 1987
6 dead in earthquake

Los Angeles
San Diego

September 25, 1978
144 killed (seven on the ground) after a mid-air collision

Pacific Ocean

In the twenty years from 1970 to 1990 **1,003,079** Americans were killed in traffic accidents

With the predominance of television, natural and accidental disasters obtained immediate nationwide prominence. This involved nationwide news reporting and monitoring of their aftermath, and the frequent replaying of their most dramatic features. Some of the visual images, as of the destruction of the Challenger space shuttle, the San Francisco earthquake, or the Waco fire became imprinted on the national memory.

POLLUTION: HAZARDOUS WASTE SITES, 1990

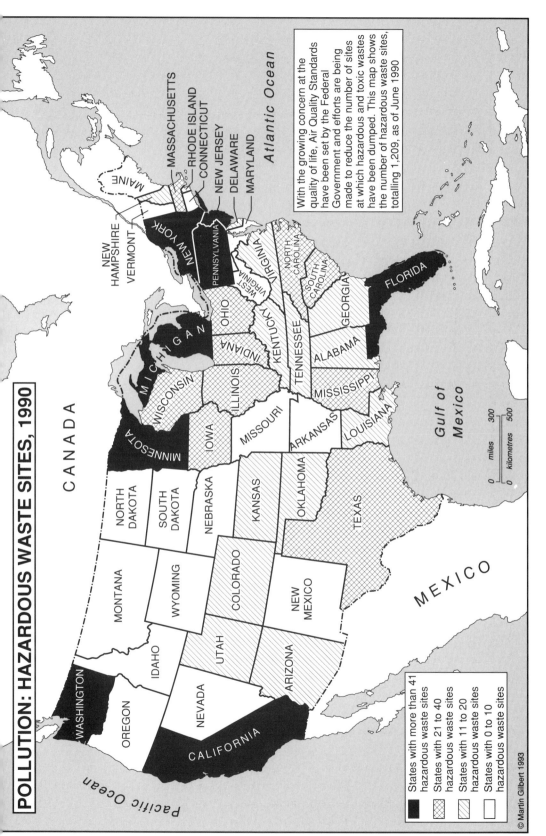

With the growing concern at the quality of life, Air Quality Standards have been set by the Federal Government and efforts are being made to reduce the number of sites at which hazardous and toxic wastes have been dumped. This map shows the number of hazardous waste sites, totalling 1,209, as of June 1990

CANADA

Atlantic Ocean

Pacific Ocean

Gulf of Mexico

MEXICO

MAINE

NEW HAMPSHIRE
VERMONT
NEW YORK
PENNSYLVANIA

MASSACHUSETTS
RHODE ISLAND
CONNECTICUT
NEW JERSEY
DELAWARE
MARYLAND

WEST VIRGINIA
VIRGINIA
NORTH CAROLINA
SOUTH CAROLINA
GEORGIA
FLORIDA

OHIO
KENTUCKY
TENNESSEE
ALABAMA
MISSISSIPPI

MICHIGAN
WISCONSIN
ILLINOIS
INDIANA
IOWA
MISSOURI
ARKANSAS
LOUISIANA

MINNESOTA
NORTH DAKOTA
SOUTH DAKOTA
NEBRASKA
KANSAS
OKLAHOMA
TEXAS

MONTANA
WYOMING
COLORADO
NEW MEXICO

WASHINGTON
OREGON
IDAHO
NEVADA
UTAH
ARIZONA
CALIFORNIA

miles   0   300
kilometres   0   500

States with more than 41 hazardous waste sites

States with 21 to 40 hazardous waste sites

States with 11 to 20 hazardous waste sites

States with 0 to 10 hazardous waste sites

© Martin Gilbert 1993

122

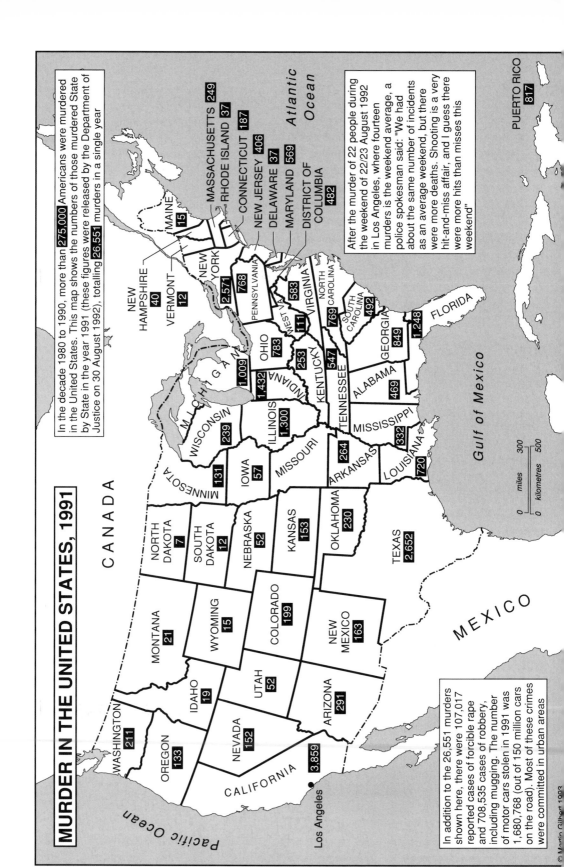

MURDER IN THE UNITED STATES, 1991

In the decade 1980 to 1990, more than 275,000 Americans were murdered in the United States. This map shows the numbers of those murdered State by State in the year 1991 (these figures were released by the Department of Justice on 30 August 1992), totalling 26,551 murders in a single year

After the murder of 22 people during the weekend of 22/23 August 1992 in Los Angeles, where fourteen murders is the weekend average, a police spokesman said: "We had about the same number of incidents as an average weekend, but there were more deaths. Shooting is a very hit-and-miss affair, and I guess there were more hits than misses this weekend"

In addition to the 26,551 murders shown here, there were 107,017 reported cases of forcible rape and 708,535 cases of robbery, including mugging. The number of motor cars stolen in 1991 was 1,680,768 (out of 150 million cars on the road). Most of these crimes were committed in urban areas

CANADA

MEXICO

Pacific Ocean

Gulf of Mexico

Atlantic Ocean

WASHINGTON 211
OREGON 133
IDAHO 19
MONTANA 21
WYOMING 15
NEVADA 152
UTAH 52
CALIFORNIA 3,859
Los Angeles
ARIZONA 291
COLORADO 199
NEW MEXICO 163
NORTH DAKOTA 7
SOUTH DAKOTA 12
NEBRASKA 52
KANSAS 153
OKLAHOMA 230
TEXAS 2,652
MINNESOTA 131
IOWA 57
MISSOURI 264
ARKANSAS 264
LOUISIANA 720
WISCONSIN 239
ILLINOIS 1,300
MICHIGAN 1,009
INDIANA 432
OHIO 783
KENTUCKY 253
TENNESSEE 547
MISSISSIPPI 332
ALABAMA 469
GEORGIA 849
FLORIDA 1,248
SOUTH CAROLINA 492
NORTH CAROLINA 769
VIRGINIA 583
WEST VA 111
PENNSYLVANIA 768
NEW YORK 2,571
VERMONT 12
NEW HAMPSHIRE 40
MAINE 15
MASSACHUSETTS 249
RHODE ISLAND 37
CONNECTICUT 187
NEW JERSEY 406
DELAWARE 37
MARYLAND 569
DISTRICT OF COLUMBIA 482
PUERTO RICO 817

miles 0 300
kilometres 0 500

© Martin Gilbert 1993

123

DEATHS FROM AIDS, 1982 - 1992

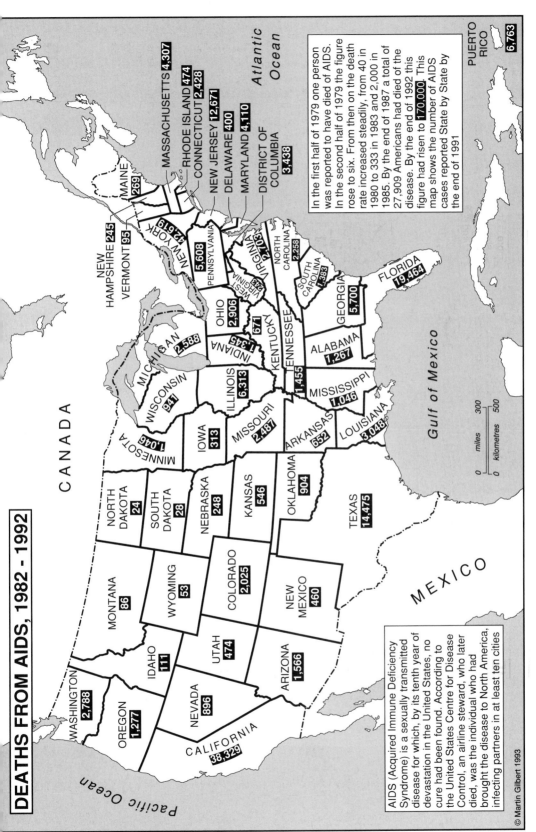

In the first half of 1979 one person was reported to have died of AIDS. In the second half of 1979 the figure rose to six. From then on the death rate increased steadily, from 40 in 1980 to 333 in 1983 and 2,000 in 1985. By the end of 1987 a total of 27,909 Americans had died of the disease. By the end of 1992 this figure had risen to 170,000. This map shows the number of AIDS cases reported State by State by the end of 1991

AIDS (Acquired Immune Deficiency Syndrome) is a sexually transmitted disease for which, by its tenth year of devastation in the United States, no cure had been found. According to the United States Centre for Disease Control, an airline steward, who later died, was the individual who had brought the disease to North America, infecting partners in at least ten cities

MASSACHUSETTS 4,307
RHODE ISLAND 474
CONNECTICUT 2,428
NEW JERSEY 12,671
DELAWARE 400
MARYLAND 4,110
DISTRICT OF COLUMBIA 3,438

MAINE 269
NEW HAMPSHIRE 245
VERMONT 95
NEW YORK 42,619
PENNSYLVANIA 5,608
WEST VIRGINIA 703
VIRGINIA 2,258
NORTH CAROLINA 2,383
SOUTH CAROLINA
GEORGIA 5,700
FLORIDA 19,464

CANADA

OHIO 2,906
INDIANA 1,845
KENTUCKY 671
TENNESSEE 1,455
ALABAMA 1,267
MISSISSIPPI 1,046

MICHIGAN 2,588
WISCONSIN 941
ILLINOIS 6,313
IOWA 313
MISSOURI 2,487
ARKANSAS 552
LOUISIANA 3,048

MINNESOTA 1,046
NORTH DAKOTA 24
SOUTH DAKOTA 28
NEBRASKA 248
KANSAS 546
OKLAHOMA 904
TEXAS 14,475

MONTANA 86
WYOMING 53
COLORADO 2,025
NEW MEXICO 460

WASHINGTON 2,788
OREGON 1,277
IDAHO 111
UTAH 474
NEVADA 896
ARIZONA 1,566
CALIFORNIA 38,329

Atlantic Ocean

Gulf of Mexico

MEXICO

Pacific Ocean

PUERTO RICO 6,763

miles 0   300
kilometres 0   500

© Martin Gilbert 1993

124

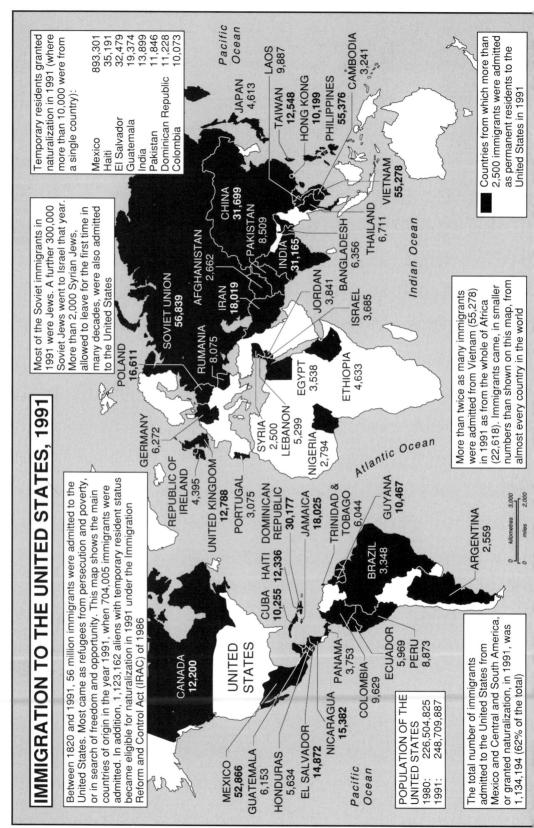

IMMIGRATION TO THE UNITED STATES, 1991

Between 1820 and 1991, 56 million immigrants were admitted to the United States. Most came as refugees from persecution and poverty, or in search of freedom and opportunity. This map shows the main countries of origin in the year 1991, when 704,005 immigrants were admitted. In addition, 1,123,162 aliens with temporary resident status became eligible for naturalization in 1991 under the Immigration Reform and Control Act (IRAC) of 1986

Most of the Soviet immigrants in 1991 were Jews. A further 300,000 Soviet Jews went to Israel that year. More than 2,000 Syrian Jews, allowed to leave for the first time in many decades, were also admitted to the United States

Temporary residents granted naturalization in 1991 (where more than 10,000 were from a single country):

Mexico	893,301
Haiti	35,191
El Salvador	32,479
Guatemala	19,374
India	13,899
Pakistan	11,846
Dominican Republic	11,228
Colombia	10,073

Countries from which more than 2,500 immigrants were admitted as permanent residents to the United States in 1991

More than twice as many immigrants were admitted from Vietnam (55,278) in 1991 as from the whole of Africa (22,618). Immigrants came, in smaller numbers than shown on this map, from almost every country in the world

The total number of immigrants admitted to the United States from Mexico and Central and South America, or granted naturalization, in 1991, was 1,134,194 (62% of the total)

POPULATION OF THE UNITED STATES
1980: 226,504,825
1991: 248,709,887

Pacific Ocean

Pacific Ocean

Atlantic Ocean

Indian Ocean

CANADA **12,200**

UNITED STATES

MEXICO **52,866**
GUATEMALA 6,153
HONDURAS 5,634
EL SALVADOR **14,872**
NICARAGUA **15,382**
PANAMA 3,753
COLOMBIA 9,629
ECUADOR 5,969
PERU 8,873
GUYANA **10,467**
BRAZIL 3,348
ARGENTINA 2,559

CUBA **10,255**
HAITI **12,336**
DOMINICAN REPUBLIC **30,177**
JAMAICA **18,025**
TRINIDAD & TOBAGO 6,044

GERMANY 6,272
REPUBLIC OF IRELAND 4,395
UNITED KINGDOM **12,788**
PORTUGAL 3,075
POLAND **16,611**
RUMANIA 8,075
SOVIET UNION **56,839**
AFGHANISTAN 2,662
IRAN **18,019**
SYRIA 2,500
LEBANON 5,299
NIGERIA 2,794
EGYPT 3,538
ETHIOPIA 4,633
JORDAN 3,841
ISRAEL 3,685
PAKISTAN 8,509
INDIA **31,165**
CHINA **31,699**
BANGLADESH 6,356
THAILAND 6,711
VIETNAM **55,278**
CAMBODIA 3,241
PHILIPPINES **55,376**
HONG KONG **10,199**
TAIWAN **12,548**
LAOS 9,887
JAPAN 4,613

0 kilometres 3,000
0 miles 2,000

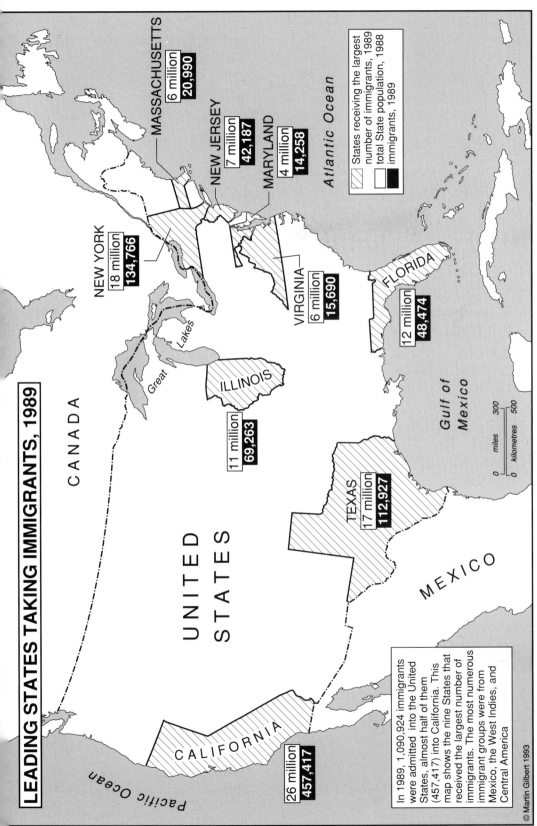

LEADING STATES TAKING IMMIGRANTS, 1989

States receiving the largest number of immigrants, 1989

total State population, 1988

immigrants, 1989

MASSACHUSETTS
6 million
20,990

NEW JERSEY
7 million
42,187

MARYLAND
4 million
14,258

NEW YORK
18 million
134,766

VIRGINIA
6 million
15,690

FLORIDA
12 million
48,474

ILLINOIS
11 million
69,263

TEXAS
17 million
112,927

CALIFORNIA
26 million
457,417

Atlantic Ocean

Pacific Ocean

CANADA

UNITED STATES

MEXICO

Gulf of Mexico

Great Lakes

0   300   miles
0   500   kilometres

In 1989, 1,090,924 immigrants were admitted into the United States, almost half of them (457,417) into California. This map shows the nine States that received the largest number of immigrants. The most numerous immigrant groups were from Mexico, the West Indies, and Central America

© Martin Gilbert 1993

NATIONAL ANCESTRY OF UNITED STATES CITIZENS

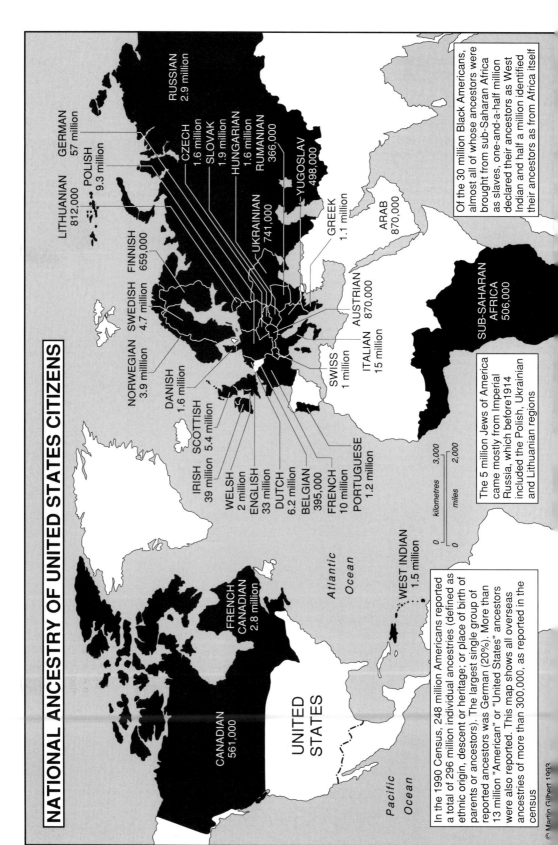

LITHUANIAN
812,000

GERMAN
57 million

POLISH
9.3 million

RUSSIAN
2.9 million

CZECH
1.6 million

SLOVAK
1.9 million

HUNGARIAN
1.6 million

RUMANIAN
366,000

YUGOSLAV
498,000

UKRAINIAN
741,000

GREEK
1.1 million

ARAB
870,000

FINNISH
659,000

SWEDISH
4.7 million

NORWEGIAN
3.9 million

AUSTRIAN
870,000

SUB-SAHARAN
AFRICA
506,000

DANISH
1.6 million

SCOTTISH
5.4 million

SWISS
1 million

ITALIAN
15 million

IRISH
39 million

WELSH
2 million

ENGLISH
33 million

DUTCH
6.2 million

BELGIAN
395,000

FRENCH
10 million

PORTUGUESE
1.2 million

Of the 30 million Black Americans,
almost all of whose ancestors were
brought from sub-Saharan Africa
as slaves, one-and-a-half million
declared their ancestors as West
Indian and half a million identified
their ancestors as from Africa itself

The 5 million Jews of America
came mostly from Imperial
Russia, which before 1914
included the Polish, Ukrainian
and Lithuanian regions

CANADIAN
561,000

FRENCH
CANADIAN
2.8 million

UNITED
STATES

*Atlantic
Ocean*

WEST INDIAN
1.5 million

*Pacific
Ocean*

kilometres 0   3,000
miles 0   2,000

In the 1990 Census, 248 million Americans reported
a total of 296 million individual ancestries (defined as
ethnic origin, descent or heritage; or place of birth of
parents or ancestors). The largest single group of
reported ancestors was German (20%). More than
13 million "American" or "United States" ancestors
were also reported. This map shows all overseas
ancestries of more than 300,000, as reported in the
census

© Martin Gilbert 1993

127

CITES WITH LARGE ETHNIC GROUPS

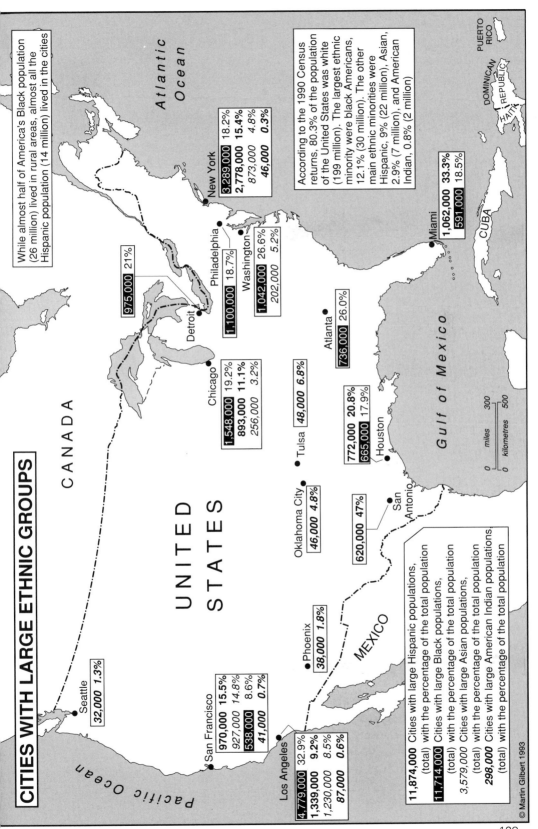

While almost half of America's Black population (26 million) lived in rural areas, almost all the Hispanic population (14 million) lived in the cities

CANADA

Atlantic Ocean

New York
3,289,000	18.2%
2,778,000	15.4%
873,000	4.8%
46,000	0.3%

According to the 1990 Census returns, 80.3% of the population of the United States was white (199 million). The largest ethnic minority were black Americans, 12.1% (30 million). The other main ethnic minorities were Hispanic, 9% (22 million), Asian, 2.9% (7 million), and American Indian, 0.8% (2 million).

UNITED STATES

Philadelphia
| 1,100,000 | 18.7% |

Washington
| 1,042,000 | 26.6% |
| 202,000 | 5.2% |

Detroit
| 975,000 | 21% |

Chicago
1,548,000	19.2%
893,000	11.1%
256,000	3.2%

Atlanta
| 736,000 | 26.0% |

Miami
| 1,062,000 | 33.3% |
| 591,000 | 18.5% |

CUBA

Gulf of Mexico

PUERTO RICO

DOMINICAN REPUBLIC

HAITI

Tulsa
| 48,000 | 6.8% |

Oklahoma City
| 46,000 | 4.8% |

Houston
| 772,000 | 20.8% |
| 665,000 | 17.9% |

San Antonio
| 620,000 | 47% |

Phoenix
| 38,000 | 1.8% |

MEXICO

Seattle
| 32,000 | 1.3% |

San Francisco
970,000	15.5%
927,000	14.8%
538,000	8.6%
41,000	0.7%

Los Angeles
4,779,000	32.9%
1,339,000	9.2%
1,230,000	8.5%
87,000	0.6%

Pacific Ocean

11,874,000	Cities with large Hispanic populations, (total) with the percentage of the total population
11,714,000	Cities with large Black populations, (total) with the percentage of the total population
3,579,000	Cities with large Asian populations, (total) with the percentage of the total population
298,000	Cities with large American Indian populations, (total) with the percentage of the total population

0   miles   300
0   kilometres   500

© Martin Gilbert 1993

128

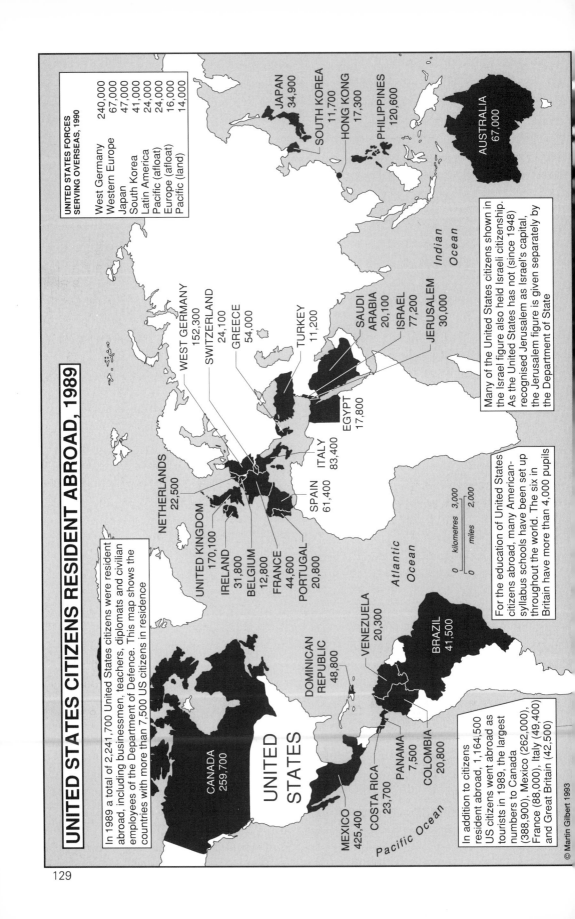

UNITED STATES CITIZENS RESIDENT ABROAD, 1989

In 1989 a total of 2,241,700 United States citizens were resident abroad, including businessmen, teachers, diplomats and civilian employees of the Department of Defence. This map shows the countries with more than 7,500 US citizens in residence

UNITED STATES FORCES SERVING OVERSEAS, 1990	
West Germany	240,000
Western Europe	67,000
Japan	47,000
South Korea	41,000
Latin America	24,000
Pacific (afloat)	24,000
Europe (afloat)	16,000
Pacific (land)	14,000

JAPAN 34,900

SOUTH KOREA 11,700

HONG KONG 17,300

PHILIPPINES 120,600

AUSTRALIA 67,000

WEST GERMANY 152,300

SWITZERLAND 24,100

GREECE 54,000

TURKEY 11,200

SAUDI ARABIA 20,100

ISRAEL 77,200

JERUSALEM 30,000

EGYPT 17,800

ITALY 83,400

SPAIN 61,400

NETHERLANDS 22,500

UNITED KINGDOM 170,100

IRELAND 31,800

BELGIUM 12,800

FRANCE 44,600

PORTUGAL 20,800

Indian Ocean

Many of the United States citizens shown in the Israel figure also held Israeli citizenship. As the United States has not (since 1948) recognised Jerusalem as Israel's capital, the Jerusalem figure is given separately by the Department of State

For the education of United States citizens abroad, many American-syllabus schools have been set up throughout the world. The six in Britain have more than 4,000 pupils

DOMINICAN REPUBLIC 48,800

VENEZUELA 20,300

BRAZIL 41,500

CANADA 259,700

UNITED STATES

MEXICO 425,400

COSTA RICA 23,700

PANAMA 7,500

COLOMBIA 20,800

Atlantic Ocean

Pacific Ocean

0 kilometres 3,000
0 miles 2,000

In addition to citizens resident abroad, 1,164,500 US citizens went abroad as tourists in 1989, the largest numbers to Canada (388,900), Mexico (262,000), France (88,000), Italy (49,400) and Great Britain (42,500)

© Martin Gilbert 1993

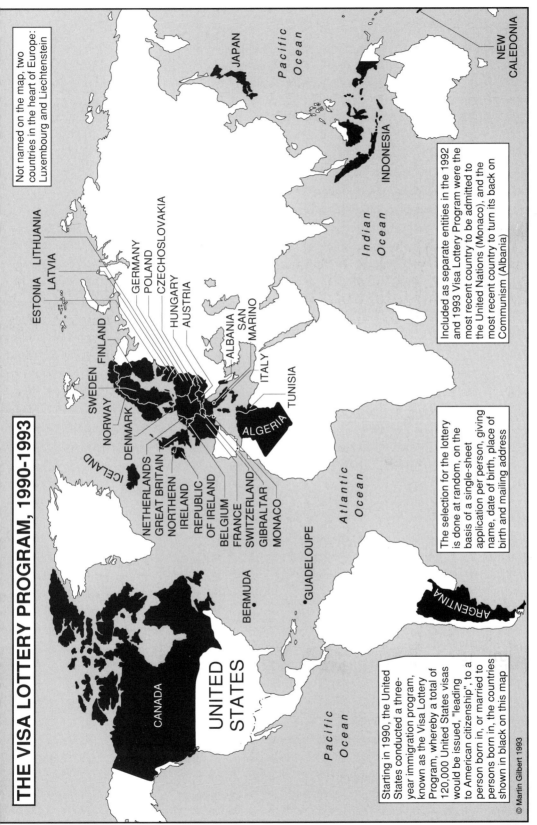

THE VISA LOTTERY PROGRAM, 1990-1993

Not named on the map, two countries in the heart of Europe: Luxembourg and Liechtenstein

Included as separate entities in the 1992 and 1993 Visa Lottery Program were the most recent country to be admitted to the United Nations (Monaco), and the most recent country to turn its back on Communism (Albania)

The selection for the lottery is done at random, on the basis of a single-sheet application per person, giving name, date of birth, place of birth and mailing address

Starting in 1990, the United States conducted a three-year immigration program, known as the Visa Lottery Program, whereby a total of 120,000 United States visas would be issued, "leading to American citizenship", to a person born in, or married to persons born in, the countries shown in black on this map

ESTONIA LITHUANIA
LATVIA
GERMANY
POLAND
CZECHOSLOVAKIA
HUNGARY
AUSTRIA
ALBANIA
SAN MARINO
ITALY
TUNISIA
ALGERIA
SWEDEN
FINLAND
NORWAY
DENMARK
NETHERLANDS
GREAT BRITAIN
NORTHERN IRELAND
REPUBLIC OF IRELAND
BELGIUM
FRANCE
SWITZERLAND
GIBRALTAR
MONACO
ICELAND
JAPAN
INDONESIA
NEW CALEDONIA

Pacific Ocean
Indian Ocean
Atlantic Ocean
Pacific Ocean

CANADA
UNITED STATES
BERMUDA
•GUADELOUPE
ARGENTINA

© Martin Gilbert 1993

130

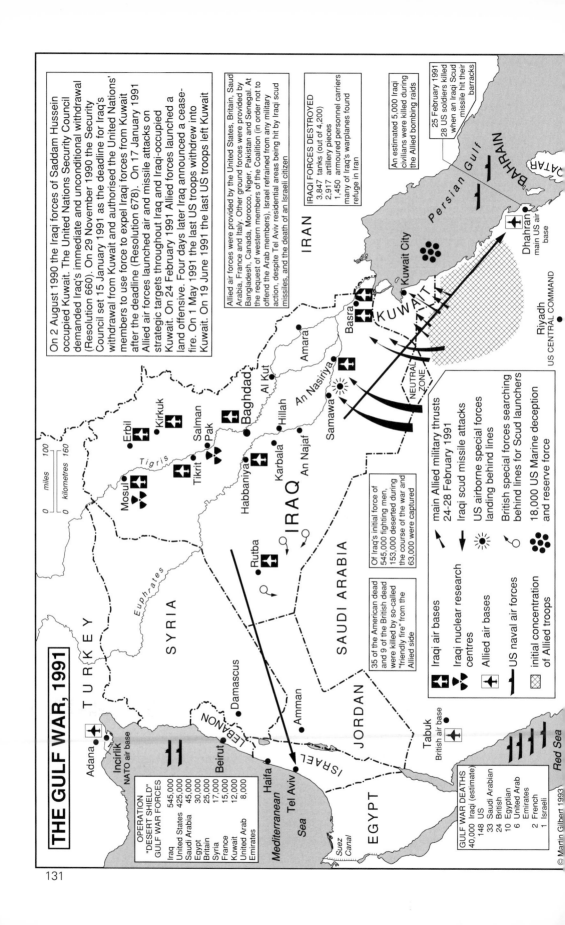

THE GULF WAR, 1991

On 2 August 1990 the Iraqi forces of Saddam Hussein occupied Kuwait. The United Nations Security Council demanded Iraq's immediate and unconditional withdrawal (Resolution 660). On 29 November 1990 the Security Council set 15 January 1991 as the deadline for Iraq's withdrawal from Kuwait and authorised the United Nations' members to use force to expel Iraqi forces from Kuwait after the deadline (Resolution 678). On 17 January 1991 Allied air forces launched air and missile attacks on strategic targets throughout Iraq and Iraqi-occupied Kuwait. On 24 February 1991 Allied forces launched a land offensive. Four days later Iraq announced a cease-fire. On 1 May 1991 the last US troops withdrew into Kuwait. On 19 June 1991 the last US troops left Kuwait.

Allied air forces were provided by the United States, Britain, Saudi Arabia, France and Italy. Other ground forces were provided by Bangladesh, Canada, Morocco, Niger, Pakistan and Senegal. At the request of western members of the Coalition (in order not to offend the Arab members), Israel refrained from any military action, despite Tel Aviv residential areas being hit by Iraqi scud missiles, and the death of an Israeli citizen

IRAQI FORCES DESTROYED
3,847 tanks (out of 4,200)
2,917 artillery pieces
1,450 armoured personnel carriers
many of Iraq's warplanes found
refuge in Iran

An estimated 5,000 Iraqi civilians were killed during the Allied bombing raids

25 February 1991
28 US soldiers killed when an Iraqi Scud missile hit their barracks

Dhahran
main US air base

Riyadh
US CENTRAL COMMAND

OPERATION "DESERT SHIELD" GULF WAR FORCES

Iraq	545,000
United States	425,000
Saudi Arabia	45,000
Egypt	30,000
Britain	25,000
Syria	17,000
France	15,000
Kuwait	12,000
United Arab Emirates	8,000

Of Iraq's initial force of 545,000 fighting men, 153,000 deserted during the course of the war and 63,000 were captured

35 of the American dead and 9 of the British dead were killed by so-called "friendly fire" from the Allied side

GULF WAR DEATHS

40,000	Iraqi (estimate)
148	US
33	Saudi Arabian
24	British
10	Egyptian
6	United Arab Emirates
2	French
1	Israeli

Legend:

Iraqi air bases	
Iraqi nuclear research centres	
Allied air bases	
US naval air forces	
initial concentration of Allied troops	
main Allied military thrusts 24-28 February 1991	
Iraqi scud missile attacks	
US airborne special forces landing behind lines	
British special forces searching behind lines for Scud launchers	
18,000 US Marine deception and reserve force	

Incirlik NATO air base — Adana

Tabuk British air base

© Martin Gilbert 1993

131

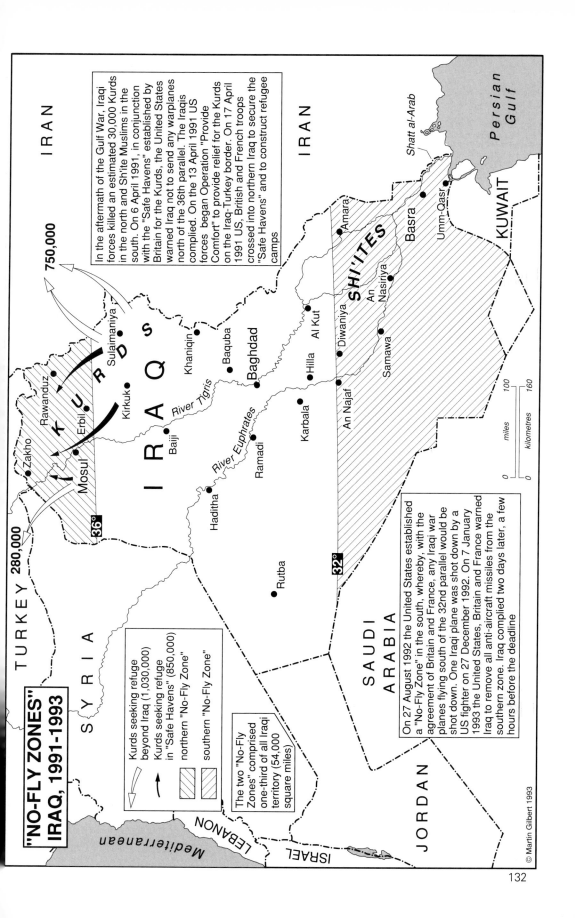

"NO-FLY ZONES"
IRAQ, 1991-1993

In the aftermath of the Gulf War, Iraqi forces killed an estimated 30,000 Kurds in the north and Sh'ite Muslims in the south. On 6 April 1991, in conjunction with the "Safe Havens" established by Britain for the Kurds, the United States warned Iraq not to send any warplanes north of the 36th parallel. The Iraqis complied. On the 13 April 1991 US forces began Operation "Provide Comfort" to provide relief for the Kurds on the Iraq-Turkey border. On 17 April 1991 US, British and French troops crossed into northern Iraq to secure the "Safe Havens" and to construct refugee camps

On 27 August 1992 the United States established a "No-Fly Zone" in the south, whereby, with the agreement of Britain and France, any Iraqi war planes flying south of the 32nd parallel would be shot down. One Iraqi plane was shot down by a US fighter on 27 December 1992. On 7 January 1993 the United States, Britain and France warned Iraq to remove all anti-aircraft missiles from the southern zone. Iraq complied two days later, a few hours before the deadline

Kurds seeking refuge beyond Iraq (1,030,000)

Kurds seeking refuge in "Safe Havens" (850,000)

northern "No-Fly Zone"

southern "No-Fly Zone"

The two "No-Fly Zones" comprised one-third of all Iraqi territory (54,000 square miles)

750,000

280,000

IRAN

IRAN

TURKEY

SYRIA

LEBANON

ISRAEL

JORDAN

SAUDI ARABIA

KUWAIT

Persian Gulf

Mediterranean

KURDS

I R A Q

SHI'ITES

Zakho

Mosul

Rawanduz

Erbil

Sulaimaniya

Kirkuk

Baiji

Khaniqin

Baquba

Baghdad

Al Kut

Hilla

Karbala

An Najaf

Ramadi

Haditha

Rutba

Diwaniya

An Nasiriya

Samawa

Amara

Basra

Umm-Qasr

Shatt al-Arab

River Tigris

River Euphrates

36°

32°

miles

kilometres

0   100

0   160

© Martin Gilbert 1993

132

UNITED STATES ARMS SALES, 1992

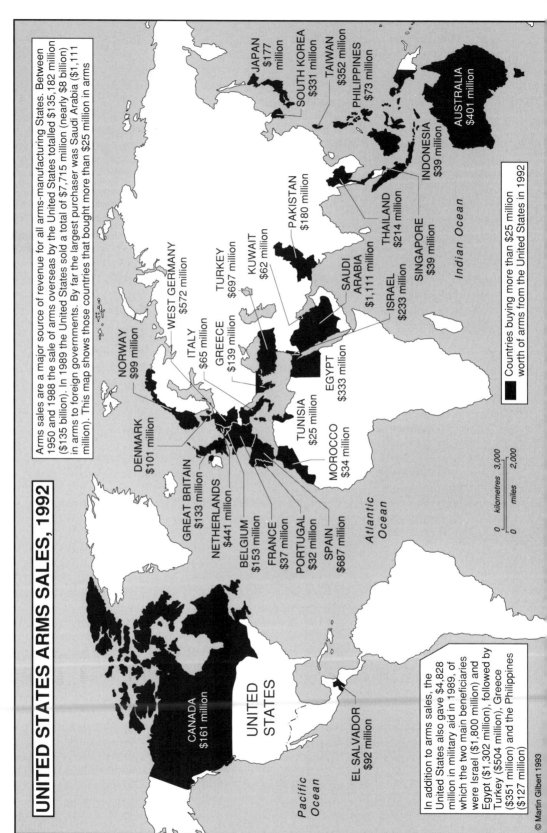

Arms sales are a major source of revenue for all arms-manufacturing States. Between 1950 and 1988 the sale of arms overseas by the United States totalled $135,182 million ($135 billion). In 1989 the United States sold a total of $7,715 million (nearly $8 billion) in arms to foreign governments. By far the largest purchaser was Saudi Arabia ($1,111 million). This map shows those countries that bought more than $25 million in arms

JAPAN $177 million

SOUTH KOREA $331 million

TAIWAN $352 million

PHILIPPINES $73 million

AUSTRALIA $401 million

INDONESIA $39 million

PAKISTAN $180 million

THAILAND $214 million

SINGAPORE $39 million

Indian Ocean

NORWAY $99 million

WEST GERMANY $572 million

ITALY $65 million

GREECE $139 million

TURKEY $697 million

KUWAIT $62 million

SAUDI ARABIA $1,111 million

ISRAEL $233 million

EGYPT $333 million

TUNISIA $25 million

MOROCCO $34 million

DENMARK $101 million

GREAT BRITAIN $133 million

NETHERLANDS $441 million

BELGIUM $153 million

FRANCE $37 million

PORTUGAL $32 million

SPAIN $687 million

Atlantic Ocean

■ Countries buying more than $25 million worth of arms from the United States in 1992

UNITED STATES

CANADA $161 million

EL SALVADOR $92 million

Pacific Ocean

0   kilometres   3,000
0   miles   2,000

In addition to arms sales, the United States also gave $4,828 million in military aid in 1989, of which the two main beneficiaries were Israel ($1,800 million) and Egypt ($1,302 million), followed by Turkey ($504 million), Greece ($351 million) and the Philippines ($127 million)

© Martin Gilbert 1993

133

MAIN RECIPIENTS OF UNITED STATES ECONOMIC AID, 1992

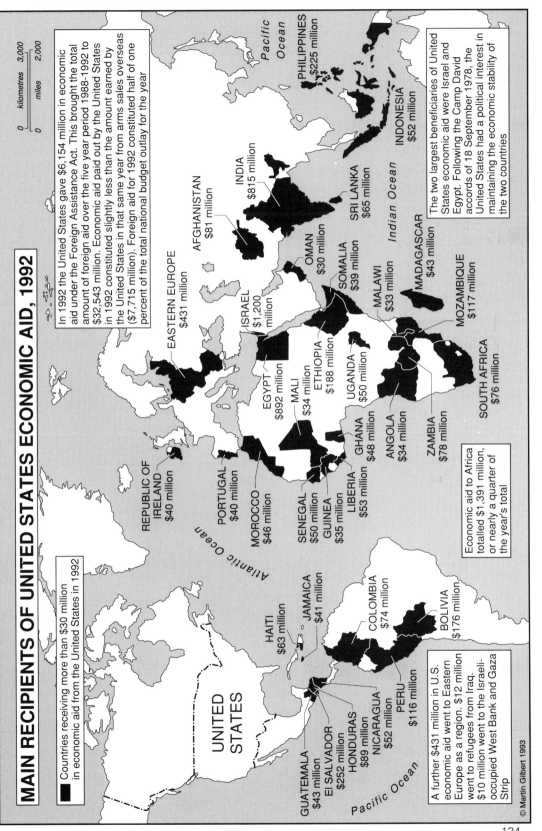

Countries receiving more than $30 million in economic aid from the United States in 1992

In 1992 the United States gave $6,154 million in economic aid under the Foreign Assistance Act. This brought the total amount of foreign aid over the five year period 1988-1992 to $32,543 million. Economic aid paid out by the United States in 1992 constituted slightly less than the amount earned by the United States in that same year from arms sales overseas ($7,715 million). Foreign aid for 1992 constituted half of one percent of the total national budget outlay for the year

The two largest beneficiaries of United States economic aid were Israel and Egypt. Following the Camp David accords of 18 September 1978, the United States had a political interest in maintaining the economic stability of the two countries

Economic aid to Africa totalled $1,391 million, or nearly a quarter of the year's total

A further $431 million in U.S. economic aid went to Eastern Europe as a region. $12 million went to refugees from Iraq. $10 million went to the Israeli-occupied West Bank and Gaza Strip

UNITED STATES

Pacific Ocean

GUATEMALA $43 million
El SALVADOR $252 million
HONDURAS $89 million
NICARAGUA $52 million
PERU $116 million
HAITI $63 million
JAMAICA $41 million
COLOMBIA $74 million
BOLIVIA $176 million

REPUBLIC OF IRELAND $40 million
Atlantic Ocean
PORTUGAL $40 million
MOROCCO $46 million
SENEGAL $50 million
GUINEA $35 million
LIBERIA $53 million
GHANA $48 million
ANGOLA $34 million
ZAMBIA $78 million
SOUTH AFRICA $76 million

EASTERN EUROPE $431 million
AFGHANISTAN $81 million
ISRAEL $1,200 million
EGYPT $892 million
MALI $34 million
ETHIOPIA $188 million
UGANDA $50 million
OMAN $30 million
SOMALIA $39 million
MALAWI $33 million
MOZAMBIQUE $117 million
MADAGASCAR $43 million

INDIA $815 million
SRI LANKA $65 million
Indian Ocean

Pacific Ocean
PHILIPPINES $225 million
INDONESIA $52 million

0   kilometres   3,000
0   miles   2,000

© Martin Gilbert 1993

134

DEFENCE PREPAREDNESS ON LAND, 1991

From 1945 to 1990 the main thrust of United States defences was in the confrontation with the Soviet Union. With the collapse of Communist power from 1990, and the demise of the Warsaw Pact, defence priorities were under continuous scrutiny. This map shows the location of Air Force Tactical Fighter Wings, and of the Strategic Offensive Forces, in 1991. Further cuts in bases were made in 1992 and 1993

- ⊙ Air Force Tactical Fighter Wings
- ◪ Strategic Offensive air bases
- ■ Strategic Offensive naval bases
- ▣ Strategic Offensive missile sites

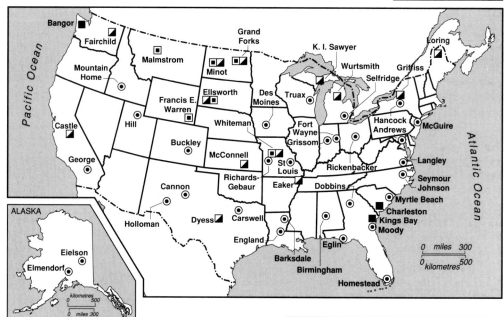

On 30 July 1991 the Department of Defence announced the shutting down of 72 United States military installations in Europe, and reduced operations at seven others

BASES TO BE CLOSED	
Germany	38
Britain	13
Italy	8
Turkey	7
Spain	5
Netherlands	1

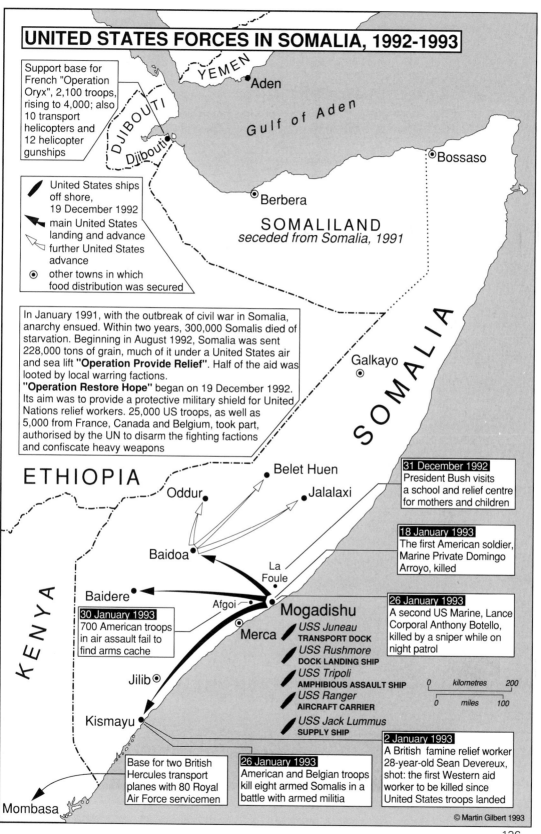

UNITED STATES FORCES IN SOMALIA, 1992-1993

YEMEN
•Aden

Support base for French "Operation Oryx", 2,100 troops, rising to 4,000; also 10 transport helicopters and 12 helicopter gunships

DJIBOUTI
Djibouti

Gulf of Aden

⊙Bossaso

/ United States ships off shore, 19 December 1992

◀ main United States landing and advance

◁ further United States advance

⊙ other towns in which food distribution was secured

⊙Berbera

SOMALILAND
seceded from Somalia, 1991

In January 1991, with the outbreak of civil war in Somalia, anarchy ensued. Within two years, 300,000 Somalis died of starvation. Beginning in August 1992, Somalia was sent 228,000 tons of grain, much of it under a United States air and sea lift **"Operation Provide Relief"**. Half of the aid was looted by local warring factions.
"Operation Restore Hope" began on 19 December 1992. Its aim was to provide a protective military shield for United Nations relief workers. 25,000 US troops, as well as 5,000 from France, Canada and Belgium, took part, authorised by the UN to disarm the fighting factions and confiscate heavy weapons

Galkayo
⊙

SOMALIA

ETHIOPIA

Belet Huen•

Oddur•

Jalalaxi•

31 December 1992
President Bush visits a school and relief centre for mothers and children

Baidoa•

La Foule

18 January 1993
The first American soldier, Marine Private Domingo Arroyo, killed

Baidere•

Afgoi ⊙

Mogadishu

26 January 1993
A second US Marine, Lance Corporal Anthony Botello, killed by a sniper while on night patrol

K E N Y A

30 January 1993
700 American troops in air assault fail to find arms cache

Merca ⊙

USS Juneau
TRANSPORT DOCK

USS Rushmore
DOCK LANDING SHIP

USS Tripoli
AMPHIBIOUS ASSAULT SHIP

USS Ranger
AIRCRAFT CARRIER

USS Jack Lummus
SUPPLY SHIP

Jilib⊙

0   kilometres   200
0   miles   100

Kismayu•

2 January 1993
A British famine relief worker 28-year-old Sean Devereux, shot: the first Western aid worker to be killed since United States troops landed

Mombasa

Base for two British Hercules transport planes with 80 Royal Air Force servicemen

26 January 1993
American and Belgian troops kill eight armed Somalis in a battle with armed militia

© Martin Gilbert 1993

136

EXPLORING THE SOLAR SYSTEM, 1962-1992

Beginning in 1962, the United States took the lead in exploring the solar system, starting with the launch of an unmanned *Mariner* spacecraft towards the planet Venus. On 3 March 1972 the unmanned, nuclear-powered spacecraft *Pioneer 10* was launched towards Jupiter: twenty years later it had travelled five billion miles from Earth

On 25 April 1990 the Hubble Space Telescope was launched, to study distant stars and galaxies, and to search for evidence of planets in other solar systems

2 March 1992
Pioneer 10 reaches five billion miles from Earth, the furthest distance travelled by any man-made object

26 January 1986
Voyager 2 passes, sends back details of planet's composition

● URANUS

3 December 1973
Pioneer 10 gives first close-up pictures
4 March 1979
Voyager 1 discovers rings and details of sixteen moons

3 February 1992
Ulysses flies to within 235,000 miles (and 416 million miles from Earth). Its signals take 37 minutes and 15 seconds to get back to Earth

1986
Pioneer 10 becomes the first man-made object to escape the solar system

29 March 1974
Mariner 10 takes 2,800 photographs

8 December 1992
Galileo, while bound for Jupiter (due 1995) passes within 200 miles of Earth. Its instruments detect signs of intelligent life on Earth!

PLUTO ●

● JUPITER

NEPTUNE ●

● MERCURY

SUN ●

· EARTH

● VENUS

14 December 1962
Mariner 2 passes 21,648 miles from surface
5 January 1969
Soviet space craft lands on surface and returns

13 June 1983
Pioneer 10 crosses the orbit of Neptune

MARS ●

8 November 1968
Pioneer 9 achieves sun orbit

28 November 1964
Mariner 4 trajectory passes Mars and sends 22 pictures from 6,100 miles above the planet's surface
13 November 1971
Mariner 9 in orbit 862 miles above planet's surface

● SATURN

November 1980
Voyager 1 sends photographs, reveals winds of 1,100 miles an hour at Equator and a total of 17 moons

○ **Sun**   RELATIVE DISTANCE BETWEEN THE PLANETS
· Mercury
· Venus   Jupiter   Saturn   Uranus   Neptune   Pluto
· Earth
· Mars

DEFENCE PREPAREDNESS IN SPACE, 1992-1993

On 31 December 1992 the United States Department of Defence awarded 6-year contracts to develop the "Brilliant Eyes" satellite. Each satellite was intended to carry sensors to monitor both space and Earth. Between 20 and 40 "Brilliant Eyes" would orbit at less than 1,000 miles above the Earth, in contrast to the 22,000-mile altitude of existing Early Warning satellites. This whole programme was cancelled by President Clinton on 13 May 1993 when he announced "the end of the Star Wars Era": a final affirmation of the end of the Cold War

In January 1992, Russian President Boris Yeltsin called for the United States and Russia to establish a Global Protection System. Following his call, talks began for the establishment of a Joint Missile Warning Centre that would receive data on missile launches

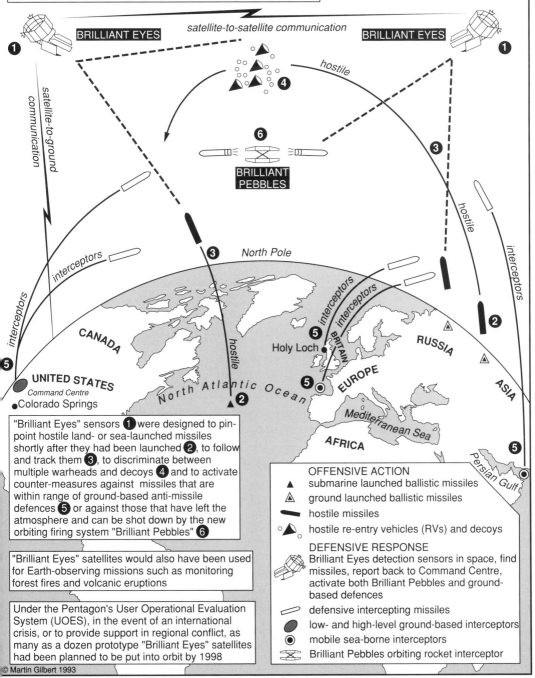

BRILLIANT EYES

satellite-to-satellite communication

BRILLIANT EYES

satellite-to-ground communication

hostile

4

6

BRILLIANT PEBBLES

3

North Pole

interceptors

hostile

interceptors

hostile

interceptors

CANADA

interceptors

interceptors

Holy Loch

5

2

BRITAIN

RUSSIA

UNITED STATES
Command Centre
Colorado Springs

5

North Atlantic Ocean

5

2

EUROPE

ASIA

AFRICA

Mediterranean Sea

5

Persian Gulf

"Brilliant Eyes" sensors ❶ were designed to pin-point hostile land- or sea-launched missiles shortly after they had been launched ❷, to follow and track them ❸, to discriminate between multiple warheads and decoys ❹ and to activate counter-measures against missiles that are within range of ground-based anti-missile defences ❺ or against those that have left the atmosphere and can be shot down by the new orbiting firing system "Brilliant Pebbles" ❻

"Brilliant Eyes" satellites would also have been used for Earth-observing missions such as monitoring forest fires and volcanic eruptions

Under the Pentagon's User Operational Evaluation System (UOES), in the event of an international crisis, or to provide support in regional conflict, as many as a dozen prototype "Brilliant Eyes" satellites had been planned to be put into orbit by 1998

OFFENSIVE ACTION
▲ submarine launched ballistic missiles
△ ground launched ballistic missiles
▬ hostile missiles
°▲. hostile re-entry vehicles (RVs) and decoys

DEFENSIVE RESPONSE
Brilliant Eyes detection sensors in space, find missiles, report back to Command Centre, activate both Brilliant Pebbles and ground-based defences
⬭ defensive intercepting missiles
● low- and high-level ground-based interceptors
◉ mobile sea-borne interceptors
⬟ Brilliant Pebbles orbiting rocket interceptor

The Twenty-First Century

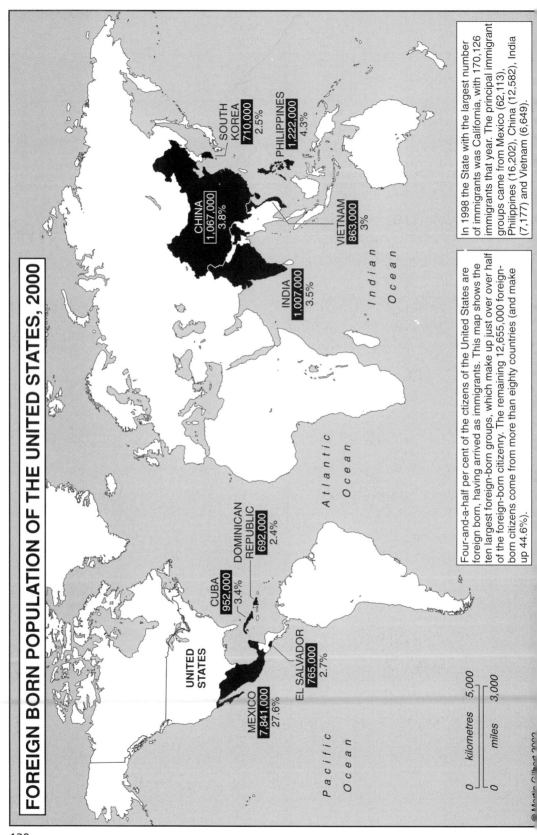

FOREIGN BORN POPULATION OF THE UNITED STATES, 2000

SOUTH KOREA 710,000 2.5%

PHILIPPINES 1,222,000 4.3%

CHINA 1,067,000 3.8%

VIETNAM 863,000 3%

INDIA 1,007,000 3.5%

Indian Ocean

In 1998 the State with the largest number of immigrants was California, with 170,126 immigrants that year. The principal immigrant groups came from Mexico (62,113), Philippines (16,202), China (12,582), India (7,177) and Vietnam (6,649).

Four-and-a-half per cent of the ctizens of the United States are foreign born, having arrived as immigrants. This map shows the ten largest foreign-born groups, which make up just over over half of the foreign-born citizenry. The remaining 12,655,000 foreign-born citizens come from more than eighty countries (and make up 44.6%).

Atlantic Ocean

DOMINICAN REPUBLIC 692,000 2.4%

CUBA 952,000 3.4%

UNITED STATES

EL SALVADOR 765,000 2.7%

MEXICO 7,841,000 27.6%

Pacific Ocean

0   kilometres   5,000

0   miles   3,000

© Martin Gilbert 2002

139

IMMIGRATION TO THE UNITED STATES, 1998

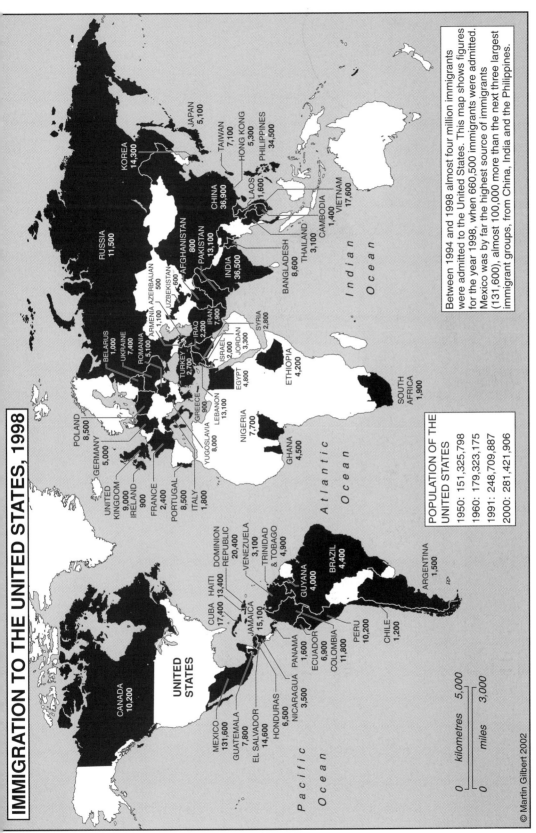

CANADA 10,200

UNITED STATES

MEXICO 131,600
GUATEMALA 7,800
EL SALVADOR 14,600
HONDURAS 6,500
NICARAGUA 3,500
PANAMA 1,600
ECUADOR 6,900
COLOMBIA 11,800
PERU 10,200
CHILE 1,200

CUBA 17,400
HAITI 13,400
JAMAICA 15,100
DOMINION REPUBLIC 20,400
VENEZUELA 3,100
TRINIDAD & TOBAGO 4,900
GUYANA 4,000
BRAZIL 4,400
ARGENTINA 1,500

POPULATION OF THE UNITED STATES
1950: 151,325,798
1960: 179,323,175
1991: 248,709,887
2000: 281,421,906

POLAND 8,500
GERMANY 5,000
UNITED KINGDOM 9,000
IRELAND 900
FRANCE 2,400
PORTUGAL 8,500
ITALY 1,800
YUGOSLAVIA 8,000
GREECE 900
LEBANON 13,100
NIGERIA 7,700
GHANA 4,500

BELARUS 1,000
UKRAINE 7,400
ROMANIA 5,100
ARMENIA 1,100
AZERBAIJAN 500
UZBEKISTAN 600
TURKEY 2,700
IRAQ 2,200
ISRAEL 2,000
JORDAN 3,300
SYRIA 2,800
EGYPT 4,800
ETHIOPIA 4,200
SOUTH AFRICA 1,900

RUSSIA 11,500
AFGHANISTAN 800
PAKISTAN 13,100
INDIA 36,500
IRAN 7,900
BANGLADESH 8,600

KOREA 14,300
JAPAN 5,100
TAIWAN 7,100
HONG KONG 5,300
PHILIPPINES 34,500
CHINA 36,900
LAOS 1,600
THAILAND 3,100
CAMBODIA 1,400
VIETNAM 17,600

Indian Ocean

Atlantic Ocean

Pacific Ocean

Between 1994 and 1998 almost four million immigrants were admitted to the United States. This map shows figures for the year 1998, when 660,500 immigrants were admitted. Mexico was by far the highest source of immigrants (131,600), almost 100,000 more than the next three largest immigrant groups, from China, India and the Philippines.

0   kilometres   5,000
0   miles   3,000

© Martin Gilbert 2002

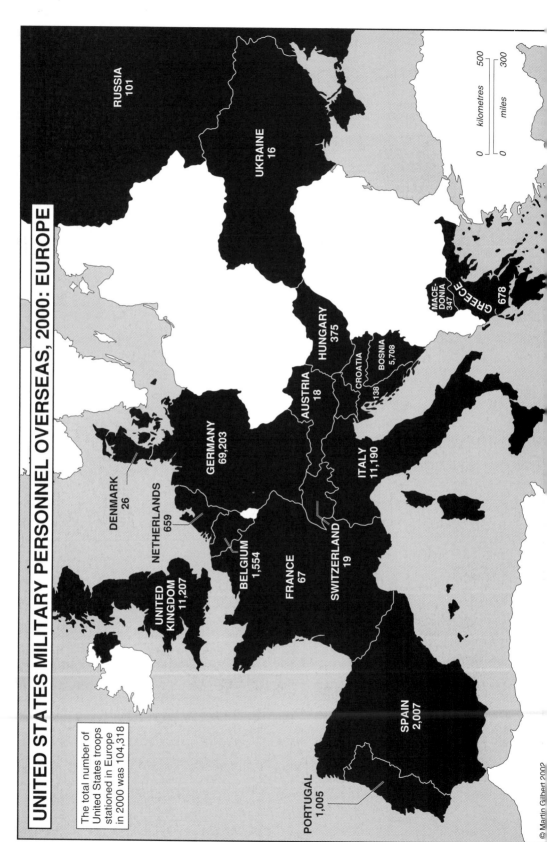

UNITED STATES MILITARY PERSONNEL OVERSEAS, 2000: EUROPE

The total number of United States troops stationed in Europe in 2000 was 104,318

RUSSIA 101

UKRAINE 16

MACE-DONIA 347

GREECE 678

HUNGARY 375

CROATIA 138

BOSNIA 5,708

AUSTRIA 18

DENMARK 26

GERMANY 69,203

ITALY 11,190

NETHERLANDS 659

BELGIUM 1,554

FRANCE 67

SWITZERLAND 19

UNITED KINGDOM 11,207

SPAIN 2,007

PORTUGAL 1,005

0 — 500 kilometres
0 — 300 miles

© Martin Gilbert 2002

UNITED STATES MILITARY PERSONNEL OVERSEAS, 2000: GLOBAL

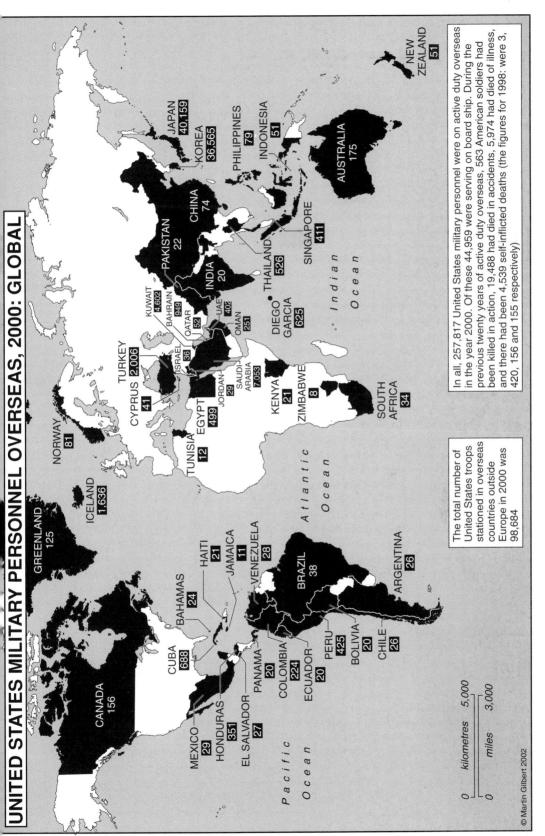

NEW ZEALAND 51

JAPAN 40,159
KOREA 36,565
PHILIPPINES 79
INDONESIA 51
AUSTRALIA 175

CHINA 74
PAKISTAN 22
INDIA 20
SINGAPORE 411
THAILAND 526

KUWAIT 4,602
BAHRAIN 949
QATAR 92
UAE 402
OMAN 251
DIEGO GARCIA 625

TURKEY 2,006
ISRAEL 36
CYPRUS 41
JORDAN 29
SAUDI ARABIA 7,053
KENYA 21
ZIMBABWE 8

NORWAY 81
EGYPT 499
TUNISIA 12
SOUTH AFRICA 34

ICELAND 1,636

GREENLAND 125

HAITI 21
JAMAICA 11
VENEZUELA 28
BAHAMAS 24
BRAZIL 38
ARGENTINA 26

CUBA 688
PANAMA 20
COLOMBIA 224
ECUADOR 20
PERU 425
BOLIVIA 20
CHILE 26

CANADA 156
MEXICO 29
HONDURAS 351
EL SALVADOR 27

In all, 257,817 United States military personnel were on active duty overseas in the year 2000. Of these 44,959 were serving on board ship. During the previous twenty years of active duty overseas, 563 American soldiers had been killed in action, 19,488 had died in accidents, 5,974 had died of illness, and there had been 4,539 self-inflicted deaths (the figures for 1998: were 3, 420, 156 and 155 respectively)

The total number of United States troops stationed in overseas countries outside Europe in 2000 was 98,684

Pacific Ocean

Indian Ocean

Atlantic Ocean

0 — kilometres 5,000
0 — miles 3,000

© Martin Gilbert 2002

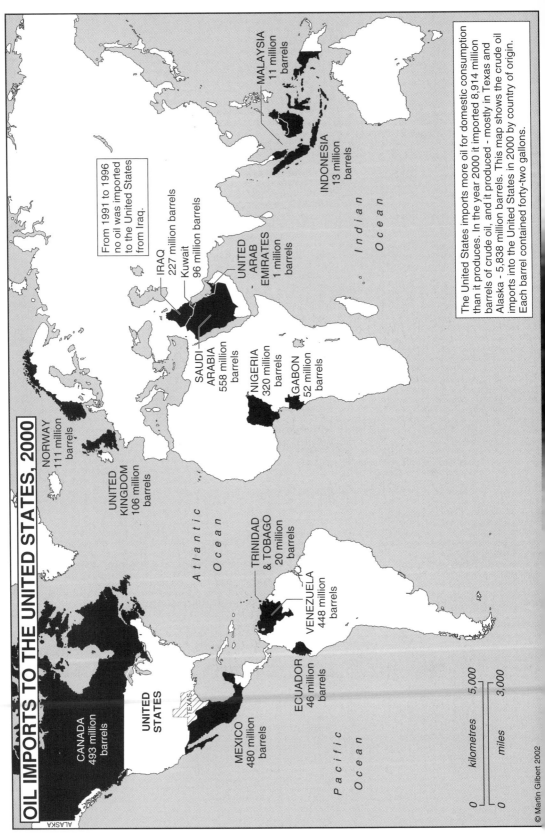

OIL IMPORTS TO THE UNITED STATES, 2000

ALASKA

CANADA
493 million
barrels

UNITED
STATES

TEXAS

NORWAY
111 million
barrels

UNITED
KINGDOM
106 million
barrels

From 1991 to 1996
no oil was imported
to the United States
from Iraq.

IRAQ
227 million barrels

Kuwait
96 million barrels

UNITED
ARAB
EMIRATES
1 million
barrels

SAUDI
ARABIA
558 million
barrels

NIGERIA
320 million
barrels

GABON
52 million
barrels

MALAYSIA
11 million
barrels

INDONESIA
13 million
barrels

*Indian
Ocean*

*Atlantic
Ocean*

TRINIDAD
& TOBAGO
20 million
barrels

VENEZUELA
448 million
barrels

ECUADOR
46 million
barrels

MEXICO
480 million
barrels

*Pacific
Ocean*

The United States imports more oil for domestic consumption
than it produces. In the year 2000 it imported 8,914 million
barrels of crude oil, and it produced - mostly in Texas and
Alaska - 5,838 million barrels. This map shows the crude oil
imports into the United States in 2000 by country of origin.
Each barrel contained forty-two gallons.

0   kilometres   5,000

0   miles   3,000

© Martin Gilbert 2002

143

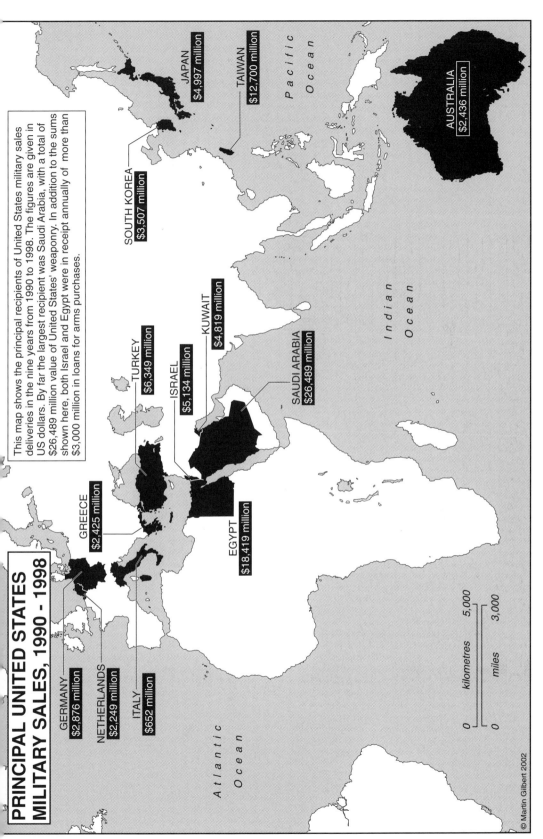

PRINCIPAL UNITED STATES
MILITARY SALES, 1990 - 1998

This map shows the principal recipients of United States military sales deliveries in the nine years from 1990 to 1998. The figures are given in US dollars. By far the largest recipient was Saudi Arabia, with a total of $26,489 million value of United States' weaponry. In addition to the sums shown here, both Israel and Egypt were in receipt annually of more than $3,000 million in loans for arms purchases.

JAPAN
$4,997 million

TAIWAN
$12,700 million

AUSTRALIA
$2,436 million

Pacific Ocean

SOUTH KOREA
$3,507 million

Indian Ocean

TURKEY
$6,349 million

ISRAEL
$5,134 million

KUWAIT
$4,819 million

SAUDI ARABIA
$26,489 million

GREECE
$2,425 million

EGYPT
$18,419 million

GERMANY
$2,876 million

NETHERLANDS
$2,249 million

ITALY
$652 million

Atlantic Ocean

kilometres 0   5,000

miles 0   3,000

© Martin Gilbert 2002

144

THE URBANIZATION OF THE UNITED STATES BY 2000

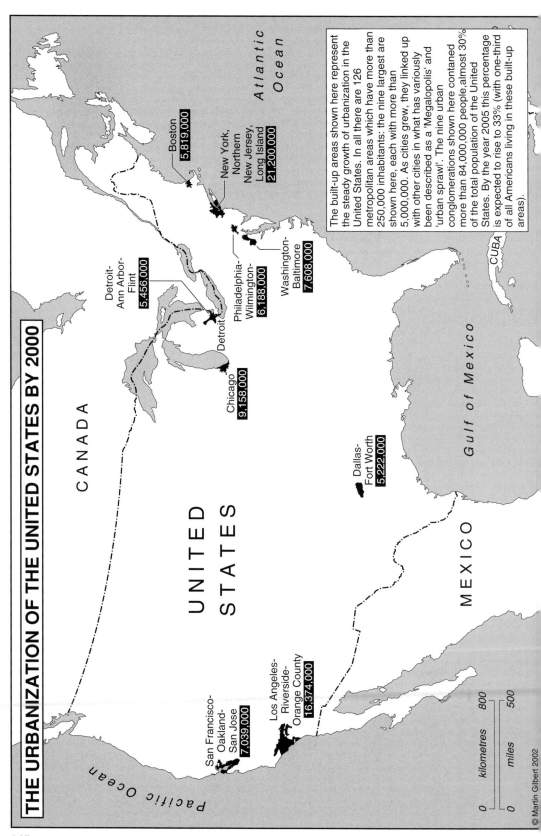

The built-up areas shown here represent the steady growth of urbanization in the United States. In all there are 126 metropolitan areas which have more than 250,000 inhabitants: the nine largest are shown here, each with more than 5,000,000. As cities grew, they linked up with other cities in what has variously been described as a 'Megalopolis' and 'urban sprawl'. The nine urban conglomerations shown here contaned more than 84,000,000 people, almost 30% of the total population of the United States. By the year 2005 this percentage is expected to rise to 33% (with one-third of all Americans living in these built-up areas).

Boston
5,819,000

New York, Northern New Jersey, Long Island
21,200,000

Philadelphia-Wilmington
6,188,000

Washington-Baltimore
7,608,000

Detroit-Ann Arbor-Flint
5,456,000

Detroit

Chicago
9,158,000

Dallas-Fort Worth
5,222,000

San Francisco-Oakland-San Jose
7,039,000

Los Angeles-Riverside-Orange County
16,374,000

CANADA

UNITED STATES

MEXICO

CUBA

Atlantic Ocean

Pacific Ocean

Gulf of Mexico

| kilometres | 0 | | 800 |
| miles | 0 | 500 | |

© Martin Gilbert 2002

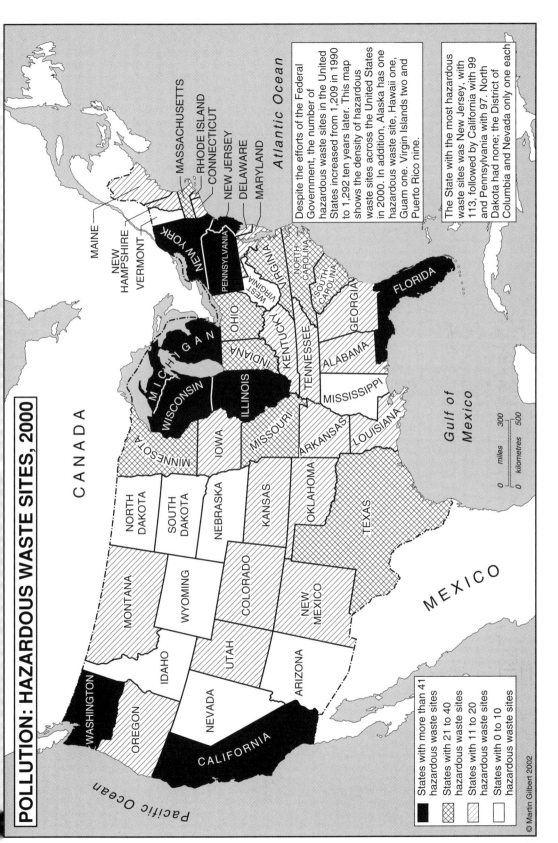

POLLUTION: HAZARDOUS WASTE SITES, 2000

Despite the efforts of the Federal Government, the number of hazardous waste sites in the United States increased from 1,209 in 1990 to 1,292 ten years later. This map shows the density of hazardous waste sites across the United States in 2000. In addition, Alaska has one hazardous waste site, Hawaii one, Guam one. Virgin Islands two and Puerto Rico nine.

The State with the most hazardous waste sites was New Jersey, with 113, followed by California with 99 and Pennsylvania with 97. North Dakota had none; the District of Columbia and Nevada only one each

CANADA

MEXICO

Atlantic Ocean

Gulf of Mexico

Pacific Ocean

MASSACHUSETTS
RHODE ISLAND
CONNECTICUT
NEW JERSEY
DELAWARE
MARYLAND

MAINE
NEW HAMPSHIRE
VERMONT

NEW YORK
PENNSYLVANIA
VIRGINIA
WEST VIRGINIA
NORTH CAROLINA
SOUTH CAROLINA
GEORGIA
FLORIDA
ALABAMA
MISSISSIPPI
LOUISIANA
TENNESSEE
KENTUCKY
INDIANA
OHIO
MICHIGAN
WISCONSIN
ILLINOIS
MISSOURI
ARKANSAS
IOWA
MINNESOTA
NORTH DAKOTA
SOUTH DAKOTA
NEBRASKA
KANSAS
OKLAHOMA
TEXAS
COLORADO
NEW MEXICO
WYOMING
MONTANA
IDAHO
UTAH
ARIZONA
NEVADA
WASHINGTON
OREGON
CALIFORNIA

0 miles 300
0 kilometres 500

States with more than 41 hazardous waste sites

States with 21 to 40 hazardous waste sites

States with 11 to 20 hazardous waste sites

States with 0 to 10 hazardous waste sites

© Martin Gilbert 2002

146

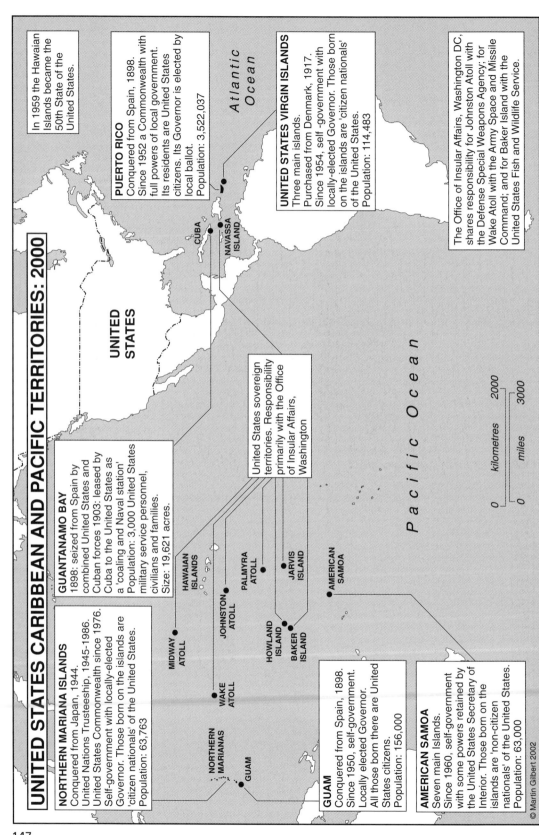

UNITED STATES CARIBBEAN AND PACIFIC TERRITORIES: 2000

NORTHERN MARIANA ISLANDS
Conquered from Japan, 1944.
United Nations Trusteeship, 1945-1986.
United States Commonwealth since 1976.
Self-government with locally-elected
Governor. Those born on the islands are
'citizen nationals' of the United States.
Population: 63,763

GUANTANAMO BAY
1898: seized from Spain by
combined United States and
Cuban forces 1903: leased by
Cuba to the United States as
a 'coaling and Naval station'
Population: 3,000 United States
military service personnel,
civilians and families.
Size: 19,621 acres.

PUERTO RICO
Conquered from Spain, 1898.
Since 1952 a Commonwealth with
full powers of local government.
Its residents are United States
citizens. Its Governor is elected by
local ballot.
Population: 3,522,037

UNITED STATES VIRGIN ISLANDS
Three main islands.
Purchased from Denmark, 1917.
Since 1954, self -government with
locally-elected Governor. Those born
on the islands are 'citizen nationals'
of the United States.
Population: 114,483

The Office of Insular Affairs, Washington DC,
shares responsibility for Johnston Atoll with
the Defense Special Weapons Agency; for
Wake Atoll with the Army Space and Missile
Command; and for Baker Island with the
United States Fish and Wildlife Service.

Atlantic Ocean

UNITED STATES

CUBA

NAVASSA ISLAND

United States sovereign
territories. Responsibility
primarily with the Office
of Insular Affairs,
Washington

Pacific Ocean

HAWAIAN ISLANDS

MIDWAY ATOLL

JOHNSTON ATOLL

PALMYRA ATOLL

JARVIS ISLAND

WAKE ATOLL

HOWLAND ISLAND

BAKER ISLAND

AMERICAN SAMOA

NORTHERN MARIANAS

GUAM

GUAM
Conquered from Spain, 1898.
Since 1950, self-government.
Locally elected Governor.
All those born there are United
States citizens.
Population: 156,000

AMERICAN SAMOA
Seven main islands.
Since 1960, self-government
with some powers retained by
the United States Secretary of
Interior. Those born on the
islands are 'non-citizen
nationals' of the United States.
Population: 63,000

In 1959 the Hawaian
Islands became the
50th State of the
United States.

0   kilometres   2000

0   miles   3000

© Martin Gilbert 2002

147

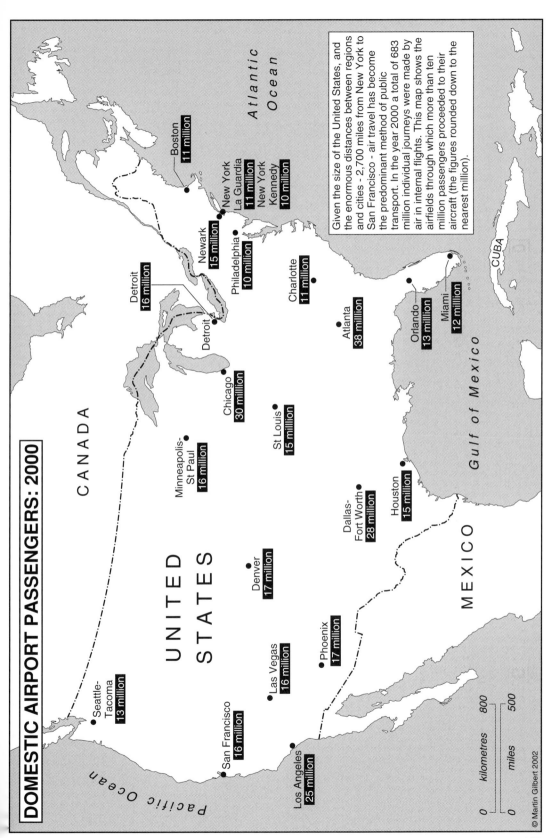

DOMESTIC AIRPORT PASSENGERS: 2000

Given the size of the United States, and the enormous distances between regions and cities - 2,700 miles from New York to San Francisco - air travel has become the predominant method of public transport. In the year 2000 a total of 683 million individual journeys were made by air in internal flights. This map shows the airfields through which more than ten million passengers proceeded to their aircraft (the figures rounded down to the nearest million).

CANADA

UNITED STATES

MEXICO

Atlantic Ocean

Pacific Ocean

Gulf of Mexico

CUBA

Boston
11 million

New York
La Guardia
11 million
New York
Kennedy
10 million

Newark
15 million

Philadelphia
10 million

Charlotte
11 million

Detroit
16 million

Detroit

Chicago
30 million

St Louis
15 million

Minneapolis-
St Paul
16 million

Atlanta
38 million

Orlando
13 million

Miami
12 million

Houston
15 million

Dallas-
Fort Worth
28 million

Denver
17 million

Phoenix
17 million

Las Vegas
16 million

Seattle-
Tacoma
13 million

San Francisco
16 million

Los Angeles
25 million

© Martin Gilbert 2002

0   800
kilometres

0   500
miles

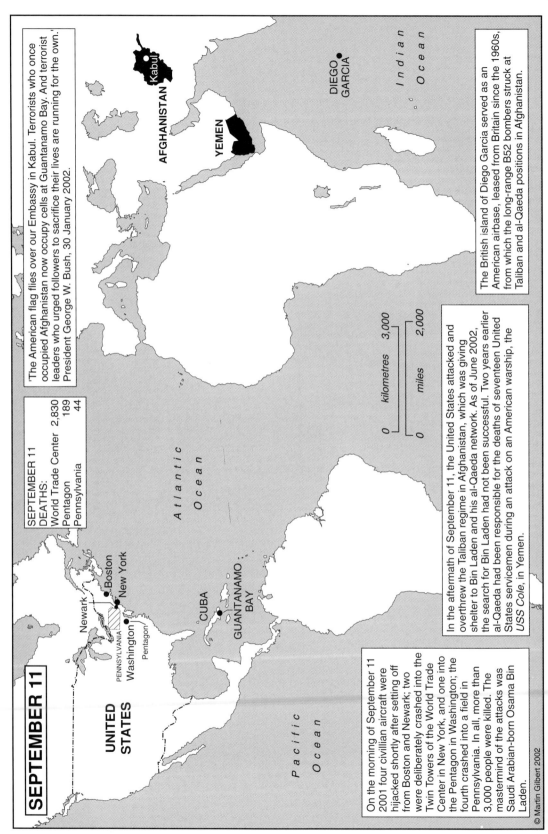

SEPTEMBER 11

SEPTEMBER 11
DEATHS:
World Trade Center 2,830
Pentagon 189
Pennsylvania 44

'The American flag flies over our Embassy in Kabul. Terrorists who once occupied Afghanistan now occupy cells at Guantanamo Bay. And terrorist leaders who urged followers to sacrifice their lives are running for the own.' President George W. Bush, 30 January 2002.

The British island of Diego Garcia served as an American airbase, leased from Britain since the 1960s, from which the long-range B52 bombers struck at Taliban and al-Qaeda positions in Afghanistan.

On the morning of September 11 2001 four civilian aircraft were hijacked shortly after setting off from Boston and Newark; two were deliberately crashed into the Twin Towers of the World Trade Center in New York, and one into the Pentagon in Washington; the fourth crashed into a field in Pennsylvania. In all, more than 3,000 people were killed. The mastermind of the attacks was Saudi Arabian-born Osama Bin Laden.

In the aftermath of September 11, the United States attacked and overthrew the Taliban regime in Afghanistan, which was giving shelter to Bin Laden and his al-Qaeda network. As of June 2002, the search for Bin Laden had not been successful. Two years earlier al-Qaeda had been responsible for the deaths of seventeen United States servicemen during an attack on an American warship, the *USS Cole*, in Yemen.

UNITED STATES

Newark
Boston
New York
PENNSYLVANIA
Washington
Pentagon

Pacific Ocean

Atlantic Ocean

CUBA
GUANTANAMO BAY

AFGHANISTAN
Kabul

YEMEN

DIEGO GARCIA

Indian Ocean

0   kilometres   3,000
0   miles   2,000

© Martin Gilbert 2002